Editors' Choice, *New York T*
Anticipated Book of the Ye
Reviewed Nonfiction of the week" (*Book Marks*)

"Delicious and infuriating. . . . Unputdownable."

—Sadie Stein, *New York Times*

"A tour de force. . . . The stories Ciuraru tells are gripping, horrific, and sometimes funny, but most of all, they are important."

—*Washington Post*

"Compulsively readable. . . . Ciuraru sketches cradle-to-grave portraits of each of her subjects, with a focus on their relationships—and the effects on the wife's work—as they devolve from initial infatuation to bitter disillusionment."

—*Wall Street Journal*

"Lively and absorbing."

—*New York Times Book Review*

"*Lives of the Wives* explores five literary marriages full of tempest and tumult, offering rich biographical portraits and examining the roles of ambition, narcissism, misogyny, infidelity, and alcoholism in relationships where imbalance seems baked in from the start."

—*The Guardian*

"Eye-opening. . . . A rare window into five relationships providing a respectful yet unflinching look inside the daily, often complicated lives of the writers and their wives. . . . The reality is often harsh—but also fascinating. An illuminating, well-rendered literary biography."

—*Kirkus Reviews* (starred review)

"A notable book about remarkable women."

—*Library Journal* (starred review)

"Witty and powerful."                                    —*People*

"Carmela Ciuraru offers scintillating, no-prisoners-taking portraits of five marriages in which at least one partner was a well-known writer."
—*Shelf Awareness*

"An intriguing analysis of the relationship dynamics between creatives."
—*Booklist*

"*Lives of the Wives* is a fascinating offering, providing a sort of testimony to the dazzling range of marriages one would not want to be stuck in, even if the other person is brilliant, and charming, and a writer."
—*East Hampton Star*

"Enthralling . . . incendiary reading. . . . These five marriages are very different in the nature of their dysfunctionality and the manner in which a talented woman is subordinated to the talented man she chooses to marry."                    —Daphne Merkin, *Air Mail*

"Ciuraru manages to reposition her wives, bringing them out from behind their great men and placing them center stage. Up close, we discern their resilience and determination and view most of them not as other halves but better halves."

—Malcolm Forbes, *Washington Examiner*

"The literary relationships featured in *Lives of the Wives* may have been tumultuous, but in Carmela Ciuraru's telling, they are never tawdry, and nobody is a victim. The women she focuses on are complex, accomplished, and witty; their relationships are fully realized and dimensional."

—*Boston University Today*, "Books to Read for
Women's History Month"

"Deliriously readable. . . . You'll want to read it in one go."
—The Center for Fiction

# Lives of the Wives

ALSO BY CARMELA CIURARU

*Nom de Plume: A (Secret) History of Pseudonyms*

# Lives of the Wives

## Five Literary Marriages

Carmela Ciuraru

HARPER  PERENNIAL

NEW YORK • LONDON • TORONTO • SYDNEY • NEW DELHI • AUCKLAND

HARPER ● PERENNIAL

HarperCollins books may be purchased for educational, business, or sales promotional use. For information, please email the Special Markets Department at SPsales@harpercollins.com.

FIRST HARPER PERENNIAL EDITION PUBLISHED 2024.

*Designed by Nancy Singer*

Library of Congress Cataloging-in-Publication Data has been applied for.

ISBN 978-0-06-235692-5 (pbk.)

23 24 25 26 27  LBC  5 4 3 2 1

For Terry Karten, who waited

*Possibly she would have been a genius if we had never met.*

—F. SCOTT FITZGERALD

*The wives . . . are buying groceries or cleaning up messes or having a drink. Their lives are concerned with food and mess and houses and cars and money. They have to remember to get the snow tires on and go to the bank and take back the beer bottles, because their husbands are such brilliant, such talented incapable men, who must be looked after for the sake of the words that will come from them.*

—ALICE MUNRO, "MATERIAL"

*Dear Natalia, stop having children and write a book that is better than mine.*

—CESARE PAVESE, POSTCARD TO NATALIA GINZBURG, 1941

# CONTENTS

# WHAT'S A WIFE TO DO?

It is a truth universally acknowledged, that a single man in possession of a good fortune, must be in want of a wife," Jane Austen famously wrote in *Pride and Prejudice*. Two hundred years later, Margaret Atwood offered a riposte from the other side: "Longed for him. Got him. Shit."

The problem with being a wife is being a wife. Historically, the primary function of marriage was to bind women to men as a form of property, and to protect bloodlines by producing legitimate offspring. Women existed to serve men, in every sense, and did. "Wives are young men's mistresses; companions for middle age; and old men's nurses," Francis Bacon wrote in 1597. The fundamental predicament of womanhood can be traced back to the myth of Adam and Eve, in which female agency poses an existential threat to paradise. The creation of Eve, from the rib of Adam—*woman* from *man*—established the notion that a woman's very existence depended upon, and was only validated by, a dominant male counterpart. In the book of Genesis, God decrees to Eve: "I will greatly multiply thy sorrow and thy conception; in sorrow thou shalt bring forth children; and thy desire shall be for thy husband, and he shall rule over thee." Eve was probably thinking, "Kill me now, God." But the template was set.

Once upon a time, women were told that someday their prince would come. Being a wife was a badge of honor, no matter how miserable the marriage. The alternative, spinsterhood, was worse. To be a wife was to be offered up as chattel, cook, housekeeper, and nursemaid, among other things. The woman vowed to serve and obey, and legally, she ceased to exist. Of the husband, little was demanded in return. (Proverbs 18:22: "Whosoever findeth a wife findeth a good thing.") The invention of marriage was a gift to men and a strategic alliance between families. Societal stability was said to depend on it. When marital relations did not go as he wished, the husband could do what he deemed necessary, apart from murder, to make things right. If he beat his wife, the law upheld his authority. He was also entitled to sex, however loveless or coerced—rape was considered a reasonable response if the wife did not comply. (In the United States, marital rape was not a crime in all fifty states until 1993.) In the thirteenth century, the English jurist and cleric Henry de Bracton, chancellor of Exeter Cathedral, declared that a married couple is one person, and that person is the husband. In 1863, Lucy Gilmer Breckinridge, a nineteen-year-old girl in Virginia—who had been keeping a journal to alleviate her boredom during wartime—fretted privately that she might never learn to love a man: "Oh what I would not give for a *wife*!"

The history of wives is largely one of resilience and forbearance, with countless women demonized, marginalized, misrepresented, and silenced. As they found themselves trapped in bad marriages, their husbands were free to roam in search of more and better sex. The wives buried their desires, hopes, and regrets for the greater good and in the interest of keeping the peace—all while serving as beaming helpmeet. When a husband went astray, the wife had the additional duty to reform him. It isn't surprising that in the index of a book chronicling the history of marriage, "*wives (and drunkenness)*" is among the entries.

Contemporary marriage, in its ideal form, is an egalitarian, sexually fulfilling, and mutually supportive alliance, comprising love and friendship. Yet for many couples, heterosexual or otherwise, this perfect union is unrecognizable. Modern marriage is a series of compromises, a relentless juggling act of work obligations, childcare demands, household chores, money squabbles, hoarded grievances, simmering hostilities, and intimacy issues. (The burdens are more extreme at lower socioeconomic levels.) Perhaps that explains the endless discourse around the "work" of marriage, a predictable result of the tedium that can set in after two people have lived together for a long time. "Arnold Bennett says that the horror of marriage lies in its 'dailiness,'" Virginia Woolf wrote in her diary in 1926. "All acuteness of a relationship is rubbed away by this."

Toss in male privilege, ruthless ambition, narcissism, misogyny, infidelity, alcoholism, and a mood disorder or two, and it's easy to understand why the marriages of so many famous writers have been stormy, short-lived, and mutually destructive. Given the extraordinary works of literature that could *only* have been produced as a result of their marital partnerships, there's a topsy-turvy aspect to assessing what it means to have had a "failed" marriage. The typical rules do not apply. (For the wife, "happily ever after" often means "happily ever after the divorce.") Yet an ending does not always provide a clear path to salvation, even when the wife is a prominent writer. In a 2013 interview with Sharon Olds, the Pulitzer Prize–winning poet was asked whether she had reinvented herself in the aftermath of a devastating divorce. "I was fifty-five," she said. "I would not have known how. What I had to do was persevere."

In traditional literary marriages, the lot of the wife is rather bleak. She must tend to the outsize needs of the so-called Great Writer, and her work is never done. Literary wives are a unique breed, requiring a particular kind of fortitude. No vade mecum exists to guide them. "Sooner or later, the great men turn out to be all alike," V. S. Pritchett once lamented. "They never stop working. They never lose a minute. It is very depressing." It is even more depressing for their wives. The phrase *I don't know how she does it* is commonly uttered about wives and mothers, with their numinous gift for serving others, but we are unlikely to hear it said of their writer-husbands. We know exactly how they do it.

With an ego the size of a small nation, the literary lion is powerful on the page but a helpless kitten in daily life—reliant on his wife to fold an umbrella, answer the phone, or lick a stamp (looking at you, Vladimir!). Those towering, mononymic geniuses of Western literature—Tolstoy, Dickens, Dostoyevsky, Hemingway, Nabokov—where would they be without their wives?

In the marriages of celebrated literati throughout history, *husband* is to *fame* as *wife* is to *footnote*. Yes, this framing is reductive, and in rare instances, the wife was the artist, served and supported by a man—or, in homosexual relationships, by a same-sex partner. But conjuring historical examples of the latter model leaves us struggling to count fingers on more than one hand. (George Eliot and Virginia Woolf come to mind.) No matter the configuration of gender or sexuality, however, the long-held and much romanticized notion of the "lone genius" persists, as does the stubborn myth of the "tormented genius." Even in instances when the writer is mediocre at best, if nothing else he is a genius at getting others—namely, his long-suffering wife—to prop him up and perpetuate the myth of his greatness. In Diane Johnson's superb biography *The True History of the First Mrs. Meredith and Other Lesser Lives*, she sets the scene perfectly:

Many people have described the Famous Writer presiding at his dinner table, in a clean neckcloth. He is famous; everybody remembers his remarks. He remembers his own remarks, being a writer, and notes them in his diary. We forget that there were other people at the table—a quiet person, now muffled by time, shadowy, whose heart pounded with love, perhaps, or rage, or fear when our writer shuffled in from his study; whose hands, white knuckled, twisted an apron, whose thoughts raced. Or someone who left the room with a full throat of sobs.

Same-sex relationships have been held up as exemplars of equitable partnerships, in which one life is not "lesser" than the other. In a 2014 interview, the researcher Robert-Jay Green said his findings indicated consistently that same-sex couples are "much more egalitarian in their relationships. They share decision-making more equally, finances more equally, housework more equally, childcare more equally. Basically, every dimension we looked at, same-sex couples are dramatically more equal in the way they function together as a couple compared to heterosexual couples." One might assume that in a lesbian relationship in which one or both partners are writers, there exists a utopia of domestic tranquility and the nurturing of intellectual and creative desires without impediment. The reality is more complicated.

"It is generally agreed that without Alice Toklas, [Gertrude] Stein might not have had the will to go on writing what for many years almost no one had any interest in reading," Janet Malcolm writes in *Two Lives: Gertrude and Alice*. By the time Stein met Toklas in Paris in 1907, she had long been convinced of her own genius. Stein's ego required care and feeding, and Toklas arrived just in time. "She banished doubt from Stein's artist's consciousness," Malcolm writes, "as she would later banish the unworthy from Stein's salon." After the couple moved in together, Toklas had a strict routine: she typically woke at six o'clock in the morning and was said to clean the drawing room herself, so that nothing would be broken. She supervised the household servants, planned meals, and typed up manuscript pages for Stein, savoring the intimacy of it: "I got a Gertrude Stein technique, like playing Bach. My fingers were adapted only to Gertrude's work. Doing the typing of *The Making of Americans* was a very happy time for me," Toklas wrote in *What Is Remembered*. "I hoped it would go on forever."

Her belief in Stein's genius emboldened the writer further. There was no mistaking the fact that Stein was the man of the house, while Toklas played bride and muse. (Stein often called Toklas "wifey.") "The division of household labor between the two women, with one doing everything and the other nothing, was another precondition for the flowering of Stein's genius," Malcolm writes, suggesting that behind every great woman is another great woman. "It take [*sic*] a lot of time to be a genius," Stein wrote in *Everybody's Autobiography*, "you have to sit around so much doing nothing, really nothing." After Stein died at the age of seventy-two in 1946, Toklas never recovered. "She tended the shrine of Stein's literary and personal legend with the devotion of a dog at the master's grave," Malcolm writes. "She would snarl if anyone came too close to the monument."

Toklas might be described as a lesbian Véra Nabokov, surely the greatest writer's wife of all time and someone whose name has become synonymous with the art of literary wifedom. Like many wives of geniuses, Toklas, who had once been a promising concert pianist, abandoned her ambitions to serve her partner. When Toklas died at eighty-nine on March 7, 1967, she was buried next to Stein in the Père-Lachaise cemetery in Paris, preserving their union in perpetuity.

Another story of a long-term "marriage" with an important lesbian writer, Audre Lorde, proves just as off-kilter in its spousal sacrifices. Born in Harlem in 1934 to Caribbean immigrant parents, the influential Black poet and activist boldly tackled racism, sexism, and homophobia in her work, along with other issues of social justice. In 1962, Lorde appeared to follow convention when she married a white attorney and good friend, Ed Rollins. Both were gay, and both wanted children. After having a son and a daughter, they divorced in 1970. Two years earlier, after Lorde was awarded a grant to become a poet-in-residence at Tougaloo College, a private, historically Black college in Mississippi, she met Frances Clayton, a white midwesterner who had come to Tougaloo as a visiting professor. They fell in love. Clayton was an ambitious and accomplished academic—the first woman in her department at Brown University to receive tenure—yet she sacrificed her enviable position for the woman she loved, moving to New York City to be with Lorde and her children. Finding a job after giving up a tenured position at an

Ivy League institution was not easy. In her former life, Clayton enjoyed a prestigious teaching job while leading groundbreaking research on animal behavior. Now she taught introductory psychology courses at Queens College. She focused her energy on domestic chores, setting up a study just for Lorde and doing all the cooking and cleaning. The relationship allowed Lorde to remain prolific, and spared her from the kinds of wifely duties that had hampererd Clayton's career.

As Lorde gained great acclaim in the 1970s, traveling and giving lectures around the world, Clayton stayed home to care for the children while taking courses to transition into a career as a psychotherapist. By 1984, following two brutal bouts of cancer, Lorde had become roman- tically involved with another woman, Gloria Joseph, whom she met at a retreat for Black feminists in 1979. Soon Lorde was traveling regularly to St. Croix, where Joseph had a vacation home. The steadfast Clayton continued to give her partner unconditional support as Lorde's health worsened, even accompanying her to a private clinic in Switzerland for treatment.

Determined to "live the rest of my life with as much joy as possi- ble," as Lorde wrote in her journal in 1986, she moved full-time to St. Croix to be with Joseph. (A doctor told Lorde that she had less than five years to live.) The breakup was ruinous for Clayton, who had given up so much to stand by her partner of nearly twenty years. In 1992, a few months before her fifty-ninth birthday, Lorde died of liver cancer in St. Croix with Joseph at her side. Clayton died in 2012 at the age of eighty-five.

Of course, our best-known stories of literary couples are heterosexual partnerships, with the Great Writer white and male. Locked in Oedipal warfare with the literary predecessors he both admires and envies—what the critic Harold Bloom called the "anxiety of influence"—the Great Writer's drive to succeed is relentless. He is charismatic and beloved, his works regarded as masterpieces, at least in his own mind. His allegiance is to Literature, but as he devotes himself to being a literary trailblazer, he also craves a stable existence at home. Someone must protect him from interruptions. As we fetishize the daily routines and rituals of famous writers—where, when, and how they like to work, what they drink or smoke to get the creative juices flowing, and so on—we ignore the ornamental wives who make everything possible, liberating their husbands from the tyranny of everyday life.

"The famous carry about with them a great weight of patriarchal baggage—the footnotes of their lives," Elizabeth Hardwick wrote in "Wives and Mistresses." Some of those footnotes, also known as women, have inspired poems "or have seen themselves expropriated for the transformation of fiction." Hardwick spoke from experience, having had her anguished letters to her former husband, the manic-depressive poet Robert Lowell, scandalously adapted as source material in *The Dolphin*. She had nursed and supported Lowell for more than twenty years, through multiple breakdowns, when he abandoned her for Lady Caroline Blackwood, the Anglo-Irish aristocrat he married in 1972. His book won the Pulitzer Prize two years later. ("It's been my experience," Hardwick once wrote, "that nobody holds a man's brutality to his wife against him.") The "attendants," as Hardwick called the put-upon and used-up women such as herself, have "written and received letters, been lied to, embezzled, abandoned, honored, or slandered. But there they are, entering history with *them*, with the celebrated artists, generals, prime ministers, Presidents, tycoons."

There they are too with the celebrated writers. The literary wife is not unlike Ariadne, who in Greek mythology aids Theseus in his epic quest to slay the Minotaur. She ensures the return of her beloved by supplying him with the means to kill the Minotaur (a sword), as well as the means of escape (a red spool of thread that will lead him to safety). She advises Theseus to tie one end of the thread near the entrance of the Labyrinth, letting it unroll as he ventures deeper in, then following it back to the entrance after slaying the monster, where she awaits him. Theseus promptly abandons her on the island of Naxos. There are many versions of this myth: one ends with Ariadne hanging herself, while another tells us that Theseus left her to die before she was rescued by the god Dionysus, who claimed her as his wife. No version ends well for her.

In the context of writers' marriages, the manuscript is the monster to be slain. The faithful wife, having given her husband the tools and conditions required to succeed in his quest, awaits the return of the brave genius like a welcoming light at the end of the creative tunnel. Like Ariadne, sometimes she too is abandoned, left for dead.

The ideal wife of a famous writer has no desires worth mentioning. She lives each day in second place. Rather than attempt to seize control of her own fate, she accepts what she has been given without complaint. Her ambitions are not thwarted because she doesn't have any. "What does it mean to be unambiguously a woman?" wrote Carolyn Heilbrun in *Writing a Woman's Life*, her groundbreaking 1988 feminist study. "It means to put a man at the center of one's life and to allow to occur only what honors his prime position." Yet the wife may sometimes feel beaten down by loneliness, drudgery, and a persistent lack of purpose. ("Marriage," Susan Sontag once wrote in her journal, "is based on the principle of inertia.") Perhaps being loved by a powerful man isn't enough. She may wonder, as she folds the laundry, pays the bills, or brings her husband another cup of coffee, whether she has wasted her life. Surely her husband cannot be held accountable for any perceived misdeeds. "Everyone is quick to say Dickens was a bit of a shit, did not treat his wife very nicely," the actor Ralph Fiennes said in a 2012 interview of the man he was portraying on screen. "But he was churning with creative imagination." In other words, Dickens may have treated Catherine, the mother of his ten children, with indefensible cruelty, but *c'est la vie*, the man was a genius.

If the literary wife is lucky, she plays a more active role in her spouse's work, perhaps as first reader or editor. Joy Davidman, a divorced Jewish American single mother who had been regarded as a child prodigy and who won the Yale Series of Younger Poets Prize in 1938, is better known, if at all, as Mrs. C. S. Lewis. She converted to Christianity and became her husband's intellectual partner, essentially serving as coauthor while he worked on his novel *Till We Have Faces: A Myth Retold.* "Whatever my talents as an independent writer," she revealed in a letter, "my *real* gift is a sort of editor-collaborator like Max Perkins, and I'm happiest when I'm doing something like that." She died from breast cancer at forty-five.

When a wife has ambitions of her own—and worse, talent—there's bound to be trouble. In 1943, while Ernest Hemingway's third wife, Martha Gellhorn, was reporting from war-torn Europe, he cabled her plaintively from his home in Cuba: "Are you a war correspondent or wife in my bed?" The Irish writer Edna O'Brien was working for a pharmacist in Dublin when she married the novelist Ernest Gébler in the summer of 1954. He was sixteen years older and this was his second marriage. Upon reading the manuscript of her debut novel, *The Country Girls,* he told her: "You can write and I will never forgive you." The threat of writerly rivalry was too much to bear. When O'Brien's book was published in 1960, she became famous at the age of thirty. (Attempting to be a good wife, she had used part of her meager advance to buy a sewing machine.) "He was very angry, very resentful, very undermined," their elder son, Carlo, later said of his vindictive and controlling father. "He felt reduced by her literary success. He felt in some way the acclaim should be pointed towards him and that he was the person who helped her to become the writer she became." Gébler sabotaged opportunities that came her way: after the publication of O'Brien's second novel, *The Lonely Girl,* in 1962, he intercepted a letter from a London theater producer who wished to adapt the book into a musical. Posing as O'Brien's agent, the nonexistent "Edward Cresset," Gébler replied to say that the rights were not available—but *The Love Investigator,* a novel by Ernest Gébler, was up for grabs and even better. The marriage ended soon after.

For some literary couples, dual egotism has its advantages. As Joan Didion's husband, John Gregory Dunne, once said, "If I weren't married to a writer, I couldn't be as self-absorbed as I am." (For her part,

Didion said in an interview that she and her husband were "terrifically, terribly dependent on one another.") Often the independent-minded women who pursue literary careers are referred to as "women writers." A male writer is just a writer. Being a *woman writer*, however, suggests something exotic and unexpected, like a monkey who can play chess or speak French.

If we think of literary wifedom as a narrative genre, it might be described as some blend of romance—turbulent, passionate, highly charged—and dystopian literature. (The *Oxford English Dictionary* defines dystopia as an "imaginary place or condition in which everything is as bad as possible.") One of the twentieth century's most famous and tragic literary relationships began the night Sylvia Plath met Ted Hughes, "that big, dark, hunky boy," at a party in Cambridge, England, in 1956. He kissed her "bang smash on the mouth," and she bit him on the cheek, drawing blood. "Such violence, and I can see how women lie down for artists," she wrote in her journal afterward. The poets married four months later. Plath went on to describe the "the big, blasting, dangerous love" of their relationship, and although her ambition matched his, she struggled with her dependence on Hughes—admitting privately that "my whole being has grown and interwound so completely with Ted's that if anything were to happen to him, I do not see how I could live. I would either go mad, or kill myself." She toggled back and forth in her journals between wanting to please her husband and craving an identity separate from his. "Make him happy: cook, play, read . . . never accuse or nag—let him run, reap, rip—and glory in the temporary sun of his ruthless force," she wrote in one entry. But in the summer of 1958, she confided: "I must be myself—make myself & not let myself be made by him." On February 11, 1963, after Hughes had left her for another woman, Plath committed suicide` while her young children slept in the next room. It was an ending in which everything was as bad as possible.

In the official marital record, who gets to be chronicler and narrator? *Lives of the Wives* is a project of reclamation and reparation, paying tribute to the women who have served as agents, editors, managers, publicists, proofreaders, translators, amanuenses, confidantes, cheerleaders, gatekeepers, and housekeepers to famous writers, providing emotional, practical, and even financial support. They were saviors and caretakers, enablers and collaborators.

Behind every great man is a great woman, or so the saying goes. (Groucho Marx famously quipped: "Behind every successful man is a woman, and behind her is his wife.") In examining the lives of famous authors, it is time to reposition the wife. We must give writers' wives their due, marvel at what they achieved and made possible, and reflect on what might have been. These remarkable wives possess what Joan Didion once described, in another context, as "a genius for accommodation more often seen in women than in men."

*Lives of the Wives* honors the paradoxes, constraints, and unexpected rewards of these asymmetrical partnerships. (Even in marriages in which both spouses were writers, women often felt eclipsed and fought to claim the right to their own success.) This is a book about marriage as fairy tale and marriage as nightmare. Many of the world's most esteemed writers were high-maintenance partners, utterly dependent on the wives who provided the support they needed to function. "It would be difficult to write about Véra without mentioning Vladimir," the artist Saul Steinberg once remarked, "but it would be impossible to write about Vladimir without mentioning Véra."

In a 2014 interview with the *New York Times*, the great short story writer and novelist Lorrie Moore pined for a Véra of her own. She spoke of the challenges of being a divorced single mother, holding a job as a creative writing professor while keeping up with her own work. "It's hard," she said. "There are some men I know who are teaching and writing who are single fathers. But not many. Most of them have these great devoted wives, some version of Véra Nabokov. Writers all need Véra." In fifty-two years of marriage, among many other duties, Véra guided her husband's career, negotiated his contracts, typed his manuscripts, and yes, licked his stamps. She famously stopped her husband from in-cinerating an early draft of *Lolita*, salvaging charred pages from the fire and telling him: "We are keeping this." More than a manuscript savior, Véra also served as his bodyguard, carrying a pistol in her handbag to protect him.

For many creative women burdened by the exigencies of family life, writing is an act of defiance. Shouldn't they be doing something else? The answer is always yes. Maybe that's why Toni Morrison began her first novel, *The Bluest Eye*, as an undergraduate at Howard University and did not complete it until after her divorce, when she returned to writing as a single mother. The poet Anne Sexton once described the difficulties of navigating marriage, motherhood, and a desire for creative accomplishment, admitting to a psychotic break when she was twenty-eight: "I was trying my damnedest to lead a conventional life, for that was how I was brought up, and it was what my husband wanted of me. But one can't build little picket fences to keep nightmares out." She committed suicide in 1974.

Unfettered writing time has often been some combination of im-possible feat and wishful thinking for many women, even bestselling authors. The novelist Ann Patchett once lamented the demands of do-mesticity: "How exhausting it is, as a woman, to always be the one who has to make the food and change the beds," she said in a 2016 interview with the *Guardian*. "No matter how enlightened, how much of a femi-nist I am, I am still doing all of it. With every book I think: well, if this one's really successful, maybe I won't have to make dinner any more." She expressed skepticism toward the sacrosanct advice about writing every day. "Don't you think men are the ones that always say that?" she said. "I'm not sure I've heard a woman say you have to write every day. They're too busy making dinner. I go through long periods of time when I don't write, and I'm fine."

Little seems to have improved over time. In a 1981 interview, Rebecca West was asked whether it had become easier for women to pursue their vocations. "I don't know," she said. "It's very hard. I've always found I've had too many family duties to enable me to write enough. I would have written much better and I would have written much more. Oh, men, whatever they may say, don't really have any barrier between them and their craft, and certainly I had." Virginia Woolf gave a name to the predicament that disproportionately afflicts women: the Angel in the House, a "certain phantom" that excels at family life and self-sacrifice, dissuading women from putting pen to paper. "It was she who bothered me and wasted my time and so tormented me that at last I killed her," Woolf wrote of the Angel. ". . . I turned upon her and caught her by the throat. . . . I acted in self-defence."

Not all writers with a Véra of their own behave without regard for their wives. Stephen King has attributed his success in part to his wife, Tabitha: "The combination of a healthy body and a stable relationship with a self-reliant woman who takes zero shit from me or anyone else has made the continuity of my working life possible." The novelist Norman Rush has also spoken about the support of his wife of more than fifty years, and when their son was young, the couple split their workday to ensure equal parenting. In a profile that appeared in the *New York Times* in 2013, the journalist Wyatt Mason wrote: "Not a literary spouse who stealthily delivers cups of tea to the genius in the attic, Elsa is what Rush calls 'a partner in the process,' which he describes as 'a battle waged in common.'"

Throughout history, many women have stepped up as creative partners while also ensuring that every spousal whim was catered to, no matter how carnal, petty, tedious, or bizarre. (Véra Nabokov cut up her husband's food for him at mealtime.) Some of these women remained loyal even as they were belittled, tormented, and abused, and as their husbands attempted to manipulate and destroy them. The British critic Kenneth Tynan encouraged his American wife, Elaine Dundy, to write, expressing confidence in her talent—then fumed as her first novel became a bestseller. Threatening divorce, he warned her not to publish another book, and in response she began writing a new novel the next morning. Similarly, Roald Dahl enjoyed basking in the glow of his movie star wife, Patricia Neal, until he despised her for earning more money than he did and felt emasculated by her fame. She was advised by a friend of his that if she wished to repair her marriage, she could go on being the breadwinner as long as her husband controlled the bank account—and she must do all the cooking and cleaning. Elizabeth Jane Howard knew that to fully devote herself to writing, she had to divorce Kingsley Amis. Throughout their marriage, Howard admired her husband's rate of production and felt that his discipline was "a marvelous example," but, as she once admitted, "I didn't have the same time to do it." Her energy was consumed by his needs, leaving her to take up gardening as her primary creative outlet. All three of these couples were enviably picture-perfect, and all were adept at keeping up appearances to mask the misery behind closed doors.

The marriage of the Italian novelists Elsa Morante and Alberto Moravia was uneasy from the start. Morante stands apart from the other wives in this book by being the least self-sacrificing and nurturing. She was nonetheless a woman overshadowed by her more famous and prolific husband, and one who struggled with creative ambition in ways that he did not. And, like many writers' wives, Morante had a spouse who often made her feel ignored, unwanted, taken for granted. She craved her husband's attention, but he was never quite present.

Although the couple shared an intellectual intensity, they were sexually incompatible and never in love. Given the insuperable problems in their relationship, there was little chance the marriage could endure. The volatile Morante often behaved aggressively toward her husband— berating him in public, humiliating him, erupting in fury at random moments. Moravia was cool and detached, as emotionally available as a rock—and his indifference and mild manner only drove his wife to further rage. She was also known to treat women with something like contempt, leading some friends to regard her as a misogynist. (Friendship did not dissuade her from unfiltered remarks: Morante once invited her editor, the esteemed novelist Natalia Ginzburg, out to dinner, only to inform Ginzburg that her new play was "fatuous, silly, sugary, affected and false.") With her turbulent emotional life, it is true that Morante could be spiteful and difficult, especially with those closest to her. Still, Moravia was fascinated by what he described as "an extreme, heart-rending, passionate quality in her character." His admiration for her work never wavered. Morante admired her husband as a writer too, but hated being called "Mrs. Moravia" and refused to share works in progress with him. Their marriage ended after two decades (they never formally divorced), but they stayed friendly and kept in touch. The relationship fed them both in unexpected ways, and during her marriage Morante's reputation grew: she produced some of her most powerful (and bestselling) fiction, won major literary prizes, and ultimately established herself as one of Italy's most important postwar writers.

It is interesting that two lesbians, Una Troubridge and Radclyffe Hall, are the most conventional—and socially and politically conservative—couple in *Lives of the Wives*. With Troubridge inhabiting the role of submissive wife and Hall the controlling husband, they did not exactly defy patriarchal norms. Both were unapologetic snobs who held problematic and deplorable views, including antipathy to Jews and fascist sympathies. Both frowned upon political protests by vociferous women clamoring for equal rights. At the same time, Hall and Troubridge lived openly as a "married" couple, doing as they pleased, which was partly a function of their privilege and wealth. Troubridge had been a precocious child who aspired to become an artist. Married as a young woman to a naval officer twenty-five years her senior, she hated being a wife and resented her husband's stifling of her creative impulses. Yet when she left her husband for Hall, Troubridge accepted a subservient role with no trace of resentment or seething envy. It was an asymmetrical union from the start, with a division of labor that left Troubridge taking care of everything. She savored her gatekeeping power—controlling

Hall's schedule and correspondence, managing household staff, and protecting Hall from negative reviews, among other duties. Occasionally Troubridge took on translation work and pursued her own interests, but her wifely responsibilities always came first.

If Troubridge was underappreciated in her lifetime, decades after her death she was praised by reviewers on the website Goodreads, in response to a biography by Richard Ormrod: *"What a fascinating woman! She seemed to want to be remembered for being the friend of Radclyffe Hall but she so easily could have had her own career as a sculptor, artist, and translator. She had an amazingly generous spirit and a passionate, loving nature. . . . After reading about her I feel I would have loved to have known her myself!"* Another wrote, *"What an incredible woman Una Troubridge was!! She really should be better known and celebrated! Several times I became so angry with Radclyffe Hall I decided [to] stop liking her but then I thought: if Una thought she was worth all the trouble, she must have been! So John, you are forgiven!"* The "marriage" of Troubridge and Hall was not without a plenitude of heartbreak, yet each woman proved a lodestar for the other. Their relationship spanned nearly thirty years, until the death of Hall in 1943. After losing the love of her life, Troubridge served as fierce guardian of Hall's legacy. Of the five marriages chronicled in this book, their relationship is the only one that endured.

*Lives of the Wives* examines how the maddening tensions between creative life and domestic life were resolved (or not) within a marriage. These are stories of vulnerability, loneliness, infidelity, envy, sorrow, abandonment, heartbreak, and forgiveness. This book is not a project of adjudication, but in our #MeToo era, it is impossible not to challenge notions of power and silence in the context of writers' marriages. We can no longer indulge or swat away misconduct because the offender crafts beautiful sentences. We must continue to interrogate the use of virtuosic literary achievement to justify monstrous behavior. Self-aggrandizing men have always done whatever they wanted because they could. As Zadie Smith has written, "[T]he unusual thing about misogyny is the elaborate intellectual superstructure that has for so long supported and celebrated it, not as blind spot or as pernicious ideology but, on the contrary, as perfect vision."

Each marriage carries its own secrets, its particular rhythms and understandings, its unique version of complicity. ("A couple's private language can develop in peculiar ways that look ordinary to the couple," as Norman Rush once put it, "but very strange to any outsider.") Marriages are messy and inscrutable and shift over time. One is never just like another. As I began this project, I marveled at the complexity of these relationships and learned that no matter how wretched the marriage, both spouses stood to benefit from their arrangement.

In choosing which couples to write about, I wanted to avoid the living since their stories are still unfolding. (Diane Middlebrook, perhaps best known for her 1991 biography of Anne Sexton, had a decidedly unsentimental view of her deceased subjects: "The dead cannot be shamed.") With the exception of Una Troubridge (born in 1887), all the wives in this book were born in the first few decades of the twentieth century. I decided to steer clear of the all-star wifely roster, captivating and irresistible as they are. That meant no Zelda, no Véra, no Nora Barnacle, no Sofia Tolstoy. And I left out the women associated with some of the most notorious misogynists in literary history: Hemingway's four wives, Bellow's five, and Mailer's six.

The wives in this book are known to a greater or lesser extent, but in revisiting their stories through the lens of marriage, I hope they will be viewed with a fresh perspective, revealing new angles, nuances, and truths. When I think about what these fascinating women have in common, the word that comes to mind is *courage.*

Each story in *Lives of the Wives* explores how women have defined themselves through or in opposition to men, and each reveals the toll of the creative process—not only on writers, but on their partners and children. This is a book about money and fame and how those elements can unite a couple when love does not. It's about power and the negotiation of power. If, as Phyllis Rose argues in her seminal 1983 book *Parallel Lives*, each marriage is not just a narrative construct but rather two narrative constructs—and, in unhappy marriages, there are "two versions of reality rather than two people in conflict"—how is a partnership sustained or harmed by the fictions we tell ourselves? What happens when fissures appear? How does a wife stay tethered to a spouse with a monomaniacal devotion to work? Does the ability to compartmentalize protect a marriage or destroy it? Why does there exist, in many literary couples, an unspoken noncompete clause for the wives? Why do women often end up as peripheral characters in biographies of dazzling men— diminished, traduced, silenced by history? How does a woman achieve self-worth when her husband proclaims himself the more valuable partner? If, as Rose writes, "living is an act of creativity," is the mastery of domestic multitasking, pushed to the extreme, itself a form of genius?

In the fall of 2020, as I walked past a storefront in downtown Manhattan, I had to glance twice at the sign to see that I had transposed the letters and misread it. Above what appeared to be a martial arts supply store was the sign BOWERY MARITAL ARTS SUPPLIES. If only such a shop existed. Marriage, at least in *Lives of the Wives*, is a kind of combat, and wives must be well equipped for battle.

# UNA TROUBRIDGE
## and Radclyffe Hall

"All I knew or cared about was that I could not, once having come to know her, imagine life without her."

The year was 1912. When Una Troubridge met the writer Radclyffe Hall at a summer reception in London, neither left a lasting impression on the other. Three years later, on the first day of August, they met again at a tea party—this time, a fateful encounter. It was love at second sight.

Twenty-eight-year-old Una had been in a rut, feeling "deeply depressed and intensely lonely." She found the dashing thirty-four-year-old woman with the silver-blond hair, intense gaze, and raffish smile "very good indeed to look upon." Her eyes were "a clear grey blue, beautifully set and with a curiously fierce, noble expression. . . . [I]t was not the countenance of a young woman but of a very handsome young man." Her hands "were not feminine hands," and were "quite beautiful." Wearing a bespoke white suit, Hall stood with a miniature fox terrier in her arms. "Her appearance was calculated to arouse interest," Una noted. "It immediately aroused mine."

Una was married to a high-ranking naval officer and had a five-year-old daughter, Andrea Theodosia, nicknamed Cubby. Hall, who had always said she felt like a man trapped in a woman's body, was known as John. Through a substantial inheritance, John was independently wealthy, and since 1907 had been in a relationship—"Head and heart and soul in love"—with Mabel Batten, more than two decades her senior and known as Ladye: witty, beautiful, married to a man, and already a grandmother. Ladye also happened to be Una's cousin, once removed, through Una's mother. It was Ladye who had affectionately christened her lover with the name John, whom she sometimes called Jonathan. A prominent arts patron, society hostess, and amateur singer of lieder, Ladye claimed Edward VII as a former lover, and he was godfather to one of her grandchildren. In 1897, John Singer Sargent painted her portrait, which is in the collection of the Metropolitan Museum of Art. The accompanying commentary on the painting notes that after first hearing her sing, Sargent "convinced Batten to pose, recording her carried away in the ecstasy of her song, head thrown back, lips parted wide, bosom thrust forward."

Following the 1910 death of Ladye's husband, George Batten, secretary to the Viceroy of India, Ladye and John moved into a flat at Cadogan Square, where Ladye had exacting standards and once fired a servant for an unkempt appearance. She slept with two hot-water bottles, even in summer, and insisted on fresh flowers daily. John adored Ladye and loved to spoil her. As a housewarming gift, she gave Ladye a Yorkshire terrier, Claude, and adopted a French bulldog soon after. (John already had a collie and a parakeet.) That year, John's third collection of verse was published, dedicated to "Mrs. George Batten." Ladye took pride in supporting John's work by copyediting manuscripts and correcting John's terrible spelling. The couple became active with the Red Cross during World War I, attending lectures, learning first aid, and supporting the war effort in other ways. Ladye, who suffered from hypochondria as well as actual ailments such as a weak heart, revised her will to provide for John. Theirs was an eternal love. What could go wrong?

Five years later, Ladye's young cousin was the interloper, and Ladye sensed the pesky problem could not be eliminated anytime soon. Much to her displeasure, Una began visiting John with alarming frequency: stopping by for tea, staying for lunch, lingering for dinner, and sometimes staying the night. Una gave John some of her sketches, and in return, John read aloud a story she had written. They enjoyed wide-ranging conversations on art, books, religion, and more. Una was not oblivious to her cousin's increasing frostiness, but later admitted having "as much consideration for her or for anyone else as a child of six." She was smitten. There was no chance of retreat.

John was thrilled by the pursuit of new sexual conquests, and she had a thing for married women. Handsome in the tailored men's suits she favored, she owned nearly a hundred neckties and smoked dozens of Dunhill cigarettes a day. Una was fascinated by John, "a mass of sharp corners, prejudices and preconceptions," finding her irresistible on every level. Their relationship was, strictly speaking, platonic, but wouldn't remain so for long: within a few months, Una and John became lovers and made little effort to hide the affair.

Until their meeting, Una later recalled, John's devotion to Ladye had "burned with a steady light. . . . [H]er fancy did stray once, it is true, but it was a trivial, passing lapse, broke no bones and left no aftermath. It is hardly worth recording, Ladye dismissed the incident with a tolerant smile, and no one but John, scourging herself for infidelity, gave it any great importance." That Una would dismiss an act of betrayal so blithely says everything about her uncritical dedication to John. The reality was messier and more painful: John had thrown herself into a full-blown affair with a married woman, leaving Ladye depressed and suffering from insomnia. Initially, John had no interest in Una beyond a casual diversion. As someone who savored and even demanded freedom in her relationships, John issued a blunt warning to her new mistress: "How do I know if I shall care for you in six months' time?" Una paid no heed, refusing to be dismissed as another fling. Her persistence would pay off.

BORN IN LONDON ON MARCH 8, 1887, THE YEAR QUEEN VICTORIA CEL-ebrated her Golden Jubilee, Una was christened Margot Elena Gertrude Taylor. Just as her cousin Mabel had been given the pet name "Ladye," her family nicknamed her "Una," the feminine form of the Italian *uno*, and the Latin *unus*. She was indeed singular. After dropping her given name in favor of the more exotic-sounding Una, she added a new middle name, Vincenzo, borrowed from Florentine relatives. ("Una Vincenzo Taylor" seemed suitably dramatic and imposing.) Una was close to her elder sister, Viola, who was her confidante and best friend.

Although Una's Oxford-educated father, Harry Taylor, was part of a distinguished social set that included Edward Burne-Jones and Rudyard

Kipling—Kipling's daughter Josephine was Una's playmate—Harry's income as a civil servant was modest. The family lived first in Kensington and later in Knightsbridge. When Harry died of tuberculosis in 1907 at the age of fifty-two, just a few days before Una's twentieth birthday, he left behind considerable debt and an estate valued at less than seven hundred pounds. Una's mother, Minna, came from an upper-class Irish family and found the lack of money shameful.

Una had been extremely attached to her father, and his death left her heartbroken. It was Harry who ensured that his daughters grew up in a cultured home, where the arts were valued, and encouraged their intellectual development, bibliomania, and love of music. (As a teenager, he aspired to become a professional pianist, but his father forced him to join the army instead.) Harry also instilled in his children a great lifelong affection for animals. Una's many childhood pets included a tortoise, a mouse, a hedgehog, and a brown owl named Merlin who was permitted to fly around the house.

Even at the age of three, Una's aptitude for drawing and painting was evident, and she produced a remarkable watercolor depiction of Adam and Eve. When Una was seven, Harry arranged art lessons for her at the Victoria & Albert Museum. He took his daughter to her first "grown-up" play when she was eleven. A few years later, Una saw her idol, Sarah Bernhardt, perform at His Majesty's Theatre in London, and returned to watch her performance many times, often bringing a sketchbook. When Una had the chance to meet Bernhardt and give the actress some of the drawings she had made of her, Bernhardt was kind and thanked her with a kiss.

At home, Una and Viola liked staging performances for family and friends. (Una was a bit of a show-off and enjoyed attention from adults.) She took dancing, singing, and piano lessons. She was fluent in French, having been left largely to be cared for by nannies—first a Frenchwoman and then a Belgian governess. Confident and competitive, Una was regarded as a prodigy with a promising future. She felt destined to become an artist, maybe a great one. No one could have guessed that this formidably bright girl would later cede the spotlight to the great love of her life and embrace a supporting role instead.

She enjoyed experimenting with androgynous sartorial choices, dressing up in boys' flannel shirts and suits and wearing patent leather Oxford shoes. That it upset her mother only pleased her more. Una admired Napoléon Bonaparte (her "number one" historical god, she said), devoured biographies, and decorated her room with portraits of him. She went through a French Revolutionary clothing phase, once appearing in an outfit that "gave realism to the illusion that I had been born 150 years earlier, of varying and uncertain sex but naturally of high degree and had with other fortunate ones of my rank managed to escape the guillotine."

In 1900, at the age of thirteen, Una decided to complete the difficult entrance examination for the Royal College of Art. Her application was accepted, and she was the youngest art student in the program by far. She worked on life studies, made bookplates for friends, and created a series of illustrations inspired by *Jane Eyre*, and her statuette of the prima ballerina Adeline Genée was shown in an exhibition. By the age of sixteen, Una enjoyed some financial independence after receiving commissions for her work. "Later on when you are famous I shall say the 'creation' was given me years ago when the artist was 'quite a girl,'" wrote one of her first "clients."

In 1907, bereft after losing her adored father, Una fell into a relationship with a paternal substitute: Ernest Troubridge, a forty-five-year-old white-haired Royal Navy captain and widower with three teenage children. Una had met him several times through a family friend. Known as "the handsomest man" in the British navy, Ernest was nicknamed "the Silver King." To his young bride, he must have seemed a solid and comforting presence, someone who made her feel safe. He came from a distinguished naval family and would serve as private secretary to Winston Churchill. "Zip," as she called Ernest, was a cultured man, interested in opera and art, and he loved singing and playing the banjo.

In the fall of 1908, the couple married at the British Consulate in Venice. Una was twenty-one. On her marriage certificate, she listed her "rank or profession" as "sculptor."

From the start, she felt no physical desire for her husband. (Una had never experienced a strong attraction to the opposite sex.) Once, while vacationing in Italy with Viola, she reported in a letter that she enjoyed plunging into the sea "just like a man," and added that, despite all the handsome men on the beach, she was uninterested—"Wch was sad as I might otherwise have had a better time."

Una tried to be a good wife, but her efforts were half-hearted and unsustainable. Nor could she forsake her artistic leanings, much to the frustration of her disapproving husband. The marital tension was heightened by Ernest's children, who disliked her, and by Ernest's sisters, who adored their brother and shunned Una.

Settling in London with Ernest in the fall of 1909, Una began taking daily singing lessons, visiting art museums, and working on her drawings and sculptures. She started exhibiting again and was registered as a sculptor in the *Dictionary of British Artists*. These independent activities rankled the rigid and controlling Ernest, who expected Una to submit more readily to her domestic chores—especially after she became a mother in November 1910, following a near-fatal ectopic pregnancy the previous year. He didn't mind his wife taking up "hobbies," harmless activities to pass the time, but serious intellectual pursuits were not appropriate. His interests should be hers. She must redirect her attention. "I have never really wished you to work at anything that would occupy you away from me," he wrote in a stern letter to his wife. "I would much rather you were not engrossed in anything else."

Una found motherhood overwhelming. She fell into a postpartum depression, realizing that as much as she wanted to bond with Cubby, "there was nothing in her whole make-up that was not alien to mine." Her sadness was accompanied by frequent headaches, insomnia, anxiety, and nausea. She felt unable to take part in her husband's interests, much less satisfy his demands for sex. Among the bright spots in her dreary life were invitations to high-status events such as the coronation of King George V and Queen Mary at Westminster Abbey. Being the wife of an important man had a few benefits, at least.

She began seeing a specialist in nervous disorders, Dr. Hugh Crichton-Miller, and undergoing psychoanalysis (which had recently become fashionable) and hypnosis. His fees were exorbitant. She threw herself into treatment for her "nerves," never talking openly about her conflicted sexuality, and remaining hopeful that her marriage would improve. She dedicated herself to "working" on the relationship as one might commit to a weight-loss regimen—all brute determination to succeed. Apart from small pleasures like going to the opera, therapy became her full-time preoccupation, and she received treatment almost daily. Meanwhile, Ernest rose in rank to become Rear Admiral Troubridge, Commander of the 1st Cruiser Squadron, aboard the Mediterranean Flagship HMS *Defence*. With his squadron based in Malta, he expected Una to join him. The thought of it left her depressed, and one night she wrote in her diary: "Tried to leave England tonight, no go—saw [Dr. Crichton-]Miller." As someone who had converted to Catholicism as a teenager, she must have believed that persevering in her marriage was the right thing to do. Years later, she revealed in a letter: "I should not have been sidetracked into marrying at all." And more than two decades after her marriage, Una wrote in her diary, "Having chosen for my husband a man old enough to be my father I set to work to try to look his age." Indeed, she dressed and looked much older than she was, a means of deflecting, rather than attracting, his attention. As Una struggled, Ladye became her cousin's confidante. (Una's sister, Viola, had marital troubles of her own to deal with.) Ladye told Una more than once that she was to blame for her marital problems, because "you yourself accustomed him, when you first married, to having no occupation but him."

Going back and forth between Malta and London, Una always felt liberated at home in England, enjoying the temporary respite from her husband. When he summoned her again to Malta in the spring of 1913, nothing about the experience gave her pleasure, including having tea with the Churchills and the Asquiths. Taking care of Cubby remained exhausting and burdensome, too. Among Una's rather unorthodox habits as a mother was to dry Cubby after a bath by hanging her out the window in a muslin bag.

Una hated her wifely duties: hosting dinner parties, attending formal events with Ernest, and having luncheons with naval wives who bored her. These social obligations felt oppressive, and none relieved her loneliness. Once again, she suffered headaches and fatigue. That summer, during a family holiday in Norfolk, she claimed time for herself by sculpting again, but the selfish pleasure was short-lived. In the fall, when Ernest returned to Malta, Una came too. Apart from doing some French translation work and studying Italian, her time was taken up with motherhood and household duties, and she was very unhappy.

In 1914, at the outbreak of the war, Ernest made a major tactical blunder on a critical mission. In pursuit of German battleships, he intended to intercept them before they could reach the open sea—but conflicting instructions from his superiors, along with poor weather, caused Ernest to let the Germans pass freely from Messina to the Dardanelles. He was recalled to England and court-martialed, and the humiliating event made front-page news. Una was sympathetic to her husband's travails but preoccupied with her own problems. She was pleased to end the year on a happy note: the bust she sculpted of Nijinsky—as the Faun in the one-act ballet he'd choreographed, *Prélude à l'après-midi d'un faune*, performed by Sergei Diaghilev's Ballets Russes—was included in a major international exhibition in Venice. (The bust is now part of the permanent collection of the V&A Museum.)

As for Ernest, despite having been exonerated by the tribunal, the damage was done. He was left in limbo with nothing to do. Even after he was named Head of the British Naval Mission to Serbia in May 1915, his pride was injured——it was an administrative post with little promise. The thrill of sea command was gone.

Alone in London with Cubby, Una kept busy with volunteer work, raising money for a hospital for British soldiers in Belgrade. She was due to join her husband in September but dreaded the thought of it. Her usual activities helped her cope: sculpting, singing, reading, getting together with friends. In her diary, Una acknowledged that her marriage had been a failed "altruistic effort." (One day, on impulse, she shook up her ennui with a drastic change, chopping off her long, flowing hair into a severe pageboy cut.) On July 30, Una received a letter from the Admiralty with her upcoming travel schedule to Serbia. The future seemed grim. Then came the tea party that would transform her life—save it, perhaps.

On August 1, 1915, Una accepted an invitation from her cousin Emmy Clarendon, Ladye's sister, to an afternoon tea party in Cambridge Square. Una met John again, and this time she paid attention. The meeting sparked a coup de foudre that would redirect the course of their lives. From that day onward, they were rarely apart, and when they were not together, John felt grumpy and tense. Ladye was made to feel like a nuisance while John and Una were thrilled to discover they had much in common: sharp, wide-ranging intellects; devout Catholicism (John, baptized a Protestant, had converted at Ladye's urging); a variety of health issues, with ailments both real and psychosomatic; a passion for shopping and travel; cold, distant mothers; fathers who had gone to Oxford and died at fifty-two; eminent grandfathers; a great love of dogs; an appreciation of finely made clothing, as well as capes and tricorn hats; a belief in drinking in moderation; and an unabashed tendency toward snobbery, with a disdain for the working class. Nor were these two seemingly radical lesbians in favor of sexual freedom. Once, having spotted an article advocating sexual liberation, a disgusted Una burned the magazine before her servants could see it. As she wrote years later: "We desire order and fidelity and the privilege of a religious and legal bond."

John was a staunch monarchist, a defender of tradition, and politically conservative to her core. Protective of her investment income, she despised the Labour Party, with its insistence on "sacrifices" and higher taxes. Her greatest allegiance was to her class. (She had more than a few things in common with Virginia Woolf's lover, Vita Sackville-West, an aristocrat who enjoyed cross-dressing, gave herself the nickname Julian when passing as a man, and never bothered challenging the political positions of the upper class.) Although John supported the right of women to vote, she had to draw the line somewhere. She was moved by social injustices—to a point—but some women took things too far. John found acts of civil disobedience threatening to societal order. Following violent demonstrations in 1912, which coincided with a miners' strike, she wrote an indignant, anonymous letter to the editor of the *Pall Mall Gazette*:

> Sir—Have the Suffragettes no spark of patriotism left, that they can spread revolt and hamper the Government in this moment of grave national danger? According to Mrs Pankhurst, they are resorting to the methods of the miners! Since when have English ladies regulated their conduct by that of the working classes?

Even as she believed in the right to live openly with a female partner, John aligned herself primarily with men and in some ways favored them. She identified as a "congenital invert," having been influenced by the pseudoscientific theories of prominent sexologists such as Havelock Ellis, whose works included an early medical textbook on homosexuality published in 1897, and the German psychiatrist Richard von Krafft-Ebing, known for his 1886 work *Psychopathia Sexualis*. (He characterized female sexual inversion as "the masculine soul, heaving in the female bosom.") John offered herself as "godfather" to the second child of Ladye's daughter, Cara, but only if the baby was a boy. She often said that she possessed a "male" mind, and she supported a patriarchal society in which women abstained from ambitions of their own. "To be a good wife and mother is the finest work a woman can do," she once told an interviewer. She very much saw herself as a husband, first to Ladye and then to Una. "John told me she expected me to housekeep in future and she seemed awfully angry about nothing, which upset me," Ladye recorded in a 1913 diary entry, feeling like a wife who did not measure up.

In September 1915, just as she was meant to be meeting Ernest in Belgrade, Una moved alone into a flat in Mayfair. Attached to the flat was a studio, where she had the freedom and privacy for drawing and sculpting. She set to work at once on an etching of John. "All I knew or cared about was that I could not, once having come to know her, imagine life without her," Una later wrote. John began dropping by regularly, Una accompanied John to church, and the gift exchanges continued—small acts to claim possession of the beloved. John gave Una the pet name "Squiggie." Slowly but surely, the admiral's wife was being seduced. An aggrieved Ladye kept an obsessive record of the couple's meetings, even noting the shop on Kings Road where John had Una's works framed. In one entry, the ever-vigilant Ladye reported that "[Una] started a statuette of John." Her insecurity descended into paranoia.

Things would soon get worse, as Una managed to invite herself and Cubby along on John and Ladye's holiday in Cornwall. Almost immediately, Ladye was tossed aside, left behind at the hotel with Cubby and her nanny while John and Una strolled along the beach. "[D]ay by day I fell more completely under the spell of her enthralling personality," Una recalled later. Feeling very much like a third wheel, Ladye attempted a brave face amid the growing intimacy between John and Una. "Had two frightening dreams," Ladye wrote in her diary. "One that my eyes were being burnt—and the other that J was drowning on a river bank, whilst I was running to the bank shouting. . . . Una photographed us."

John bought a bulldog pup for Una, and the two "friends" took long walks in Hyde Park. John still made half-hearted attempts to keep up relations with Ladye, taking her out to lunch at the Ritz for her fifty-ninth birthday. But around that time, with expenses rising because of the war, John decided to downsize by selling her Cadogan Square flat, as well as White Cottage, a home she owned in Malvern Wells, Worcestershire. She and Ladye moved into a hotel suite, not far from Ladye's daughter. On November 29, 1915, John traveled down to her cottage to take inventory and remove the belongings she needed. Una came too, leaving Ladye feeling "done up, sad and rotten." After John and Una arrived at White Cottage in the afternoon, they had sex for the first time. "I can shut my eyes now & recall the luncheon she had prepared for me—& trying to eat while I summoned my resolution to leave immediately," Una wrote years later, the memory still vivid in her mind.

She started seeing John and Ladye for lunch every day. Sometimes she also had breakfast with John alone, after John had spent the night with her. In the ongoing power struggle with Ladye, Una did not mean to be cruel but felt unable to control herself—she was greedy for John's attention. "I was swept along on a spate of feeling," she explained later. Yes, she was stealing another woman's wife, but with good reason: she had to have her. Una's love for John was ferocious. Time would not diminish it.

Even in the blissful early days of their relationship, however, Una could not help noticing an "intolerance" in John, a "violent" temper that was "so quickly spent, and her penitence if she thought she had given pain, so extreme." Ladye too had endured more than her fair share of John's dark side. "I find Jonathan delightful to be with," she once wrote in a letter to Cara. "Of course, her temper is hotter than Tabasco and she is very impulsive—but what does that matter?"

John's temper was indeed violent and handed down from both her parents. Marguerite Antonia Radclyffe-Hall was born on August 12, 1880, in Bournemouth, England. Just weeks after her birth, her sister, Florence, older by a year, died of mysterious convulsions, and her parents were in no state to care for this new infant. Her mother, an American woman named Mary—who later called herself Marie and had been married once before—was left a single mother when her philandering, physically abusive husband, Radclyffe Radclyffe-Hall (aptly known as Rat), abandoned the family. His daughter would inherit her father's love of dogs, his knack for infidelity, and his fits of rage. Marie and Rat divorced a few years later.

John despised her vain, selfish, neglectful mother, who made sure her maternal rejection was keenly felt. As a young girl, she angered Marie after shedding the name "Marguerite" and asking to be called Peter by her friends. Like her former husband, Marie had a frightening temper and bullied and beat her daughter. Bruised both emotionally and physically, John would later describe her mother as "brainless . . . a terribly crafty and cruel fool, for whom life had early become a mirror in which she saw only her own reflection."

John was a shy, sensitive, and lonely child. She sought refuge with her protective grandmother, a beloved nanny, household servants who supplied her with affection, and her first pet, a pug named Joey. As for Rat, John saw him less than a dozen times over the years, with a final meeting occurring shortly before his death in 1898 of pulmonary tuberculosis.

Marie would marry a third time, moving the family from provincial Bournemouth to London, where she fell in love with her Italian voice teacher, Alberto Visetti, who taught at the Royal College of Music. At the age of nine, John was forced to live with her neglectful mother and newly acquired stepfather, settling in Earl's Court. (Like his predecessor, Rat, Alberto enjoyed cheating on his wife at every opportunity.) Alberto had no interest in bonding with his wife's daughter. He ignored her aptitude for music, and worse, dipped into her trust fund to satisfy his own lavish tastes.

By the time John was an adolescent, Marie suspected that her daughter was not "normal," and that she harbored deviant desires. Meanwhile, Marie was blind, willfully or not, to Alberto's sexual abuse of John. It is unclear how long it went on, but apparently John suffered at least one violent encounter. (Decades later, a few years after John's death, Una confessed in her diary to having removed dozens of pages from the biography/hagiography she was writing of her beloved: "I have deleted the sexual incident with the egregious Visetti lest we have psycho-analytic know-alls saying you [John] would have been a wife and mother but for the experience.")

For any number of reasons, John could not escape home soon enough. At the age of twenty-one, she came into a large inheritance from her grandfather, and money meant freedom. She would never have to work a day in her life, nor did she intend to. She bought expensive clothing, wrote poems whenever the mood struck, traveled when she felt the urge, played the piano, cultivated a passion for riding and hunting, and smoked and smoked. In 1906, she bought her cottage in Malvern Wells. She also paid for the publication of her first volume of poetry, *'Twixt Earth and Stars*, which included lines hinting at forbidden love: "A little sigh, and—was it wrong? / A kiss, both passionate and long." The collection received a few favorable, if minor reviews, and was later set to music. Although the positive reception was enough to encourage John as a writer, it did not motivate her to commit to a writing routine. She could afford to do nothing.

After John met and fell in love with Ladye, she published her second book, *A Sheaf of Verses*, in 1908. (These poems referred obliquely to homosexual love.) She published three more volumes of poetry over the next seven years, including *The Forgotten Island* in 1915. There was no indication of the novels to come, but she tried her hand at short stories (all destroyed by Una after John's death). She received encouraging words about her stories from William Heinemann, who became her publisher, but he urged her to write a novel instead. Although John hoped to justify his faith in her, he died in 1920, four years before her first novel was published.

Slowly, as she applied herself to her work, John gained confidence as a writer. She was on the verge of a bona fide literary career, and Una, not Ladye, would help her achieve it.

Soon after falling in love with John, Una knew the trajectory her life must take: to remain with her beloved until one of them died. Of course, Ladye was a major problem to contend with—but not, in Una's mind, an insurmountable one. Other obstacles, such as Una's daughter, were treated as inconveniences. To be fair, whenever her child experienced a health crisis, Una rushed to her side. Yet Cubby was often left with friends, relatives, nannies, and neighbors, and at one point, Una even asked Dr. Crichton-Miller whether Cubby could live with his family. (He declined.)

Once John and Una became a couple, John spent generously on Cubby and could be tender toward her—teaching the girl how to ride a bicycle, buying her gifts, playing games with her, and paying her school fees. More often, John played the role of stern, distant stepfather, ignoring or resenting the girl's presence. (She tried getting Cubby to address her as "Uncle John," with no luck.) Sometimes John's black moods could be set off by something as mundane as the clutter of Cubby's toys around the house. She did not want the girl around. Una, ever eager to please John, decided to ship off her nine-year-old daughter to a boarding school in Sussex. Later Cubby went on to study at Oxford, but Una was appalled when she left without a degree. The mother-daughter relationship continued to deteriorate over time. Cubby would become an actress, marry twice, and die in a car crash in 1966.

With Ladye very much still in the picture, for Christmas 1915 John gave a platinum ring to Una. It was engraved with both their names, a sign of commitment, and Una was ecstatic. She was also happy to have her days free to work in her studio, getting closer to the bohemian life of the artist she had always craved. She spent New Year's Eve dining with John and Ladye at their hotel—surely not the New Year's Eve Ladye had envisioned. That night, Ladye wrote in her diary that she was feeling "depressed and very sad."

The situation was distressing for all. As the friction grew between John and Ladye, even Ladye's presence could set John off. ("Atmosphere sad beyond words," Ladye wrote one night.) After she and John bought a new flat at Cadogan Court, near Sloane Square, Ladye considered leaving John. "Thought seriously of going to live by myself," she confessed in another diary entry. John wanted to break free too. That spring, Ladye experienced debilitating health issues: bouts of blurred vision, chest pains, high blood pressure, and difficulty breathing.

One night, John returned home late after a brief getaway with Una. She had a nasty row with Ladye, who had been ill that day and felt abandoned by John. After retreating to her bedroom in distress, Ladye suffered a seizure and fell unconscious. Una rushed over that night with a doctor, but there was nothing to be done. Ladye had suffered a cerebral hemorrhage. Ten days later, on May 25, 1916, she was dead.

Where did this leave Una? Still competing for John's affections, but now with a dead woman. The old love triangle was stronger than ever, yet the roles had been reconfigured: John in pursuit of Ladye, Una in pursuit of John, and Una's dead cousin the obstruction between them. This turn of events was, in every way, unexpected: rather than run joyfully into the arms of her lover, John wanted to be alone. Her grief was profound. In the ten-day period that Ladye had rallied by emerging from her coma—though she lay in bed, paralyzed on one side of her body and barely able to speak—John was desperate for Ladye to recover and felt hopeful that she would. She wanted to declare her love for Ladye once more, and prove her devotion, so all would be well again. But Ladye was dead. There would be no forgiveness, no relief for John. Tormented by guilt, convinced that her selfish behavior was to blame for Ladye's death, she contemplated suicide. Una did not attend Ladye's funeral.

John paid for a grand memorial, with a requiem mass at Westminster Cathedral and a large catacomb chamber in Highgate Cemetery. (She also reserved a space there for herself and for Ladye's daughter, Cara.) John had Ladye's corpse embalmed, with a silver crucifix blessed by the Pope laid upon it. She said that losing Ladye meant losing "the shield between myself and the world." But no matter what she did or said as penance, her attempts to make things right failed to move Cara. "Because she has gone, I am no longer all myself," John wrote to her. "How can I ever hope to be happy again. . . . The only thing I do see is that I must never fail her. From now on no interest shall ever lower her memory for me." She confessed an overwhelming guilt at the thought that "any peevish words of mine" were the cause of Ladye's death. "I shall never forgive myself that I allowed her to be annoyed over Una's constant presence," she wrote. (Ladye had been humiliated and brokenhearted, not "annoyed.")

Una tried getting closer to John in this time of grief, but John was cold and distant. Knowing that John resented her for being allowed to "trespass" in John's relationship with Ladye—"Thereby marring the happiness of Ladye's last months on earth"—Una burned her diaries from the years 1915 and 1916, destroying whatever damning disclosures may have been recorded. For her, Ladye's death was a different kind of tragedy: it made "an almost total shipwreck" of her relationship with John. They had plotted their union for so long, and Ladye had to ruin everything by dying. Una's sole concern was to regain her lover's affection. Given John's maudlin displays of grief, it would be no easy task. Unreachable in her sorrow, John kept pushing her away, and Una admitted that "we frayed each other's nerves." A fervent believer in psychic phenomena, John announced one day that she wished to "find" Ladye by communicating telepathically through a medium. She was desperate for contact, to feel Ladye's presence beyond the clothing, jewelry, and other possessions she had kept. The thought of reconnecting with Ladye filled her with hope, and if nothing else, this all-consuming endeavor would be a welcome distraction. Una had no choice but to feign support and accompany John on what was to be a strange and even scandalous journey.

Through the Society of Psychical Research (SPR), the couple found a medium named Gladys Leonard (the author of *My Life in Two Worlds*) to serve as their liaison to the dead. Notes were taken on the proceedings, and each meeting was transcribed. Soon they were seeing Gladys several times a week. Unsure of what she was getting into, John hired a private detective to verify that the psychic was getting her information honestly, and directly from Ladye, rather than from the public records office.

During the séance sessions, which served almost as couples' therapy sessions, Una was the dutiful secretary, taking copious notes and suppressing her impatience as "Ladye" spoke to them through the writhing, possessed Gladys. It almost didn't matter whether Gladys was a fraud or an authentic conduit to the afterlife—she satisfied a yearning in John that had to be pursued. And the news from the dead was consoling: according to Gladys, Ladye was enjoying the afterlife immensely— horseback riding, gardening, and communing with Christ. The posthumous Ladye spoke often of her love for John and even her fondness for Una, insisting she had not suffered on the night she died. Of Heaven, she said: "You will love it when you come."

These sessions did not have the effect that Una hoped for. "J very depressed & in vile temper," she confided in her diary in 1917. "Not a nice evening and I cried much after I was left alone." Both lives were at a standstill: John wasn't writing much and Una had no time to devote herself to art. John had become, Una confessed, "the be-all and end-all of my life." She loved John and believed wholly in her genius. Although Una had essentially traded in one husband for another, self-sacrifice now seemed liberating rather than suffocating. She was happy to surrender her own creative aspirations to support John's career, but even so, she knew she had failed to live up to her early promise, and to others' expectations of her as an artist. In a posthumous tribute to her former mentor at the Royal College of Art, Una wrote: "He lived to see me throw overboard with such complete indifference the talent that he had nurtured and on which he had built such high hopes."

After the war ended in 1918, Ernest found out that Una and John had bought a house together, Chip Chase, in Hadley Wood, Middlesex— "Rather like the sort of castle that you would buy in Harrods' toy department," as Una described it. He threatened litigation, accusing John of being a home-wrecker and "a grossly immoral woman." This was dumb, useless rage. Legal action presented no threat. John did as she pleased and answered to no one. With abundant sums of money at her disposal, she could settle in comfortably for a prolonged court battle with Ernest, one that would prove ruinous for him. Plus, unwanted media attention was the last thing he needed. Embarrassing private matters would be exposed—for instance, Una's medical evidence that he had infected her with syphilis. He knew it was best to retreat quietly. Still, he managed to strike one vengeful blow with a revised will. He declared that in the event of Una's death, his daughter would "under no circumstances be left under the guardianship or care of Marguerite Radclyffe-Hall."

Further injury was still to come for Ernest. After he was knighted, the wife who abandoned him was nonetheless given a title: Una, Lady Troubridge. She intended to use it. Even the household servants were instructed to call her Lady Una. This should have come as no surprise, since both she and John had an imperious manner in the presence of staff, and for years dismissed a succession of worn-out maids, cooks, chauffeurs, gardeners, and butlers. ("John and I up after breakfast and had to turn out the cook for insolence and drinking all our brandy," Una recorded in one diary entry.) Theirs was a residence of high staff turnover and low morale.

Happily for Una, she and John were lovers again. She wrote an elliptical message in her diary ("J.s.I've m.L and I've m.y."): "John said I have married Ladye and I have married you." The couple's immersion in the paranormal had strengthened their partnership. Around this time too, they became friendly with the poet W. B. Yeats, who had a keen interest in psychic phenomena. "Yeats came and talked all evening till 11 o'clock about the *Psychic Telegraph*," Una noted in a journal entry, referring to the newspaper he hoped to publish with her, but it never came to fruition.

After Una and John wrote a research paper detailing their experiences contacting Ladye, John was invited to deliver a private lecture at the Society of Psychical Research. The event received such an enthusiastic response that in the summer of 1917, John was invited to speak again. She wore a man's suit jacket paired with a skirt and a cravat. Some SPR members were excited by the presence of a bold lesbian in their midst, while others found it off-putting that Una and John would "flaunt" their status as a couple in public. (How they committed this offense was unclear.) One audience member, St. George Lane Fox-Pitt, a friend of Ernest and a disgruntled SPR member, had shown up to cause trouble. Finding John's un-womanly appearance objectionable, as well as her ideas, he walked out of the lecture in disgust and reported back to Ernest, who was newly enraged at John for coming between him and his wife.

While Una's estranged husband had his own agenda—proving that John had a dangerous influence on Una, leading to the breakdown of their marriage—Fox-Pitt had issues of his own. Although the SPR had invited John to serve on its council, he complained, saying she was unfit to serve. Without being explicit, the meaning was clear enough. As he traduced John further—insulting the memory of Ladye, whom he deemed "most objectionable," and dismissing John and Una's investigations as scientifically unsound—John responded forcefully and would sue Fox-Pitt for slander in 1921. (She was elected to the council, and Fox-Pitt resigned.)

The litigation occurred just as John started taking herself seriously as a writer, showing more discipline and turning her attention to writing a novel, tentatively called *Octopi*. (Una would later retitle it *The Unlit Lamp*.) She had begun working on the manuscript at Chip Chase, where she and Una had also discovered a new obsession in the previous year or so: professional dog breeding. They were exceedingly good at it, setting up kennels and entering into competitions with their dachshunds, griffons, and more. (Una showed far more affection toward her dogs than she had ever given Cubby.) At the dog shows they attended, Una and John were hard to miss in their fedoras, capes, and boots. The formidable couple won trophies at nearly every show, quickly achieving fame and admiration at Crufts, the international dog show held annually in the United Kingdom. The always-competitive John savored the thrill of winning prizes, but with her troubling snobbery—and support for eugenics—there was a creepy aspect to being rewarded for raising genetically "perfect" canine champions.

In 1921, the couple sold Chip Chase, fired their servants, and gave up dog breeding because, as Una put it, "we could not bear to sell our produce and see them go off to an unknown future." But they still enjoyed attending dog shows and there would always be dogs in their lives—"An endless series, ranging from a Great Dane weighing some five stone to a Yorkshire terrier who turned the scales at one pound and three quarters," recalled Una, "and who taxed even my neat fingers by the necessity for collecting his head furnishings daily into five tiny plaits tied with silk." John was a fellow of the Royal Zoological Society, and it was not unusual for the couple to have "willingly toiled half across Europe burdened with cages of rescued victims," for Una to wander a French village "clasping to my breast a dove that [John] had spotted on the fourth floor of a slum house," or to show up at a seaside hotel "accompanied by two dachshunds and a canary." Years later, when Tulip, one of John's favorite dogs, died, she wept and wept, revealing a sentimental, vulnerable side that she rarely showed Una. One of their other dogs, Mitsou, seemed to pick up on John's sorrow and stayed faithfully by her side. Una wrote in her diary: "When I said to her, 'Mitsou, where's father?' she turned her head and gazed adoringly at John." Wherever John and Una called home, there were dogs, as well as parrots, cockatoos, and more.

After selling Chip Chase, John and Una moved into a rented flat in Knightsbridge, where Una supervised the new household staff, ensuring that everything ran smoothly so John could keep going on *Octopi*. Because daily structure had never been imposed on her by financial need, John had to cultivate discipline and now she treated writing more like a real job. (Her drive was such that she even asked the ghost of

Ladye not to disturb her during working hours.) Una had to leave John alone for the entire day, and sometimes the night—with some quiet resentment—but they always had breakfast and read the newspapers together. Being the traditional "man of the house," John took pride in not knowing how to do any chores, such as cooking or cleaning. As a friend once recalled of John: "It was her boast that she knew nothing about housekeeping. She must have regarded this as a sign of virility, because she so often referred to it. 'Couldn't boil an egg,' she would proclaim gruffly." In her darkest moods, John would lash out at Una for wifely incompetence ("we agreed the stew had been a failure & I wept in John's arms")—comparing her unfavorably with the flawless domestic skills of Ladye.

That summer, the couple traveled to Italy, where John could work, swim, and unwind by gambling. At their hotel at the end of each day, Una read aloud from each day's material, several times if needed, and commented on the work. John made corrections and revised. Occasionally during these recitations, John would lash out in anger if she felt Una wasn't truly giving it her all. "Having been asked whether I was tired and told that I was reading abominably, and sometimes informed that my ineptitude was ruining the beauty of what I read," Una later recalled, "the manuscript would be snatched from my hands and torn to shreds or thrown into the fire."

Back in London, John wrote in a beautiful ground-floor study with a woodburning fireplace. She smoked all day, both pipes and cigarettes, and wore a brocade smoking jacket. She was fastidious about the objects in her study, using only a gold-nibbed fountain pen or a pencil at her oak desk. A large crucifix hung on the wall, and in one corner was a shrine to Ladye. John's paper had to be white, on lined notepads made in Milan. (Blue paper was for letters.) She was even particular about her paper clips. Una was impressed at how John sometimes "wrestled vainly, hour after hour, against an inspirational blackout," but pushed through. With her support, John was able to complete not one, but two novels, in quick succession. Throughout, Una managed the editorial process: a draft would be sent to a typist, then returned to Una for review, and typically there were several rounds for a single chapter. It was never a smooth process. John was dyslexic, had never learned to type, and wrote illegibly. She struggled with spelling and tended to ignore punctuation. Yet Una knew how to manage John's ego, remain calm, and keep everything on track. The typist had no such support. "Radclyffe Hall was a perfectionist," recalled her typist at the time, Winifred Reed, "and she had a fiendish temper which was exacerbated by Lady T!"

First John completed *Octopi* (now *The Unlit Lamp*), which she dedicated to "Mabel Veronica Batten, in deep affection, gratitude and respect." The story follows Joan Ogden, a sensitive, lonely girl who yearns to leave her controlling, manipulative mother and life in a stultifying English seaside town. She develops a close relationship with Elizabeth, who is first her governess, then her "passionate friend." Joan dreams of getting a flat in London with her "friend" and living happily ever after, but things turn out rather grimly for her. With its suggestively lesbian subject matter, it was a tough book to sell, and ten publishers rejected it. John believed she was doing God's work in telling such a story, but John's literary agent, Audrey Heath, urged her to be pragmatic and publish something more lighthearted and marketable first.

In just six months, John wrote *Chains*, a comedic novel that Una painstakingly transcribed and corrected, then delivered by hand to Heath in June 1923. (Once again, Una changed a book title, this time to *The Forge*.) The agent's instincts were right, and the publisher J. W. Arrowsmith offered John a contract that fall. Dedicated "To Una, with love," *The Forge* was published on January 25, 1924. In celebration, the women went out on the town, going out to dinner and taking in shows on the West End. Both dressed flamboyantly, with John in diamond and onyx cuff links, a black sombrero, and a cape, and Una in a monocle and leopard-skin coat. Within a few months, the novel had already been reprinted and landed on the bestseller list. There is no question that John could not have achieved this success without Una, who privately admitted feeling worn down at times: "Long hours of my reading, perpetual assurances that what she was writing surpassed all that had preceded it," she wrote in her diary. Yet she was proud to play such a critical role in building John's career: "a life of watching, serving and subordinating everything in existence to the requirements of an overwhelming literary inspiration and industry." It was a privilege to serve a genius, after all.

On May 29, John decided to purchase a home at 37 Holland Street in the Holland Park neighborhood in Kensington. The author felt she deserved a grand house. Not only was *The Forge* a hit, but John had also completed her third novel a few days earlier. The Holland Street residence, where the couple would live for four years, was just one in a series of real estate purchases after the sale of Chip Chase—houses that John and Una would furnish beautifully, decorate, and eventually sell. Each one seemed perfect until it wasn't, and then it was time to move on. The women loved to flit from flat to flat.

In the summer of 1924, with renovations underway, John and Una took off for Paris and then Normandy. They received good news by telegram from Audrey Heath: Cassell & Co. had agreed to publish *The Unlit Lamp*, offering John an advance of fifty pounds, fifteen percent of royalties on the first three thousand copies sold, and twenty percent beyond that. When the novel came out in late September, the reviews were positive. John and Una were pleased that all the copies at Harrods sold out on the first day, and they loved seeing the giant ad display Cassell & Co. had paid for on the clock at St. Pancras station. With each new book, the couple established a ritual of having lunch together and then dashing through as many bookshops as they could, checking for prominent window displays, counting the number of copies in stock, and talking with booksellers.

In 1925, John published her third work of fiction, *A Saturday Life*, and a year later, *Adam's Breed*, which took its title from "Tomlinson," a Rudyard Kipling poem: "I am all o'er-sib to Adam's breed that ye should give me scorn." (Yet again, Una saved John from a bad title, *Food*, and came up with *Adam's Breed* instead.) By day, Una served as publicist, schmoozing on John's behalf at social events and sending out hundreds of promotional postcards. She mailed review copies to critics. To protect John's time, Una took care of her correspondence, answering all letters and requests, and coordinated her schedule. Una also tracked press coverage, good or bad, and wrote review summaries for John, always taking care to shield the author from vitriolic pieces. *Adam's Breed* became a bestseller, selling twenty-seven thousand copies and going into a fourth printing within the first few weeks. It was acclaimed by critics, translated into several languages, and won two literary prizes: the Prix Femina and the James Tait Black Prize. Only one other novel, E. M. Forster's *A Passage to India*, had won both. Samuel Goldwyn was set to adapt the novel into a film, though in the end the deal came to nothing. Una was delighted about the book's reception, noting proudly that at one dinner, "John was much lionised." Being well respected and commercially successful was a rare feat for any author. She was photographed out and about, looking handsome in her cape and bow tie. "Isn't it amusing that I should have become quite a well known writer?" John wrote in a letter to her cousin. "I sometimes cannot understand it myself."

In January 1926, Ernest died at the age of sixty-three. He had never recovered after being abandoned by Una—and for a woman, no less. His death was a relief to Una, leaving her a widow in name only and free to live as she pleased, without interference. Because she and Ernest never divorced, Una was entitled to a lifelong pension. She found the annual sum inadequate and successfully appealed to have it increased.

Una's life was now all about serving John, but she kept up with her own interests when she could find the time: writing book reviews and freelance articles, reading manuscripts for a literary agency, and working on the English translation of a French romance novel. Una also translated Colette's *La Maison de Claudine*, bringing the author's work to an English readership for the first time. (A French bulldog Una bought for

John was named Colette.) She began writing autobiographical sketches, too. "John wants me to do a book of them," she noted proudly in her diary. "J worked till after 2:30 and so did I!"

As John's literary career took off, she and Una had a whirlwind social life. They had tea at the Savoy, dinners at London's finest restaurants, attended theater openings, and drank and danced into the night. Their friendship with the American expatriate painter Romaine Brooks led them to other remarkable women, including the American writer Natalie Barney—witty, beautiful, and rich—renowned for the lively salons she hosted in Paris for lesbian painters, poets, and writers at 20 rue Jacob. Men were also permitted, and over the years, James Joyce, Ezra Pound, and Paul Valéry were guests. Barney, whom Brooks described as having "an unusual mind of the best quality," called Paris "the sapphic centre of the western world." Her relationship with Brooks spanned more than fifty years, but it was nonmonogamous. Alice B. Toklas once remarked that Barney was so seductive she could pick up lovers in department store powder rooms.

In 1924, Brooks had invited Una to sit for a portrait at her studio in Chelsea. The result was not flattering. Una is shown sporting a monocle and standing with two of her prized dachshunds, Thor and Wotan. Her hair is cropped short and she wears a cravat and a formal, tailored jacket. She appears headstrong and controlling, aristocratic, androgynous, frowning, and dour. ("Am I really like that?" Una wondered.) It took nine sitting sessions for Brooks to complete the portrait, and Una was unhappy with what struck her as a grotesque caricature. "Una is funny to paint," Brooks wrote in a letter to a friend. "Her getup is remarkable. She will . . . perhaps cause future generations to smile." John refused to purchase the painting, which is in the collection of the Smithsonian American Art Museum.

Other women John and Una met and spent time with included Rebecca West, Tallulah Bankhead, Djuna Barnes, and Isadora Duncan. It was an exciting time. The playwright Noël Coward became a good friend, later drawing on John's psychic dabbling for his 1945 play *Blithe Spirit*, while John would base a gay male character in *The Well of Loneliness* on Coward ("Stephen was never able to decide whether Jonathan Brockett attracted or repelled her"). Una was fond of the playwright, writing of him in her diary: "He is one of the only people I know who succeeds in being chronically and excruciatingly witty without victimising anyone."

The American writer and journalist Janet Flanner, Paris correspondent for the *New Yorker*, was also part of John and Una's social circle. In 1978, shortly before her death, she participated in a literary conference panel at Rutgers University. Afterward she was approached by the pioneering cultural anthropologist Esther Newton, who was thirty-eight at the time and excited to tell Flanner that she hoped to write a biography of Radclyffe Hall. "Didn't you know her?" Newton asked. "Oh, don't spend the effort on *her*," Flanner replied. "[She and Una] were so . . . conventional." Then, smiling, Flanner added: "She was always the perfect gentleman."

John may not have been such a perfect gentleman, actually, but she always looked the part, wearing her tailored suits, men's socks, and thick-soled shoes, and having her hair done at a gentlemen's hairdresser on Bond Street. Among her and Una's distinguished circle of friends was Sir John Gielgud, who would meet the eccentric couple at The Ivy occasionally, after which they would head to his flat for drinks: "John was usually in her black hat and black-and-white pinstripe coat and skirt with a black stock over a white shirt," he recalled, and Una with her monocle, bobbed hair, and starched shirt, and sometimes a dramatic hat. He described them as "both eye-catching personalities." Another acquaintance, Alec Waugh, elder brother of Evelyn, saw John and Una as "an austere Edwardian couple who expected conventional behaviour from their guests and hosts." He liked them both, but found John humorless and preferred Una.

A fellow guest at a cocktail party in London once recalled their power-couple appearance: "Radclyffe Hall wore a beautifully cut man's dinner jacket and shirt, a stiff shirt and bow tie. . . . Lady Troubridge wore the most glorious dress, and looked like a bride." One of the couple's former housekeepers remembered them as dressing for dinner, even at home, with John "quite stunning" in a "frilly shirt, man's suit . . . always very smartly dressed," while "Lady Troubridge wore evening dresses." Dining out with Una, John was a demanding customer who insisted that the waiters make her wife happy: "Lady Troubridge would like this" and "Lady Troubridge would like that." Especially now that John was a celebrated author, they were a happy couple enjoying their life together. After the breezy success of *Adam's Breed*, Una and John were not prepared for the scandal that would accompany *The Well of Loneliness* in the summer of 1928.

"I WOULD RATHER GIVE A HEALTHY BOY OR GIRL A PHIAL OF PRUSSIC acid than this novel," declared James Douglas, editor of London's *Sunday Express*, just weeks after *The Well* was published in Britain on July 27. Describing it as an "insidious perversion of the English novel," he dismissed it as an "outrage," "an unutterable putrefaction," and claimed it was "not fit to be sold by any bookseller or to be borrowed from any library." He demanded a ban of the novel "without delay." Somehow a mere work of fiction by an award-winning writer had bloomed into a public health crisis, and Douglas was sounding the alarm. He would launch a campaign to destroy it.

Lesbianism was not illegal in the UK, only immoral. Still, *The Well of Loneliness* had violated the Obscene Publications Act of 1857 and would be removed from circulation. The problem of the book was not sex—there was none. Nor does the word "lesbian" or "homosexual" appear in the book. The problem was merely the novel's *depiction* of same-sex desire. ("She kissed her full on the lips like a lover" is about the extent of it.) "In England hitherto the subject has not been treated frankly outside the regions of scientific text-books," read the jacket copy, "but that its social consequences qualify a broader and more general treatment is likely to be the opinion of thoughtful and cultured people."

John had turned to the works of Richard von Krafft-Ebing and Havelock Ellis, among others, in her research on inversion, and Ellis contributed a brief Commentary to the novel:

> [I]t is the first English novel which presents, in a completely faith-ful and uncompromising form, one particular aspect of sexual life as it exists among us to-day. The relation of certain people—who, while different from their fellow human beings, are sometimes of the highest character and the finest aptitudes—to the often hostile society in which they move, presents difficult and still unresolved problems.

In her Author's Note, John explained that the characters "are purely imaginary, and if the author in any instance has used names that may suggest a reference to living persons, she has done so inadvertently." This claim was false. The novel was a thinly disguised telling of her life story, with the female protagonist, Stephen Gordon, as her stand-in. Like John, Stephen is a novelist who comes from a wealthy family; hates being a girl ("Do you think that I *could* be a man, supposing I thought very hard—or prayed, Father?"); has a cold, distant mother; and adopts a masculine wardrobe, wearing suits, neckties, and men's shoes. Like John, Stephen feels like a man trapped in a woman's body. At twenty-one, Stephen falls in love with a bored married woman, Angela, and is eventually rejected for a man. Later, the tormented Stephen falls in love with another woman, Mary, but drives her into the arms of a man after deciding that Mary deserves a "normal" existence.

The author and Stanford University professor Terry Castle has pointed out how awkwardly Hall grapples with her heroine's identity. "Does being an invert mean wanting to be a man? Certainly Stephen seems to yearn—excruciatingly—for some kind of real or symbolic 'manhood.' How does this yearning relate to her equally powerful craving for the sexual love of other women? Is being an invert the same as being a lesbian?" Castle writes in the afterword to *Palatable Poison*, a collection of academic writings on *The Well*. "And what does it mean to 'want to be a man' anyway? To wish outright for a male body? Or merely for the social and psychic freedom to dress and behave mannishly?" Castle asserts that the author seems "painfully unsure about the precise relationship between body and desire, gender identity and sexual orientation." (At times, John seemed conflicted about gender roles in her own life: in 1925, the publisher Rupert Hart-Davis recalled that at dinner parties, "Johnny Hall . . . found it hard to make up her mind whether to go with the women or remain with the men.")

John had intended to call her novel *Stephen*, but Una came to the rescue again, changing the title to *The Well of Loneliness*, and it stuck. They worked intensively on the manuscript, with John cranking out chapters day and night, and Una making line edits and reading the chapters to Audrey Heath. The three women collaborated on how the story ought to proceed. Despite Heath's enthusiasm, no publisher would take it. Some said it was not "commercial" enough; others said they simply could not publish such a provocative book. One publisher, saying that he admired Radclyffe Hall, turned down the book because he feared it would ruin his list. Una tracked all the rejections in her diary.

In the spring of 1928, Jonathan Cape said he wanted to publish *The Well*. (Little did he know that in publishing it, he would be charged with violating the Obscene Publications Act, the same charge that sent Oscar Wilde to prison.) Over lunch with John, Una, and Heath, Cape offered an advance of five hundred pounds. He planned to issue a first edition of around a thousand copies, and to indicate the novel's highbrow intent with a plain, unadorned jacket and somber black binding with gilt lettering on the spine. Anticipating a backlash, Cape was willing to split legal costs with the author, but he would not cover them himself.

In the United States, Blanche Knopf, the wife of Alfred Knopf and president of the publishing company they'd cofounded, offered a contract with the stipulation that John would be liable for any litigation against the book. (Knopf later terminated the contract.) Una recorded in her diary that the offer was offensive and raised a "thousand alarms." John's attitude toward Blanche Knopf was weirdly sexist, as evident in a letter to her American agent, Carl Brandt. Noting that she liked Blanche personally, John complained: "I am accustomed to dealing with men in business, to going perfectly straight for a point. . . . I find it both difficult and tedious to deal with a woman and this I have several times told her quite frankly. . . . [I]t is better for women to keep out of business negotiations."

John and Una were happy about the deal with Cape, but John insisted that any changes or omissions to the manuscript would be considered a breach of contract. "I have put my pen at the service of some of the most persecuted and misunderstood people in the world," she wrote. "So far as I know nothing of the kind has ever been attempted before in fiction."

However grandiose this seemed, her hopes for the book were undeniably poignant: "[t]o encourage inverts to face up to a hostile world in their true colours, and this with dignity and courage" and to bring "normal men and women of good will to a fuller and more tolerant understanding of the inverted." She wanted to reach a large readership, well beyond "inverts" such as herself, hoping that readers would acknowledge the need to "cease tormenting and condemning their offspring and thus doing irreparable harm to the highly sensitized nervous system that is characteristic of inversion." John was ready to be vilified and welcomed the opportunity to serve as a martyr for the cause. She believed absolutely in her mission: "Hitherto the subject has either been treated as pornography, or introduced as an episode, or veiled. I have treated it as a fact of nature—a simple, though at present tragic fact."

Despite the expectation of controversy, John believed she would achieve financial and critical success. She bought new suits for herself, hats and fur coats for Una, and new uniforms for the household staff. Una ordered expensive furniture. John wanted to make a splash, much bigger than with *Adam's Breed*, and was prepared to invest in herself. She contributed her own money toward Cape's advertising budget, and promotional ads appeared in several major papers, including the *Times Literary Supplement* and the *Sunday Times*. She advocated on her own behalf in a letter to the editor of the *Observer*, James Garvin, who was a relative of Una's. Confessing that she had written *The Well* "from a sense of duty which I dared not disobey," she asked for his support so the novel would be received "in the proper spirit, the spirit of desire for impartial justice and understanding towards an unhappy and very important section of the community." Garvin did not reply, and no review appeared in the newspaper.

Apart from doing everything they could to get ready for the book launch, including going to mass to pray for success, John and Una could only wait. Una also kept busy with her own work, translating a French novel by Charles Pettit for Boni & Liveright. In the evenings, she read aloud to John from Oscar Wilde's *De Profundis* and *Ballad of Reading Gaol*.

Una's influence was such that at one point John had even asked for her spouse's blessing in going forward with *The Well*. She wrote: "[John] pointed out that in view of our union and of all the years we had shared a home, what affected her must also affect me and that I would be included in any condemnation. Therefore, she placed the decision in my hands and would write or refrain as I should decide." Una did not hesitate. As with everything, they were in this together: "I told her to write what was in her heart, that so far as any effect upon myself was concerned, I was sick to death of ambiguities, and only wished to be known for what I was and to dwell with her in the palace of truth." Publishing *The Well* would nearly wreck their lives, but Una stood by John, "shoulder to shoulder." Unfortunately, but not surprisingly, John received no support from her mother. "You can't touch filth without getting filthy," Marie told her.

*The Well of Loneliness* was released in an impressive year for fiction, including Virginia Woolf's virtuosic, gender-bending *Orlando*, *Decline and Fall* by Evelyn Waugh, and *Lady Chatterley's Lover* by D. H. Lawrence, which was banned in the UK, but privately printed in Italy by a Florentine bookseller. (It was published in abridged, censored form in the United States by Knopf, then banned a year later, with the author denounced by a Republican senator as "a man with a diseased mind.")

*The Well* got off to a fine start, with the first printing quickly selling out. The jacket copy addressed the subject matter delicately, describing the book as "a poignant and beautiful novel, telling the story of a woman, masculine by nature, who developed into maturity in accordance with that nature. It is a courageous treatment of a difficult psychological and social problem." In just one day, a library in London got more than five hundred queries about *The Well*. John and Una were inundated with congratulatory telegrams and flowers, and the couple set out early on publication day for their traditional sweep of local bookshops. Within weeks, Harrods and others were sold out of *The Well* and had already placed reorders. And as John and Una went around visiting bookstores, they were pleased to find the book prominently displayed. The *Daily Telegraph* hailed *The Well* as "truly remarkable . . . finely conceived and written," and the *Evening Standard* praised it as "honest, convincing, and extremely courageous." Vera Brittain, writing in *Time and Tide*, deemed the novel "very moving," describing it as "a plea, passionate yet admirably restrained, and never offensive, for the extension of social toleration, compassion, and recognition to the biologically abnormal woman."

Yet Janet Flanner found *The Well* "innocent and confused." Leonard Woolf dismissed it in his review as bombastic and "sincere." (John found his review "a really dastardly attack.") Virginia Woolf, in a letter to Lady Ottoline Morrell, remarked on "the dullness of the book . . . one simply can't keep one's eyes on the page." It was "stagnant and lukewarm and neither one thing nor the other." Nor could Woolf abide the purple prose. Still, she remained an ally in defending its publication. In the *New Statesman*, Cyril Connolly wrote that it was "a long, tedious, and absolutely humorless book." In the *Saturday Review*, L. P. Hartley could not conceal his revulsion: "Miss Radclyffe Hall calls her book a novel, but it is also a tract and an apologia . . . a study of abnormal relationships between women; Miss Radclyffe Hall insists on this throughout with the greatest frankness, and those to whom such a subject is abhorrent would do well to leave the book alone."

Whether its subject matter served as propaganda, as several critics claimed, or was merely provocative, *The Well* was an important book for its time. Yet John displayed none of the literary mastery and formal inventiveness of Virginia Woolf. The novel was shrill in parts, moralistic, melodramatic, sentimental, and rather formulaic in its narrative of love and loss, with dialogue teetering at the edge of romance fiction:

Stephen would ask her: "Do I content you? Tell me, is there anything you want in the world?"

Mary's answer was always the same; she would say very gravely: "Only you, Stephen."

The final lines are a plaintive cry for freedom: "Acknowledge us, oh God, before the whole world. Give us also the right to our existence!"

Whatever its shortcomings, and despite the unhappy ending, *The Well* spoke to outcasts of all kinds. It insisted that lesbian lives were worthy of recognition, and their stories deserved to be told. Patricia Highsmith's novel *The Price of Salt*, published pseudonymously in 1952, was the first to offer a positive portrayal of lesbian love, without being a doomed affair or ending in suicide. But for the era in which it was written, John's novel was a radical exploration of lesbian yearning and societal rejection. It was published in a summer of sweeping societal change for women: with the Equal Franchise Act of 1928, all British women over the age of twenty-one were able to vote, achieving the same rights as men at last. (Previously, this right was extended in 1918 only to women over thirty who met minimum property qualifications.) *The Well* was not great literature, yet it was essential reading. It outsold any other book by or about lesbians for decades to come, and today it is the only one of Hall's novels to remain continuously in print.

The contemporary novelist Jeannette Winterson has compared *The Well* unfavorably with *Orlando* ("the first trans novel in English"), arguing that it "reinforces every depressing stereotype about gender and sexual desire," and the prose is "terrible." Terry Castle has similarly acknowledged that like "many bookish lesbians," she has done her fair share of making jokes about *The Well*, which is "crammed full with so many ghastly passages one is hard-pressed to choose one's favorite hideousness among them." With its "turgid, pimple-ridden, sumptuously ungrammatical love scenes," this "often monstrously overwrought parable of homosexual *Bildung*" nonetheless stirs complex feelings in Castle: despite "an aesthetic shame-reflex," she confesses to having succumbed to the novel's "uncanny rhetorical power," and ultimately lands on "intransigent love for this book and its author." Moreover, she praises Hall as "the first modern writer to say love between women was good—and to do so simply and courageously." Regardless of whether *The Well* fails as a work of art, Castle has argued that "[v]irtually every English or American lesbian novel composed since 1928 has been in some sense or another a response to, or trespass upon, *The Well of Loneliness*." Generations of feminists have honored, mocked, and dismissed the book, yet it has never been ignored. The historian Lillian Faderman has noted that "[t]here was probably no lesbian in the four decades between 1928 and the late 1960s, capable of English or any of the eleven languages into which the book was translated, who was unfamiliar with *The Well of Loneliness*."

Perhaps if James Douglas hadn't attacked a sapphic work of fiction as a "plague stalking shamelessly through public life and corrupting the healthy youth of the nation"—along with decrying the "unutterable putrefaction" of homosexuality—the novel might have faded into obscurity and fallen out of print. Yet Douglas kept up his vicious denunciations, warning that "murderers only slay the body, while these perverts destroy the soul." His attempts at suppression had some unintended effects, provoking a frenzy of orders from bookstores and generating plenty of publicity. He had inadvertently elevated a depraved lesbian into a brave pioneer. Radclyffe Hall the outcast was assured her place in literary history.

As legal proceedings were initiated against the novel on grounds of obscenity and indecency, the presiding magistrate, Sir Chartres Biron, declared that whatever literary merit *The Well* possessed only strengthened the case for its destruction: "The more palatable the poison, the more insidious." He condemned "unnatural practices between women," which were "horrible and disgusting." On December 14, 1928, following a failed appeal—the verdict was rendered after less than ten minutes, with no witnesses or evidence presented—*The Well* was officially banned. All extant copies were to be seized and destroyed. An alarmed John decried the ban as "an attack on personal freedom." The president of PEN in Great Britain—the writers' organization dedicated to authorial rights and freedom of expression—claimed he was too busy to advocate on her behalf. (Apparently, literary freedom was a worthy cause, but not for a lesbian novel.) In response to this cowardice, John withdrew her PEN membership.

Although she had braced herself for trouble ("I am by nature a fighter"), after enduring a trial in which the outcome was preordained, John was exhausted and depressed. In court, she had issued a statement lamenting "the lack of proper understanding of inversion" and proclaiming her Catholic faith, yet she remained defiant: "I do not regret having written the book. All that has happened has only served to show me how badly my book was needed." Her unwavering belief in the virtue of her novel was bolstered by thousands of supportive letters from fans. She had heard from many homosexual readers asking whether societal tolerance would ever come, including one young woman: "I am just 23—do you think it will be very long?"

John and Una decided to sell their house in London to help cover their substantial legal costs—all for a cause that was hopeless in the end. As Una later recalled, Sir Biron had "refused to hear any of our fifty-seven witnesses in [the book's] favour, had condemned it to death as an obscene book." She was also not convinced that anyone on the prosecutorial side had read *The Well*.

Yet all was not lost. In a subversive move, Jonathan Cape arranged for a special edition to be printed in Paris. These bootleg copies, published in English, with promotional material noting the novel's exploration of "the phenomenon of the masculine woman in all its implications," went out to local bookshops, while other copies made it to English booksellers via postal service and the suitcases of British travelers. Sales in both French and British bookstores were brisk, and unsurprisingly, censorship made the novel even more sought after, turning it into an underground success. At one point, police raided a London bookshop, followed by Cape's office a few days later. (His quick-thinking secretary directed the police to a stash in the basement, then sat on the only remaining copy until they left.) By February 1929, sales of the French edition had reached nearly ten thousand copies. In the United States, a small New York publishing firm, Covici-Friede, released a (censored) American edition after Knopf had dropped the book. A number of leading writers, including Ernest Hemingway, F. Scott Fitzgerald, Sherwood Anderson, Upton Sinclair, and Edna Ferber, signed a statement of defense for *The Well*—but a New York court ruling declared the novel obscene, noting that it would "debauch public morals." The publisher vowed to keep fighting and cleverly moved the printing plates out of state. Just as it had in the UK, the book drew tremendous media coverage and stirred up a frenzy of curiosity, and sales in the US increased by thousands of copies. More good news came in April 1929, when an appeals court overturned the obscenity charge in America and sales surged once again. The following month, the poet Ezra Pound told John that for "humorous reading" in future international editions of her novel, she should include the complete text of each country's obscenity laws.

That spring, John became the first female author on the Gallimard list after the publisher, Gaston Gallimard, offered to issue a French-language edition of *The Well*. (The translation was carefully vetted by Una.) Still, all the public attention, scrutiny, and judgment got to John. As she confessed to Audrey Heath in a letter, sometimes she fantasized about being anonymous, perhaps "a retired ironmonger with a fat bank account, a wife and four children."

In 1930, John bought a beautiful fourteenth-century house in Rye, a small town in East Sussex. The novelist E. F. Benson, a local resident, welcomed the couple warmly. Henry James had once lived in Rye, too. Having earned tens of thousands of pounds in royalties from US sales of *The Well*, which also boosted sales of her previous novels, John wanted to spoil her devoted wife. The house was a gift, purchased in Una's name, and just as John had guessed, Una was excited to oversee the renovation, which would include gutting the interior down to the studs. (In the process, the couple uncovered a fresco, a Henry VIII gold coin, and other wonderful treasures within the walls.) The renovation took several months, so John and Una moved into a local inn and, later, a rented cottage. A woman who worked at the inn later recalled the bad-tempered John addressing her not by name, but as "you fool!" Even so, she preferred John to Una, whom she described as "finicky," and she recalled that John was "like a husband, always asking for things for Lady Troubridge."

John spent every day writing, while Una, clad in overalls, supervised the construction workers. After moving in, the couple settled into the familiar routine of a respectable married couple, with Una protecting John's time and attention. She catered to her every need, answered fan mail, and supervised the cook, the gardener, and the maids. One maid was let go for being pregnant, another for leaving her key in the door and wanting time off.

Una also embarked on a new writing project: "I have determined, after many years of intermission, to keep a diary of sorts in order to supplement the daybooks that I have kept regularly for sixteen years," she wrote in the first entry. "In these I can and do state merely the facts of our daily engagements, John's and mine, and there is no room for any detail such as might later be amusing to re-read and remember." Ultimately these diaries would span thirteen years and total sixty volumes, chronicling the couple's mundane activities, major life events, and even weather reports, both from Rye and their many travels.

By 1933, having made frequent visits to London, they were beginning to feel restless back in Rye. John bought a flat in London so they could enjoy the best of both. "The book sought in the Country will always be in London and vice versa," wrote Una. "A summer season spent in London will mean missing the fruit blossom, the cuckoo, the bluebells, the nightingale; a season in the Country will mean no Russian Ballet, no Opera, no Wimbledon."

The previous year had been challenging. John's latest novel, *The Master of the House*, flopped, leaving John resentful that she hadn't received the praise she deserved. Una had done her best to help, as always: when the *Master* proofs arrived, she read them aloud to John for more than ten hours straight, and designed the advertisements, and again came up with the title (this one taken from the New Testament).

At forty-five years old, Una had endured her share of health problems over the years, but now she had excessive menstrual bleeding and was diagnosed with fibroids. Following an emergency hysterectomy, she suffered life-threatening complications and was hospitalized for a month. As the crisis passed, only one consolation sustained her—the strength of John's love. John pampered her with flowers, fruit, and other gifts while bedridden. In all their years together, Una wrote proudly in her diary, there was never "any new excitement, any emotional stimulus that made her less careful of my every need, less solicitous of my safety and comfort." But things were shifting for John and had been for some time.

John was menopausal, exhausted, and jittery, and she was smoking too much. Although she had been a patient caregiver to Una after the surgery, the nurturing role was uncomfortable for John, who was accustomed to being waited on and cared for. A distressed Una was having bad headaches, heart flutters, and hemorrhoids. The worse she felt, the more John wished to retreat. John found her unpleasant to be around. (Like Ladye before her, Una was a bit of a hypochondriac: on her thirty-first birthday, she'd insisted on getting a colon X-ray, even though a doctor found nothing wrong with her. She celebrated afterward by treating herself to a new suit.) The other issue, however superficial, was that in midlife, Una appeared older than she was. As John become more distant, Una seemed to willfully ignore any cracks in their domestic bliss. John was her soul mate, and that was that. Looking back, though, it was possible to see that of the two, Una was the more ardent spouse. It was she who was disappointed, early in their relationship, when John did not seem to care that their menstrual cycles had synced. (Una recorded the significant event in her diary.) Whereas Una recognized their menorrheal harmony as an indication of a profound physical and spiritual bond, this was lost on John.

In the summer of 1934, at Una's insistence, they had a vacation in France. Una would undoubtedly regret the trip for the rest of her life. Having visited Colette, Natalie Barney, and other friends in Paris, at the end of June the couple went on to Bagnoles, a favorite old vacation spot of theirs. A few days into their stay, Una came down with a painful gastrointestinal infection. Sensing that she could not expect John to play nurse again, she suggested they hire a real one. Weeks later, a thirty-two-year-old Russian émigré entered their lives.

Evguenia Souline's third language was English, and she didn't speak much of it, but John was enthralled from the start. She slept in Evguenia's room, supposedly so that Una could get her rest. Although nothing physical happened between them, John didn't bother hiding her intentions from Evguenia, who may or may not have been attracted to John. (It was unclear whether the young woman was a lesbian or even bisexual.) Nonetheless, after Una's recovery, John was desperate to see Evguenia again and arranged a meeting in Paris. In a hotel room, John kissed her on the mouth. After they parted, she began writing impassioned letters to her beloved, whom she called Souline, informing her of which colors of clothing or lipstick she must never wear.

John reassured Souline in more than one postscript that Una would not intercept any mail ("I shall get any letters you write myself—and open them myself"). She was quick to correct her would-be lover, noting in one early missive that "your darling stiff little letter came yesterday," and that her English had gone wrong: "[I]n my country one would not—in the circumstances—have begun: 'My dear Miss Hall.'! Try to get it into your head that never again can I be 'Miss Hall' to you." The cadence of John's letters increased from about every two days, to daily, to more than once a day. This was no infatuation. It was a full-blown obsession that happened to coincide with the decline of her literary career.

John was fifty-four years old and had been with Una for nearly twenty years. One night she confessed that she had fallen for Souline and described the subsequent altercation in a letter the next day. Expressing gratitude for Una's devotion during her *Well of Loneliness* "persecution," John wrote, "Una stood shoulder to shoulder with me, fighting every inch of that terrific battle. She has given me all of her interest and indeed of her life," but the empathy ended there:

> It has been very terrible, she has reminded me of the operation,
> of every illness she had through the years. She has told me that
> she is very ill now, that [her doctor] warned her to avoid all emo-
> tion, that if I do see you everything will happen between us, and

that then she could never be happy again but would fret herself until she died. She says that she will not tolerate our meeting. When I said that I would control myself only if I could see you again, she would not believe me, and this morning, after a scene which lasted all night, she suddenly hurled herself on the floor as though she were going demented. I think it may very well be that her operation has made her more excitable—women are like that after that operation.

Una, who regarded Souline as "a devoted and admirable nurse," had helped the young woman secure a nursing job at a local hospital. Now she was a nuisance. Una expected Souline to be merely "a bird of passage" in their lives, as she recalled years later in *The Life and Death of Radclyffe Hall*. "But the utterly unexpected does happen," Una wrote. Souline, who had found a sugar daddy in John, was not going anywhere.

A shattered Una was astonished to find herself in the position that Ladye had occupied all those years ago: a third wheel who would endure any amount of humiliation to avoid abandonment. In light of John's agonizing belief that her infidelity had hastened Ladye's death, this new affair was especially galling. (Also, in one letter, John wrote to Souline: "Had I been a man, I would have given you a child.") At least Una, like Ladye, was a stable source of support, a great believer in John's work—perhaps to a fault—and in her "genius." Souline was a spoiled brat. Impulsive, selfish, manipulative, and demanding, she ran hot and cold, mostly the latter. "[S]he was indeed as violent and uncontrolled as a savage," Una wrote. "John's work was to her a matter of no interest and could only, in her view, be a very subsidiary consideration, and indeed a matter for resentment." Una was perhaps injured more by Souline's indifference toward John's work than by her sexual relations with John. "She had less than no appreciation of the conditions essential to the production of creative work and was intensely bored whenever John was immersed in it." Worse, she added, unable to hide her disgust, "I have reason to believe that even after a number of years, Souline hardly knew the names of the characters that John had created."

John saw Souline as a muse, lust object, and vulnerable child in need of maternal protection. Una saw them as "oil and water," and their affair a series of "storms and reconciliations." After Souline developed "lung trouble," Una swallowed her "inevitable jealousy" and allowed John to pay for her lover's medical care. "From the first to the last she was an impossible patient," Una reported, "as difficult to control as a bucking bronco, headstrong and wild and inconsistent, with alternating moods of incoherent rage, of abysmal gloom and crazy optimism." From then on, to a greater or lesser extent, this mercurial woman went wherever John and Una did, either staying with them or in her own place nearby (funded by John, of course). "While it had its disadvantages," recalled Una, "it was in the long run the best solution."

Why subject herself to this degradation? "Life with John was by no means always easy," Una recalled in her memoir, "but her variety was infinite and it was always interesting." (After John's death, Una confessed, "I had lost my occupation as well as my infinitely beloved companion.") Although she still satisfied her creative urges with translating and editing work, Una's latest creative project, adapting Colette's novel *Chéri* for the stage, was a failure. The reviews were terrible, and she took it hard. Living with John and through John was all she had.

Una worked to procure a UK visa for Souline, forcing herself to trust John's empty declarations of devotion—"*You* are permanent"—and saying nothing while John gave Souline a generous allowance to cover rent and living expenses. Even more damning, John gave Souline a bulldog pup. (For John and Una, there was no token of affection greater or more meaningful.) Una spent much of her time alone, not by choice but because John was not around. Once she sat in their London flat while John went off to a hotel with Souline for a few nights, without apology or explanation. Una wrote to Souline: "You have made me a stranger to what was once my life."

She ruminated over her sad predicament, and how the past had come back to haunt her. "Ladye holds my hand day and night," Una wrote in her diary. "I feel her presence and help as never before. . . . All that I did to hurt her she has repaid by helping me in almost exactly similar circumstances." Recalling the painful circumstances of "our Threeship," as Ladye described the women's dynamic, Una admitted, "I was utterly selfish and cruel to her." Nothing could shake Una's devotion to John. Just before Christmas 1934, she protected John from an American fan who showed up on their doorstep ("a raving nymphomaniac with delusions!"), desperate to meet John. And Una refused to fall into an affair herself, even when a woman came over for lunch and flirted with her. Una was flattered and left it at that. "She is a darling and very attractive," Una wrote in her diary, "but my focus is fixed and has been since Aug. 1st 1915."

Once, after being dragged along on a trip to Paris to visit Souline, Una returned alone to the hotel to find a gift from John—an azalea plant—which only depressed her more. Even as John insisted that theirs was an eternal love, she was telling Souline how intensely she craved her body, and how "I'd kiss you until you asked for mercy." She tossed off insensitive comments in Una's presence, such as mentioning that she could never tolerate having a brainy mistress. (Una found Souline's inferior intellect particularly grating.) John would alternately lash out, blaming Una for her misery, and then seek comfort in her arms after a bad row with Souline. Una put on a brave face. Privately, she was in agony: "[S]eeing the devotion that for twenty years was all mine, overflowing for someone else, a woman years my junior and who has never been to John all that I have been, hurts and hurts and hurts and is never for one waking moment out of mind and heart."

Like Ladye before her, Una engaged in wishful thinking by telling herself that John's obsession was mere infatuation, and that John would one day drop Souline from her life and never speak of her again. Despite Souline's ugly manipulations, and her sulking, storminess, and childlike dependence, her grip on John remained firm. John seemed to have forgotten that it was only because of Una's unwavering support that she had achieved fame and success, or that she had a literary career at all. Una took care of everything and made it seem easy, even when it wasn't. "I shall not forget occasions when I told her that it was hell to live with her when a book was in progress," Una wrote in her memoir, "and I also remember saying that I did not know when she was more intolerable: when she was overworking or when she was unable to work!"

Whatever kind of a muse John had fashioned Souline into, her mistress was quite useless and not the least bit supportive. Whenever John was ill, Souline was impatient, and when she spoke of her work, Souline felt bored. In the fall of 1935, after a long period of creative struggle, John managed to finish writing what she claimed was her finest novel to date. It wasn't. She said she felt inspired by Souline, who fired up her imagination. Yet it was Una, not Souline, who read carefully through the final draft and called it "sheer genius." And once again, Una came up with the book title: *The Sixth Beatitude*. When the book was published in the spring of 1936, it was a failure. Now Una had to deal with John's stormy moods, and she was forced to travel with John and Souline through France and Italy, feeling "exhausted in spirit, mind and body" as the lovers argued, broke up, and reconciled. Also along for the trip was an anxious miniature pinscher. As Una recalled in her memoir,

> Yet another dog this time: Mary Rose. She was a German, a little black and tan dwarf pinscher whom I bought in a Paris shop because she looked so frightened. She very soon stopped being frightened, however, and began a career of frightening other people. She bit the vet and she bit our cook, she attacked a nun and so many other people that she broke my nerve and I gave her to an elderly Italian countess, who admired her temper as evidence of devotion.

While Una traipsed around Florence like a good housewife, "in search of bedding, cutlery and pots and pans" for their rented flat, John argued with Souline, who wanted to go back to Paris. She made threats, behaved petulantly, and demanded that John leave Una. The affair—which satisfied John through sex, and Souline through money—was starting to falter. John offered to raise Souline's allowance, using it as a means of leverage and control. But her mistress expressed a desire for more independence. Emotional pleas fell flat ("[I]f you go on tormenting me I may suddenly not love you anymore"), and Souline was unmoved by John's vague threats of suicide. By 1939, sexual relations had ended between them, but the push-pull dynamic continued, and somehow Souline went on traveling with them. Una recalled one miserable road trip in a hired car, with the trio stuck together in the back seat and Souline sucking on hard candy "interminably," like an irritating child.

The only happy event for John and Una was their adoption of a white poodle, Fido, who was given "a tiny bedroom to himself and slept in the bed with his head on a pillow." Otherwise, John's creative output had dried up—she would not live to publish another novel—and she was depressed and suffering from various physical ailments.

On September 1, 1939, Hitler invaded Poland. Although John enjoyed her "one or two really dear Jewish friends," she believed that Jews "hate us and want to bring about a European War and then a World Revolution in order to destroy us utterly." Una too harbored a loathsome antisemitic streak, once describing neighbors as "the nice type of Jews." John began losing her eyesight and suffered from colitis, hemorrhoids, and double pneumonia, Una was upset to see John in such a terrible state. She wrote to Souline, begging her to send letters to John to lift her spirits. In March 1943, John was diagnosed with colon cancer. On October 7, she was dead.

Together for twenty-eight years, Una was at John's bedside when John drew her final breath. She described her beloved as "very peaceful, very calm," and looking exquisitely handsome, like "a young airman or soldier . . . Not a trace of femininity; no one in their senses could have suspected that anything but a young man had died." The preceding months had been awful for Una to witness, as John managed pain and nausea with injections of morphine and then heroin. Yet her wifely loyalty paid off. In the end, John belonged only to her. Although Souline made a few half-hearted visits to John in the hospital, her lack of compassion was obvious. Una tended lovingly to John in her last few months and had never felt closer to her. "I want you, you, *you*," John declared one day. "I want only you in all the world." As for John's will, drafted days before her death: everything was for Una.

Now Una's reason for living was gone. She relied on her faith to sustain her, along with her conviction that someday she would be reunited with John. She threw herself into every aspect of the funeral arrangements, including a requiem mass and the display of John's coffin in Westminster Cathedral before being laid to rest at Highgate Cemetery, in the same vault where Ladye was buried. On the doorway to the joint tomb, Una had a marble plaque installed with an inscription from the poet Elizabeth Barrett Browning:

RADCLYFFE HALL

1943

AND, IF GOD CHOOSE,

I SHALL BUT LOVE THEE BETTER

AFTER DEATH.

UNA

Una realized that as keeper of John's legacy, her devotion could assume a new form. She regarded herself as "guardian of the lamp" of

John's "genius" and "our enduring love," a mission that would sustain and console her. The grieving widow began by destroying the half-finished manuscript of John's final novel, which Una claimed was honoring a promise she had made to John. (As a thinly veiled account of John's obsession with Souline, it seemed unfit for publication.) She was careful to protect John's reputation by largely erasing Souline from their story line, destroying hundreds of her letters to John. Only one still exists.

Souline had not lost a great love; she had lost a necessary patron, and she had no intention of simply carrying on with her life. She demanded to be taken care of, even after John's death. Attempting to stir up trouble over John's estate, she claimed that John would have wanted her to live comfortably, if not luxuriously. Una dismissed Souline's claims as "entirely fictitious." In her will, John made only a vague mention of her former lover, allowing for a minimal amount of money to be given at Una's discretion. There was no legal obligation to be kind.

Because Una now occupied a position of power and control, she continued sending the incorrigible woman a basic allowance, even after Souline married a Russian factory worker, Vladimir Makaroff, in 1946. They lived in a single, dilapidated room. She expressed no gratitude for Una's generosity and begged for more money to pay off her debts. Each new letter from her provoked rage in Una, who grew tired of the constant demands. "I am not a perpetual running fountain of cash," Una wrote in her diary. Knowing that with her "venomous tongue," Souline was capable of saying or doing anything, Una sent just enough to shut her up for a while, and to keep her from causing trouble. At one point, Una asked for details of her salary and expenses, her husband's income, receipts from doctors' bills, and more. "I will not have her getting away with deliberate dishonesty in addition to her chronic moral dishonesty," Una wrote.

When Souline was diagnosed with cancer in 1956, she saw a private physician and insisted that Una pay the bill. (She refused.) A lawyer representing Souline wrote to demand funding for medical treatment and nursing care, claiming that Una was violating the terms of John's will. He also noted that Souline had begun typing up all of John's letters to her for posterity. Una, perceiving the attorney's letter as blackmail, would not budge. Souline died at fifty-three in the summer of 1958. "I do not feel that I can blame myself where she was concerned," Una wrote, reflecting on the "abominable cruelty" Souline had inflicted on John for years. "She has always been disastrous in both our lives. I imagine the husband did not notify me as he hoped to get a couple of extra installments of the allowance."

With Souline's death, Una felt free to pick up a project she'd begun years before. In 1945, Una worked feverishly on a tribute to John and a memoir of their nearly thirty-year union: *The Life and Death of Radclyffe Hall*, completing it in just over a month. Yet she waited until 1961 to publish it, noting that Souline's death "of course clears the way for publication of my book." Also Una may have been waiting for certain family members and former acquaintances to die before she felt she could set the record straight about her life with John.

In 1945, with the end of the war, Una decided to leave England for good. Four years later, a small publisher, Falcon Press (which later became Hammond, Hammond & Co.), took a chance by releasing a new edition of *The Well* and testing whether the Home Office law would again strike it down. (The novel had been selling well in the United States and elsewhere for nearly twenty years.) A funny thing happened: there was no challenge this time, and *The Well* sold steadily and successfully in the UK. It was a proud moment for Una, who had long wished for this to happen.

She settled into a new life in Florence in November 1946, finding a large garden flat near the Ponte Vecchio. She created a shrine to John: shelves and shelves of multiple editions of John's books, and photographs of John everywhere. In the evenings, alone in her flat, she wore John's dressing gown. The sixty-two-year-old woman with the gray bob and severe expression lived an austere life, with just one maid—who wore a uniform, of course—to do the cooking and cleaning. Una read, attended mass daily, shopped for antiques, went to the cinema, saw a few Florentine friends, and took on translation work. She owned a vast record collection, and spent hours listening to music. She enjoyed going to concerts and operas, often wearing John's black pinstripe suit, bowtie, and diamond and onyx cuff links.

In 1951, an encounter in Milan would transform the final chapter of her life. After meeting the opera singer Nicola Rossi-Lemeni at La Scala ("To hear him is one of the greatest pleasures I can have"), they formed a fast friendship. He asked for her help with a production he was preparing for, *The Emperor Jones*, adapted from the Eugene O'Neill play, and Una began translating the libretto into Italian. She became a confidante to the thirty-year-old Nika, as she called him, and he leaned on her for support following his divorce. His companionship helped her keep "the devil of depression" at bay—she missed John terribly, a wound that would never heal.

For Una, Nika became a platonic version of John: he was the star whom she could worship, serve, fuss over, adore. She answered fan mail, made travel arrangements, helped with publicity, and accompanied him on tours throughout Europe and America. She was in San Francisco for Nika's US debut as Boris Godunov in 1952, for his first performance a year later at the Metropolitan Opera House in New York, and with him to open the Chicago Lyric Opera's first season with *Don Giovanni* in 1954. Later, when he recorded several operas with Maria Callas, Una beamed with a kind of maternal pride.

Sometimes she stayed up late with Nika, giving him massages and rubbing his feet. After all her years with John, this was Una's idea of fulfillment. "It is a blessed thing that he wants and depends on me," she boasted in her diary. "He loves me more than his mother." She loved being needed by him: "Nika could not do without me, would never be able to do without me." In 1956, when he married his second wife, Virginia, a well-known soprano, the new bride got another mother-in-law in Una, who would become godmother to their son, Alessandro. A year later, after loaning Nika money for a down payment on an apartment in Rome, Una rented a flat next door to the couple. (It is unclear whether Virginia objected to any of this.) Once again, a triad. Just as John had been the center of her life, now there was Nika. "He does realize that *he* is my occupation," she wrote. His career was "the prevailing interest of my old age."

Nika was grateful for her friendship and flattered by her admiration. As he wrote years later, "For Una there were three 'idols': Nijinsky, Radclyffe Hall . . . and me!" Along with many other acts of generosity, Una encouraged Nika to write poems, which he did, eventually winning a poetry competition and publishing five books of verse. He described her as a "walking encyclopedia" and marveled at "how our friendship was absolutely unique. . . . We shared the same interests for art, for antiques, for religious and philosophical problems—it was a constant contact and she was for me an endless source of knowledge and inspiration."

The relationship gave Una the intellectual and emotional nourishment she needed at the end of her life. Her days had structure and meaning. When Una met up in Milan one day with an old novelist friend, Micki Jacob, she was delightful company: "Una Troubridge, with her knowledge of music, art, and literature, with her ability to *use* that knowledge, commands my admiration; while her ability to make a new life for herself, to be . . . amusing, interesting—and interested in you!—adds to my affection and respect for her."

Settled in Rome with a new maid, Nada, Una surrounded herself with relics of her former life with John, and each day she placed fresh flowers in front of a picture of John displayed in the living room. "Allowing for the passing of years, I have remained in almost all things the same person," she wrote in 1962. Her health began to decline as she suffered falls, injuries, lethargy, and loss of appetite, and was generally feeling "*very* weak and shaky." She had liver cancer.

On September 24, 1963, Una died at seventy-six in the arms of her maid. Nika bought a burial plot for her in the "Catholic Foreigners" section of the Campo Verano Cemetery in Rome, where many notable Italian actors, directors, and politicians have been laid to rest. On her coffin, the inscription read: *Una Vincenzo Troubridge, the friend of Radclyffe Hall.*

# ELSA MORANTE
## and Alberto Moravia

"Literary couples are a plague."

Elsa Morante had an idea. It was 1938. In Rome, Hitler and Mussolini were due to pass below her apartment, riding together in a convertible limousine in a parade. She boiled a pot of oil on her stove and planned to open the window and pour it on their heads as they went by. Her lover of one year, a fellow writer named Alberto Moravia, convinced her not to. It was a bad idea.

Seven years later, Hitler and Mussolini were dead: Hitler by suicide, and Mussolini by machine-gun fire, his corpse displayed in the Piazzale Loreto in Milan to be kicked, beaten, and spit upon. By then, Elsa was living with Moravia, who had already experienced literary success and fame in 1929 with the release of his first novel *Gli indifferenti* (*The Time of Indifference*)—begun when he was just eighteen years old and published to wide acclaim when he was twenty-one. The book, a scathing critique of the Roman bourgeoisie, essentially established him as Italy's leading writer of fiction and is still considered by many to be his best novel. It was reprinted four times before a second edition in 1934. Decades later, Alberto recalled, with no trace of humility, "It was a great success. In fact, it was one of the greatest successes in all modern Italian literature. The greatest, actually; and I can say this with all modesty," he said. "There had never been anything like it. Certainly, no book in the last fifty years has been greeted with such unanimous enthusiasm and excitement."

His novel *La mascherata* (later published in English as *The Fancy Dress Party*), with its farcical portrayal of a dictator in an imaginary Latin American country, was written in 1941 and confiscated and banned by the fascist regime. Newspapers were under orders not to commission him to write anything, so for years he had to write under the pen name Pseudo. He was a man in trouble. Elsa and Alberto were forced into hiding in the summer of 1943, when the half-Jewish (by his father) Alberto was placed on the "wanted" list of arrests by the fascist police. Under Mussolini, all manuscripts had to be submitted to the Ministry of Popular Culture, and Jews were thrown out of the army, the navy, and any governmental positions, and forbidden to publish books. "Censorship is an awful thing! And a damned hardy plant once it takes root!" Alberto once said. "Censorship is monstrous, a monstrous thing!"

Like Alberto, Elsa was born in Rome, and like him, she had a Jewish parent. Her mother, Irma Poggibonsi, was a teacher from a Jewish family in Modena, and she married a Sicilian, Augusto Morante, who worked at a boys' reform school. Following the loss of a son, Mario, who died shortly after his birth, Elsa was the eldest of her siblings: Aldo, Marcello, and Maria. (Perhaps haunted by Mario's absence, Elsa always said she wished she had been born a boy.) Irma routinely mocked and humiliated her husband, forcing him to eat all his meals alone and to sleep in the basement. The only reason she didn't leave Augusto was that she believed he would kill himself, so she must have felt something like relief when he became ill and died after the Second World War. It was only in the final stage of Augusto's sad, lonely life that Irma tossed him small crumbs of kindness—allowing him a sleeping upgrade from the basement to the living room sofa, upon which he would die. The fact of Augusto's impotence meant that he had been the children's father in legal terms only. Their biological father turned out to be a family friend, a handsome Sicilian postal worker named Francesco Lo Monaco. Elsa had correctly guessed this secret well before Irma revealed the truth to her children.

The Morante household was drab and tense. The children were fearful of their mercurial mother, who was prone to rages and frequently critical. Working full-time as a schoolteacher while raising four children and having to cook, clean, iron, and deal with household bills might have pushed anyone over the edge. For Irma, some of the bitterness and anger she harbored was rooted in her unfulfilled desire to become a writer. To satisfy this dream in her own way, she liked to compose poems and song lyrics, and once published a story in an Italian magazine. Later, Irma would live vicariously through Elsa, whom she envied, and she placed enormous pressure on her daughter to succeed.

The two youngest children, Marcello and Maria, sensed that Irma preferred Aldo and Elsa, and they were right. She loved them less. Elsa especially was prized—she had her own room, where she would retreat from family arguments and write compulsively. Considering Irma's frustrated literary ambitions, it's no wonder she was invested in Elsa and determined to see her achieve greatness. Elsa's talents were also supported by her wealthy godmother, an aristocrat named Donna Maria Guerrieri Gonzaga, who would invite her to stay at her beautiful villa in the northwestern quarter of Rome.

Going back and forth between the dingy Morante home and the sumptuous environment of Donna Gonzaga's villa gave Elsa a lifelong ease among both the rich and the poor, grandeur and squalor—and moreover, this exposure would shape the depictions of class tensions in her work. By the age of five, the imaginative girl was writing poems in small, neat handwriting and drawing impressively detailed pictures. Elsa did not attend elementary school, but she was a greedy reader, always hungry for books, and loved inventing stories and games. A collection of her fantasy children's stories, written in adolescence, would be published (along with her illustrations) when she was nearly thirty: *Le bellissime avventure di Caterì dalla trecciolina e altre storie*. As a girl, she loved the poems of Baudelaire and taught herself French to read them.

In 1922, enrolled in middle school, Elsa wrote her first play. The headmistress, astonished that the impressive work had been written by a child, referred to her as a "genius." Elsa was not a popular girl, and regarded herself as ugly, yet she was a top student and her peers were keen to be liked by her. (They brought her gifts of candy and chocolate so they could copy her work.) She went on to attend a top high school in Rome, Visconti e Mamiani, where she studied Greek and Latin and again excelled academically. At the age of eighteen, she published her first story in *Corriere della Sera*, one of Italy's oldest newspapers and the most widely read. Rather than attend university, Elsa decided to leave home and make her way in the world as a writer. (In her early years of fiction writing, she said that Kafka was the only author to influence her work, but she later repudiated Kafka and fell in love with Stendhal.) As well as declining to continue her formal education, she rejected a job offer for a teaching position with a secure income.

This decision left her living alone, in penury, renting a tiny room near Piazza Venezia. She scraped by giving private lessons in Italian and began to publish poems and stories in various magazines (some of which she wrote under the pseudonym Antonio Carrera). She was so poor that she often did not have enough to eat. And she was so lonely that she used to phone a number that gave the current time, just to hear a human voice.

The next several years were a struggle for Elsa, financially and emotionally. She had love affairs, but nothing stuck. One spring evening in 1937, she went out to dinner with friends, and among the group was Alberto, a known womanizer. According to his account of their meeting, after the meal he was saying good night to Elsa when she slipped her house keys to him. He was thirty; she was twenty-five. He was intrigued by this intellectual young woman with "a big mushroom of hair above a round face," "beautiful eyes with the dreamy gaze of the near-sighted," and "a little nose, and a big, willful mouth." There was neither love nor lust at first sight. "I never managed to lose my head," Alberto recalled in a book-length interview with the writer Alain Elkann. (It was published in 1990 as *Life of Moravia*, a memoir of sorts. The intensely private Elsa left behind no autobiographical account.) "I wasn't in love, but I was fascinated by an extreme, heart-rending, passionate quality in her character." He described her as "an angel fallen from heaven into the practical hell of daily living. But an angel armed with a pen." Asked whether Elsa was ambitious, he replied, "Ambitious is putting it mildly. Writing was her life."

A year later, Elsa recorded in her diary one day that Alberto told her that they should end their relationship. He fled to Greece. When he returned a few weeks later, it was Elsa who wanted to end the relationship. Somehow the couple endured. There was, however, the ongoing issue of money, and the lack of it. Despite Alberto's growing literary reputation, he was not yet financially successful and still lived at home with his parents. His paternal cousins, Nello and Carlo Rosselli, founders of an anti-fascist resistance movement, were murdered in Paris under orders from Mussolini. In 1941, he also suffered the loss of his younger brother, Gastone.

Early on in his relationship with Elsa, it stung Alberto to be poor, but he was not one to panic: "I thought that poverty might be an interesting experience," he recalled. "I've been protected all my life by my indifference." He was also protected by his Jewish Venetian father, Carlo, who recognized that his son must be a writer and nothing else. Carlo was among the first in Rome to have a car—a fifteen-horsepower Fiat—and even a chauffeur who would drive him and his wife to the opera. The family was affluent enough that Carlo did not feel compelled to pressure his son to get a job. As an architect and an amateur painter, he was "aware of the value of art," Alberto said. (He was born Alberto Pincherle, and later adopted Moravia, a family name, as his writing surname.) Despite his prosperous background—Alberto recalled himself as a boy "who plays with his sisters and goes to bed early and speaks French with the governess"—he was familiar with suffering early on, having been diagnosed at the age of nine with tuberculosis of the bone. It left him with one leg several inches shorter than the other and a permanent limp. For years after the diagnosis, he was bedridden at home and later sent to a sanatorium in the Italian Alps. "To understand my character," he revealed in his memoir, "you must keep in mind that I was ill in infancy, and because of it I was alone, completely alone, until I was 18. I never went to school. I never had other children to play with. Solitude entered my soul so deeply that even today I feel a profound detachment from others." He filled his days by reading Dostoyevsky, Shakespeare, Dante, Molière, Rimbaud, and many others. By the time he was a teenager, he was fluent in French, German, and English. And as he once told a reporter, "It was that long illness that made me start to write."

When he met Elsa, Alberto was suffering from spasmophilia, a form of nervous colitis. "I was filled with air, I didn't eat, I became very thin," Alberto recalled. The couple began spending their evenings in typical Roman fashion, meeting friends at a local trattoria and talking for hours. They bonded over their mutual horror of fascism, and their social circle included painters and writers. Alberto did not spend his nights at Elsa's flat, instead choosing to go back to his parents' home. Though Alberto was attracted to the force of her personality ("so original, so strong"), he said he felt no "violent desire" for her. "In love-making," he said, Elsa was "almost hostile to the transports of physical love. In sum, she was very passionate but not very sensual, if by sensuality you mean allowing your body complete freedom." They married in April 1941 for practical reasons: Alberto said he hated the long walks to and from her flat in the freezing winter. Living under one roof would solve that problem.

At the wedding, Elsa had a purse with a stain, which she hid by holding the purse against her skirt. The couple had four witnesses, and at Alberto's request, his family did not attend. "I remember my wedding as something not exactly happy," he later recalled, "oppressed as I was by the war, lack of money, my family, and not least, the great and proper importance that Elsa attached to the ceremony." Alberto's mother, Teresa, invited the couple over for dinner. This too proved an unpleasant experience—in fact, Alberto remembered it as "downright catastrophic." When Teresa attempted to give her new daughter-in-law some maternal advice, Elsa replied dismissively. The women argued.

"Elsa's character was unworthy of her intelligence," Alberto said. "She should have understood that my mother was simply a bourgeois lady and let it go at that." The women never saw each other again. Carlo, who was quite ill at the time, never met Elsa and died in hospital the following year.

Alberto didn't want to ask his parents for the money to buy Elsa a wedding ring, and he did not ask if the couple could live in the large apartment of a house owned by his family. But he did request the two-room attic, a space hardly sufficient for two writers, let alone their egos. After the war, they would buy a much nicer apartment just off the Piazza del Popolo. But for now, they were stuck in a tiny flat whose sole virtue was the great view of the Borghese Gardens and the Borghese Museum.

They were able to go on a honeymoon of sorts, thanks to the fifteen-thousand-lire contract Alberto had signed to write a screenplay for the film director Mario Soldati: *Tragica notte*, released in 1942 and based on a 1928 novel by Delfino Cinelli. He loved films, once describing cinema as his favorite art after literature and painting. As a boy, Alberto often watched two movies a day. He was pleased with the money from his contract but described the scriptwriting process as "annoying." He said that the scriptwriter was a kind of governess who raised a child and was then dismissed. He was resentful over "giving something precious, for money, to someone who would exploit it for his own ends," and found the collaborative nature of the writing to be tedious: "It wrecked your life. You would sit for hours and hours with the other writers, smoking, drinking coffee, now and then telling obscene or anti-fascist jokes. A constant tug-of-war." Nonetheless he went on to write several screenplays before giving up on writing for movies. Later in life, Alberto boasted, "I knew everybody, and everybody knew me. I'm part of the Italian cinema because first of all, I've written about two thousand articles of film criticism and also because at least twenty films have been based on my novels." Indeed, his novels *The Conformist* and *Contempt* became classic films by Bernardo Bertolucci and Jean-Luc Godard, respectively.

In any case, the screenplay for Soldati allowed Alberto and Elsa to travel to Siena, where they stayed at the Villa Scacciapensieri, a beautiful manor house converted to a hotel and still operating today. From there, they traveled to Anacapri, a town on the island of Capri, where they drank, smoked, walked, argued, and wrote.

The couple's routine was simple. Each morning they woke around seven, and Alberto would work on his novella *Agostino*, while Elsa was writing what would become *Menzogna e sortilegio* (*House of Liars*). She had published a book of short stories in 1941, *Il gioco segreto* (The Secret Game), along with the collection of her childhood poems, stories, and illustrations that same year. But *Menzogna e sortilegio*, which would take four years to complete, was her first novel.

They did not share work with one another, and did not discuss works in progress. "Absolutely never," recalled Alberto. "Elsa and I were absolutely not a professional writing couple who read each other's manuscripts, talk about books, debate the virtues and faults of the authors they are reading," he said. "We were really a man and a woman involved in a very difficult, very personal relationship." Elsa kept her writing life separate from her married life. "Literary couples are a plague," she once wrote to a friend. Alberto and Elsa did, however, treat the subject of love with similar pessimism in their fiction. As Lily Tuck notes in *Woman of Rome: A Life of Elsa Morante* (the first Morante biography in any language), for Elsa, love "always consumes and usually turns into hate; it is rarely joyful or peaceful." In Alberto's work, love was suffered rather than enjoyed, and it failed to relieve the alienation or apathy of his characters. In *Alberto Moravia*, her 1974 survey of the author's work, Jane E. Cottrell notes that "in Moravia's world men never seem to understand women. The female is always portrayed as more complicated than she at first appears, and she remains mysterious to her lover no matter how much he tries to probe her secrets and to possess her." He wrote bluntly, openly, and frequently about sex, once saying, "There can be sex without love, but there can be no love without sex. That is to say, that you can very well have a quick sexual relationship, even a very happy one, without love. However, the opposite is not possible."

Elsa was very protective of her work and did not welcome criticism, especially from Alberto. Just once, when she took a chance and shared a story with her husband, he admitted that he didn't like it, and she responded by tearing it up. He once said that she would have certainly loved him less, or ceased to love him at all, if his opinion of her work hadn't been "extremely favorable"—as it typically was. "Elsa was something of a totalitarian: either you were with her or against her," he recalled. "For me it was and still is today easy to accept negative opinions on my work. With her, you had to be careful."

Alberto wrote the entire manuscript of *Agostino* in a month—August, inspiring the book's title—and later regarded it as an important work that served as the "hinge" between *Gli indifferenti* and his later novels. (*Agostino* was also made into a 1962 film.) While writing the book, he said that it seemed only to be "a well-made story" and that what he had achieved was not apparent to him at that time. He wrote, he claimed, only to amuse and express himself.

*Agostino* follows a boy and his widowed mother on an idyllic summer holiday at a Tuscan seaside resort, spending their mornings together on a rowboat: "He rowed with deep pleasure on the smooth, diaphanous, early-morning sea, and his mother, sitting in front of him, would speak to him softly, as joyful and serene as the sea and sky, as if he were a man rather than a thirteen-year-old boy." His mother is "a beautiful woman still in her prime," and the boy is "filled with pride" to be in the rowboat with her, while "the bathers on the beach seemed to be watching, admiring his mother and envying him." He struggles with "the turmoil of his infatuation" and is keenly aware of his mother's body: "As his mother, she had no sense of shame; but to Agostino it seemed that she was wantonly provocative. He would hear her calling him and would go to her room to find her at her toilet, in her negligee and with her breasts half-uncovered." He is both attracted to and repelled by his mother, and when she begins an affair, Agostino—feeling neglected, and afflicted by something akin to unrequited love—warily seeks acceptance in a local gang of troubled, violent boys. Published during the Nazi occupation in 1944, this tale of frustrated longing, class tension, Oedipal conflict, and innocence lost became a bestseller, and the following year it gave thirty-eight-year-old Alberto the first literary award of his career, and Italy's first postwar literary prize, the Corriere Lombardo.

In his conversation with Elkann, Alberto described beautifully the experience of a novel flowing for him during the writing process. Inspiration, he said, is like a skein "already wound up, which unwinds quickly and easily. . . . You pull and pull, and it all unwinds easily, never stopping." In contrast, he had struggled to write his 1935 novel, *Le ambizioni sbagliate* (*Mistaken Ambitions*), for seven years, and said it was "an enormous tangle of threads." He also shared with Elkann some of his favorite contemporary authors, which included several Americans: Saul Bellow (who was also a friend), Raymond Carver, Carson McCullers, Mary McCarthy, Truman Capote, and Elsa.

Unlike the monthlong creation of her husband's manuscript, Elsa spent years on her strange and complex novel, which stretched over eight hundred pages. Alberto was highly disciplined, with a strict daily writing routine and a set number of working hours each day. He seemed completely at ease with his process, as he revealed in his *Paris Review* interview:

I have never taken notes or ever even possessed a notebook. My work, in fact, is not prepared beforehand in any way. I might add, too, that when I'm not working, I don't think of my work at all. When I sit down to write—that's between nine and twelve every morning, and I have never, incidentally, written a line in the afternoon or at night—when I sit at my table to write, I never know what it's going to be till I'm under way. I trust in inspiration, which sometimes comes and sometimes doesn't. But I don't sit back waiting for it. I work *every* day.

He also said that he reworked each of his books several times over. "I like to compare my method with that of painters centuries ago, proceeding, as it were, from layer to layer," he said. "The first draft is quite crude, far from being perfect, by no means finished; although even then, even at that point, it has its final structure, the form is visible. After that I rewrite it as many times—apply as many 'layers'—as I feel to be necessary."

Elsa's habits were erratic. She could go for long stretches doing no writing at all, but when she worked, she did so intensively, day and night. "I move very slowly," she once explained, "and only when the sentence is really well closed and jointed and the words are those that must be and not others suggested by rush, only then do I move onto another paragraph. I do the same with the chapters." While she was working, she wouldn't take a break to go out, whereas Alberto went to the movies at least once a week and sometimes daily. Elsa once said that the long stretches between writing bouts led people to believe she wasn't doing much at all. But as she explained in a letter to a friend, "Yes, I am working, although not always [on] novels; and so most people consider this work of mine a *non-work*." When she didn't have a novel in progress, she wrote poems, essays, and stories in her tiny penmanship. She said in an interview once that "working on a story becomes an addiction, like a drug." Even when she wasn't writing stories, she said, there was always one fermenting in her mind, and she was quite sentimental toward her characters, referring to them as "my people." She was always reading: Melville, Cervantes, James, Chekhov, and Proust were among her favorites. In *Woman of Rome*, Tuck describes Elsa's writing process:

> Morante always wrote in longhand in large, black, unlined note-
> books that she bought at Zampini, a stationer on via Frattina not

far from her apartment. She wrote on every other page, leaving the intervening pages blank for notes and corrections. The notes she wrote to herself remain as guidelines to how she worked and many of her edits show that she was striving to achieve more simplicity in the text. . . . Several of the pages have large passages crosshatched and crossed out. She used different colored pens and she often doodled or drew pictures of cats and stars on the side of the page.

Although Elsa denied that *House of Liars* was autobiographical, she later described having written it to exorcize her own torments. In the novel she laid bare the similarities to her life: the narrator-protagonist (and alter ego), Elisa, has a name close to her own, and Elisa's father has a name, Francesco Monaco, that recalls that of Elsa's biological father. Haunted by vivid dreams and hallucinations after the deaths of her parents when she was ten and of a prostitute friend who cared for her like a second mother, Elisa sits alone in her small room, with only her cat for company. She recounts the story of the breakdown of her family and the "ancient sickness" they have passed on to her, attempting to come to terms with a "poison of lying and deception" that runs through the generations. *House of Liars* is, as Tuck described it, "a strangely anachronistic and lugubrious novel" with a convoluted plot.

In 2009, reviewing Tuck's biography along with four Morante novels in the *New York Review of Books*, the author and translator Tim Parks, who has lived in Italy since 1981, wrote of *House of Liars*: "Morante's achievement in this bizarre and marvelous novel is her ability to play off overheated melodrama (drawing on southern Italian tropes of mother love and masculine honor) against profound, wry, sometimes even mocking reflection on the mind's inexhaustible appetite for self-deception, lies generating 'spells,' or altered mental states that fester for years." In 2019, Parks noted in the *London Review of Books* that Elsa was writing at the height of Italian neorealism, at a time when many of Elsa's friends and peers, such as Pier Paolo Pasolini—and even her own husband—"were all in different ways seeking to describe postwar desolation in spare, chastened prose. Morante was having none of it. Her own writing is more reminiscent of the fin-de-siècle grandiloquence of [Gabriele] D'Annunzio." Politically, she could not have been more removed from the man whose nationalist ideas were influential to Mussolini.

However strange and flawed Elsa's novel may have been, Alberto admired what his wife had achieved, telling Elkann in his book-length interview that Elsa was "obsessed" while writing it, and marveling that the novel was conceived "with the imaginative capacity of genius," he said, "after [Elsa] spent only three days in Sicily, which is where part of the novel takes place!"

He once made an interesting observation about his wife's relationship to realism: "In Elsa's novels, without even much transfiguration, you find Elsa herself and the people in her life and her relations with these people," he said. "What I'm saying is that realism is a very imprecise word, and . . . the realism that so horrified Elsa took its revenge in her surprising ability to depict every day and autobiographical reality." Even "reality" is a slippery term in relation to Elsa. As the critic (and dear friend of Elsa) Cesare Garboli noted, "In Elsa Morante's creative experience there is no fissure between what is real and what is invention." (He would eventually serve, along with the actor Carlo Cecchi, as coexecutor of Elsa's estate.)

Alberto once remarked upon Elsa's habit of telling lies about herself, inventing anecdotes simply because she could. When she met him in 1937, Elsa made up a wild story about having been in love with a young homosexual English lord and claimed to have witnessed his murder by his lover. The story was undoubtedly invented to grab Alberto's attention, yet Elsa was often attracted to young gay and bisexual men—so that part, at least, was true. "She hated to give information about herself, and she rarely said the same thing twice; instead, she liked to create something that was real but not necessarily true, or the other way around—that was true but not real," as Tuck explains in *Woman of Rome*. There is a revealing passage about the notion of truth in *House of Liars*, in which Elsa's alter ego describes her aspiration: "To become a worshiper and anchorite of falsehood! To meditate on lies and make them one's wisdom! To reject all experience, not just painful experience, but moments of happiness too, denying any possibility of contentment outside untruth! That's how I have lived."

In July 1943, Mussolini was overthrown and imprisoned. Pietro Badoglio was installed as prime minister, but with the shift in power, chaos ensued, and Badoglio fled, along with the Italian royal family. The Germans seized the opportunity to reinforce their power, and thus began the nine-month occupation of Rome. For those who remained, an ordeal commenced of torture, hunger, imprisonment, murder, brutality, and oppression, along with the subsequent mass deportation of Jews in October of that year. That summer, rather than returning to Capri, Elsa and Alberto had remained in Rome, but upon learning that he was due to be arrested, they fled the city. Alberto had fifty thousand lire in his pocket and a bag filled with cans of sardines.

The couple embarked on a frightening and peripatetic journey to elude capture. They encountered their first obstacle on a train to Naples: at a certain point, the train stopped at a deserted station and the conductor ordered everyone to disembark—there were no more train tracks because they had been bombed.

Next, after spending a few days in Fondi, halfway between Rome and Naples, they were forced to escape once again when the Germans began rounding people up. Moving swiftly from one secret location to another, seeking refuge but not finding it, the two headed south to the remote mountain village of Sant'Agata. For nine months, they lived in a one-room hut, built against the side of a rock, waiting for the Allies to save the day.

As Elsa recalled many years later, "On the way, the people we had to be afraid of were the middle classes, teachers, civil servants—the prejudice was with them, they would have reported us to the Gestapo. We were finally given shelter by a peasant family. To them, Jewish or non-Jewish, we were all *cristiani*." In *Life of Moravia*, Alberto recalled:

> The place where we lived can still be seen: it's exactly as it was. A little room, huddled against the wall of the *macera*, a wall of live rock, that is, with a little roof of sheet metal. Inside, you could barely turn around. There was a big bed, made of two iron supports and three planks, and on the planks a sack filled with cornshucks, which creaked and shifted every time I moved. On this cornshuck mattress there were two sheets, one beneath and one above, of rough handwoven linen. There were no blankets. . . . But the room was so small and we were so close when we slept that I never suffered the cold. There was no flooring, just packed earth. When it rained the water came in and I stood with my feet in the water. For nine months I sat on the bed; we didn't have a chair.

Their flat in Rome must have seemed like a palace in comparison. Now Alberto and Elsa had nothing to do but wait in their hut for life to change. They brought two books, *The Brothers Karamazov* and the Bible, but had no pens. "Lacking toilet paper," Alberto recalled, "we used the pages of Dostoyevsky." One day was the same as the next. Hunger, boredom, cold, and filth defined their lives now. They might have a piece of bread in the morning, and each afternoon around five, in the hut of a peasant family, they had their only meal of the day—typically a pot of boiled beans steeped with bread. (Food became more scarce over time.) With no light in their "pigsty in the mountains," as Alberto called their hiding place, in the evenings they simply sat in the dark. Each morning, Alberto would drop a bucket to the bottom of a well, filling it with icy water, which Elsa used to wash herself daily, while he did so once a week. A few times, the monotony was disrupted by "dogfights in the sky" between the Germans and the English, Alberto recalled. Their wartime experience would inspire his 1957 novel *La ciociara* (*Two Women*), chronicling a widowed mother and her teenage daughter as they endure the horrors of the war. The novel was adapted into a film a few years later by the neorealist director Vittorio De Sica, for which Sophia Loren won an Academy Award for Best Actress.

Alberto was impressed by his wife's resilience throughout their time in hiding. "Elsa behaved with great courage and great serenity through-out the stay at Sant'Agata," he said. "In those conditions she revealed qualities that didn't appear often in the routine of daily life." He felt that she gave the best of herself in "exceptional situations, in emergencies." Elsa was tormented by the thought that she might have left her manuscript for *Menzogna e sortilegio* behind at a friend's flat in Rome. She also wanted to make sure they would be prepared for the brisk weather to come. That fall, as Alberto recounted in *Life of Moravia*, Elsa astonished him by doing something he described as generous and brave:

> By now we were well into October, we were in summer clothes, it was beginning to turn cold. I had bought a pair of shoes from some Italian deserters, real army boots. But my summer suit was no protection. Then at a certain moment Elsa decided to go to Rome, collect our winter clothes, and return to Sant'Agata. To understand Elsa's courage on that occasion, you must bear in mind on the one hand the discomfort we suffered in the mountains and, on the other, that she had come only to be with me: she wasn't wanted by the police, she could easily have stayed in Rome instead of living in that horrible discomfort.

Elsa returned to their flat and filled a suitcase with winter clothing. Then she stopped by her friend's place to check on *Menzogna e sortilegio*, just as one might check upon a sleeping child, and—confident that it remained safe—made her way back. "All she cared about," Alberto said, "was me and the manuscript."

IN MAY 1944, THE RESCUE THEY'D BEEN AWAITING CAME AT LAST, AND with the help of an American lieutenant, Elsa and Alberto were able to make their way back to Rome. There was political turmoil, along with shortages of housing, petrol, food, and more, but businesses were starting up, the arts were flourishing, and the city was buzzing with creative energy. "Early post-war Italy was glorious," Sybille Bedford recalled in her memoir, *Quicksands*. "One embraced the people for whom the springs of life were flowing again." And as Jhumpa Lahiri has written of that period, "The Second World War and its aftermath drastically and irrevocably altered Italian society, penetrating the collective consciousness, traumatizing it, but eventually reinvigorating it culturally and economically."

Alberto and Elsa were grateful to be home. There was no reason to feel nostalgic about their bleak months in hiding, yet Alberto later remarked in *Life of Moravia* that the experience of extreme deprivation freed him of the "bondage" he'd always carried as "a child of the bourgeoisie," and that Italy's liberation from fascism "was mirrored in the liberation of my spirit from that element of the bourgeoisie that it contained." The time in Sant'Agata, he recalled, would also prove to be a high point of his marriage:

> The period in the mountains was the time of my greatest intimacy with Elsa. After that our relationship slowly cooled. . . . In life Elsa preferred the exceptional, impassioned moments, the sublime in other words, and she was, on the contrary, strangely awkward in dealing with daily routine. At Sant'Agata she had found herself in her element: danger, devotion, sacrifice, contempt for life. In Rome, on the other hand, daily life made her lose patience and become difficult, intolerant, and even cruel.

By the time the war ended the following year, the couple settled into their old apartment again and focused on their writing endeavors: Alberto on short stories, another novel, and writing for Italy's leading newspapers. Elsa worked on *Menzogna e sortilegio*.

In 1948, an editor at the distinguished Italian publishing house Einaudi, in Turin, received the manuscript for *Menzogna e sortilegio* after Elsa had written a letter to ask whether she could submit it for consideration. The editor happened to be Natalia Ginzburg, whose first novel, *La strada che va in città* (*The Road to the City*), had been published in 1942 under the pseudonym Alessandra Tornimparte, when writings by Jews were banned. Ginzburg and her husband, Leone, had also edited an anti-fascist newspaper before he was arrested and tortured. He died in prison in 1944.

Like Elsa, Ginzburg would rank among the most significant Italian writers of the postwar generation—and later, Ginzburg cited Elsa as the writer she most admired of their peers. (Neither would tolerate being diminished by that all-too-common qualifier, "most significant *women* writers.") In Lily Tuck's biography, the author shares a recollection from Ginzburg, describing her response after receiving the manuscript for *Menzogna e sortilegio*. She read it straight through in one sitting: "I liked it immensely," Ginzburg recalled, "although I can't say that then I clearly understood its importance and greatness. I knew only that I loved it and it had been a long time since I had read anything that gave me such life and joy." (In a 2019 anthology of Italian short stories edited by Jhumpa Lahiri, she calls Morante the "literary queen" of Rome, praising the author's "virtuosic prose" and "grand, tragic vision," and describing *Menzogna e sortilegio* as "a sprawling masterpiece, demonic in its energy.")

The war had interrupted Elsa's work on the novel, but her persistence paid off: in 1948, along with Aldo Palazzeschi's *I fratelli Cuccoli* (The Cuccoli Brothers), *Menzogna e sortilegio* was awarded the prestigious Viareggio Prize for fiction. (Ginzburg won in 1957, sharing the fiction prize with Italo Calvino and Arturo Tofanelli.)

Ginzburg loved *Menzogna e sortilegio*, so of course she had advocated strongly for it to win the Viareggio. "My friendship with Sibilla is definitively over," she reported in a letter to Elsa from a literary conference, referring to the poet and writer Sibilla Aleramo. "She's been shooting darts at me all week." Apparently, Aleramo feared that Elsa would steal her thunder at the award ceremony. Previously, only one woman had won the prize, but that year Elsa won for fiction, and Aleramo for poetry.

Unfortunately, the novel was polarizing and did not turn out to be a commercial success. Yet for Elsa, the literary award gave her the imprimatur she needed to establish herself as a major author, with her best work yet to come. And with the recent publication of Alberto's *La romana* (*The Woman of Rome*)—written in four months, a critically acclaimed bestseller, and adapted into a 1954 film starring Gina Lollobrigida—the couple experienced fame and opportunity in their professional lives, but in their personal lives, the steady deterioration of their marriage.

In the summer of 1948, Alberto and Elsa celebrated their success with a house rental on Capri, then traveled to France and England, and they quarreled often. When they returned to Rome, Alberto sold their flat and bought a large, elegant flat in via dell'Oca. They furnished it comfortably, hung paintings on the walls, and were able to provide plenty of space for Elsa's cats and kittens. She adored cats, especially Siamese cats, wrote about them often in her letters, and (though she rarely gave interviews) even struck some reporters as *una gatta* herself. In a profile ("Talk with the Moravias") that appeared in the *New York Times* on August 3, 1952, the reporter Hedy Maria Clark observed of Elsa that "her very myopic eyes, which widen and get narrow, according to her mood; the tiny triangular face, her gestures, her walk, even her slow, shy movements, are catlike." Nine years later, a journalist from the magazine *Afrique Action* interviewed Elsa, describing her (rather perceptively) as "a strange woman who has a catlike face and, who, like a cat, has that deceptive lethargy . . . which allows her to relentlessly observe quotidian reality. Like a cat, Elsa Morante gives herself over to the piti-less dissection of life so as to be able to act slowly and seldom, but with absolute certainty."

Settled in their new home, and having achieved financial stability, Alberto and Elsa hired a cook and a housekeeper. Alberto bought his wife a fur coat, and purchased a small flat in via Archimede for her to use as a writing studio. As he later explained to a visiting reporter, "She says I am too noisy, too nervous, that she needs privacy. Can you understand that? I can write in a hotel lobby, or with someone playing [the bass] in the chair near me." Elsa admitted she was "a little ashamed" to require complete privacy to work—"After all, I have produced so little!"—but she said that "if I had to write near Alberto, I probably would not write at all. And I would be unhappy."

On November 19, 1948, Elsa signed a contract to have *Menzogna e sortilegio* translated into English for an American readership, published by Harcourt, Brace. She was excited that *Menzogna e sortilegio* would reach a larger, international readership. In the contract, the designated translator was Frances Frenaye, a distinguished, award-winning transla-tor of French and Italian authors, including Balzac, Carlo Levi, Natalia Ginzburg, and Antonio Tabucchi. She was praised by a contemporary for not confining herself to literal translation, but also "capturing both the sense and the spirit of the author's intention." (Frenaye died in 1996.) It is unclear why Frenaye did not translate Morante's novel, based on the initial agreement, but in the end *House of Liars* was translated by Adrienne Foulke, who had translated works by the Sicilian writer Leonardo Sciascia, among others. Harcourt, Brace cut nearly two hun-dred pages from Elsa's novel, leaving her furious.

On October 20, 1951, the critic Serge Hughes reviewed *House of Liars* in the *Saturday Review*: "At first glance the novel would appear to be a belated realistic novel of the late-nineteenth century. But it does not require much reading to become aware that the psychology which mo-tivates the characters is completely, darkly modern, and that in using a somewhat dated setting and technique, the author has achieved a horror effect, like that sometimes provoked by a surrealist painting in which a familiar, everyday object is placed in an utterly incongruous position." Hughes ended his piece by asserting that Morante's novel "makes Zola look jovial by comparison."

Reviewing the novel in the *New Yorker* in February 1952, Maeve Brennan described Elsa as "a young Italian writer of extraordinary emotional power. Miss Morante, it is clear, is not afraid of romantic dénouements. Neither is she afraid of passion or melodrama, or of the extravagant, elaborate phrases she handles so superbly. She seems afraid of nothing, except, possibly, the dullness and resignation of a sensible solution."

In the *Atlantic*, the critic C. J. Rolo wrote: "At the start, *House of Liars* struck me as contrived and over-extravagant. But the characterizations turn out to be rich, vivid, and arresting, and Anna's obsession is made sufficiently persuasive." And the Italian literary critic Paolo Milano, writing in the *New York Times Book Review*, noted, "Elsa Morante is the wife of novelist Alberto Moravia. Her work, however, does not betray the slightest trace of conjugal affinity or influence. She is not interested in psychological realism nor in the conflicts of urban life. . . . The impact of the novel grows continuously upon the reader and remains memorable."

For Elsa, the abridged, 565-page edition was a betrayal on every level, and she could take no pleasure in positive appraisals. She described the cuts to her work as a "mutilation." She disliked the translation. And she did not choose the book's American title, which to her should have read *Lies and Sorcery*. She learned of the editorial intentions of Harcourt, Brace, in January 1949, but was helpless to do anything to stop it. Elsa wrote an angry letter to Giulio Einaudi, the head of her Italian publishing house:

> It seems bizarre to me that an author has to defend rights that are
> so obvious and natural. I don't see how these foreign publishers

fail to realize that the weight and complexity of a work, especially books that are not just light reading but written as works of art, do not come about just by chance but are the fruit of long thought and effort, and only the author can know its reasons and its aims. That is why allowing a book to be cut without the permission of the author damages that author morally and materially and thus becomes an abuse publishable by law.

Despite Elsa's threat to take legal action, nothing came of it. (Both Einaudi and Ginzburg were sympathetic to her position.) As an author at the beginning of her career—naive to the offenses that might be committed against her work without her permission—she was powerless. After all, nothing in her contract disallowed or limited editorial cuts. The text was unalterable only in her mind.

The explanation from the book's American agent was matter-of-fact. Sanford Greenburger—a prominent literary agent and foreign publishers' representative whose clients included Franz Kafka, and who was a key figure in obtaining international publication for Faulkner and Hemingway—said that *House of Liars* was far too long for American readers and could not have been published without the edits. On January 3, 1952, a depressed and defeated Elsa wrote again to Einaudi, saying that the US edition was "unrecognizable" to her, and that its publication was one of the most hurtful things to have happened to her in the previous year. "They've massacred it," she wrote, "and what is strange is that instead of lightening it they've made it heavier. If as you say the book has been well noticed in America despite having been treated so badly, it means that it has within it treasures that are indestructible."

After this painful experience, Elsa took a hard-line approach to protect her work in subsequent book contracts, insisting on a clause prohibiting arbitrary cuts or changes to the text, and even specifying typographical changes that could be made. As she explained in a letter to her publisher, she had a particular narrative rhythm in mind. All the elements in her work were carefully considered, and "*prendono un valore non solo tipografico, ma anche poetico*" ["take on a value that is not merely typographical but also poetic"].

Tim Parks indirectly touched on this in a 2010 interview. "I think there's partly a desire on the author's part that his work arrives unmediated all over the world," he said, "and that his special individuality is not seen as culturally conditioned or conditioned by his language but that he is a supreme individual everywhere, as it were." He was referring to the act of translation in general, yet his remark captures something about Elsa's determination that her words go out into the world precisely as she wrote them.

Alberto once noted of his wife that "she had a poetics of her own and anyone who criticized that poetics was automatically wrong. She was intransigent in an almost religious way." For her, he said, "it was a matter of literary ideals." (Perhaps, along with dedication and sacrifice, this quality marks the true artist: a purity of ideals, immune to external factors.) Her rigidity extended to readings of other authors. Alberto recalled that when Elsa read *Ulysses*, despite recognizing the significance of the work, she covered the pages with "unfavorable" comments: "Joyce didn't fit into her poetics."

The "massacred" edition of *House of Liars* included another grievous blow, with flap copy noting that "this long and distinguished novel, winner of Rome's literary prize—the Viareggio—is the first work of Elsa Morante, who in private life is Mrs. Alberto Moravia." Even the vaguest suggestion of Elsa as "the wife of" could set her off. She once admonished her favorite nephew, Daniele Morante, for addressing a letter to "*Elsa Moravia*."

The eminent translator William Weaver—who over the course of his long career translated works by Italo Calvino, Primo Levi, and Umberto Eco, among many others—was in his late twenties when he befriended Elsa and Alberto (he went on to translate works by both), and discovered that socializing with them required a delicate approach:

"I quickly learned the protocol to adopt in inviting Elsa," he once said. "The important thing NOT to do was issue a double invitation. You were never to say, 'Could you and Alberto come—?' Even the use of the plural *voi* was a grave infraction of Elsa's personal rules. Sometimes Elsa's reply would be a simple no. More often she would say curtly, 'Ah, you want Alberto? Call him at—' And she would supply the number of his studio." The trick was then to mention to her, as casually as possible, that if Alberto was free, he was also welcome to join. "Elsa hated to be thought of as Mrs. Moravia," Weaver said.

He was living in Rome not long before *Menzogna e sortilegio* was published, but when he first met Elsa, he had no idea she was a writer, and knew her simply as Alberto Moravia's wife. ("Fortunately, she was unaware of this ignorance," he recalled.) When her novel came out, Weaver went out to buy the "thick Einaudi volume" and brought his copy along to dinner one night for the author to sign. After confessing that he had not yet read it ("I braced myself for her ire"), Elsa's response surprised and amused him. "Oh, how I envy you!" she said. "How I wish I could read my book with a fresh mind! What a wonderful experience you have in store for you! You're really lucky!" He did not fault her passion, describing her love for the book as "childish, innocent, pure and complete."

Widely considered the greatest of Italian translators, Weaver, who died at the age of ninety in 2013, became lifelong friends with many of the authors whose works he translated. Born in Virginia, he spoke with a faint Southern drawl and attended Princeton University before dropping out to join the American Field Service as an ambulance driver during the war, traveling between Naples and Monte Cassino. A pacifist, "I was in uniform, but I was, happily, not allowed to carry a gun," he said decades later. With no thought of becoming a translator, he fell in love with the country and its people, settled into a pensione in Rome after the war, and began teaching himself Italian. He was very much a beginner when he got to know Elsa and Alberto in the winter of 1947, not yet the expert translator who would work painstakingly to preserve the rhythms, cadences, and nuances of the originals. The couple had recently moved to their via dell'Oca apartment, close to where Weaver lived. Often when he ran into Alberto on the street, he would join his friend for neighborhood perambulations, as Alberto loved to take long walks in the afternoon—often as long as six miles a day. On these strolls, he claimed that he was simply looking at people and shop windows, not thinking about his work or anything else. "Probably because of my long isolation due to my illness, most of the time my head is completely empty," Alberto said. "I'm in a state of contemplation or, if you prefer, of totally spontaneous distraction."

Whenever Weaver was invited to stroll with his friend, he was pleased. "[A] born Roman, he knew every brick of the city; even the most drab apartment block or the scruffiest little church could set off a sparkling train of associations and memories," Weaver recalled. Alberto's style of conversation would "[flow] naturally, with fascinating shifts and turns, unexpected aperçus," and he had a wonderful laugh.

Sometimes Weaver had a night out with Elsa, Alberto, and other friends, and on rare occasions he went out with just the two of them. These more intimate nights were "fraught with risk," and by that he meant one was never quite sure when a quarrel might erupt, what had caused it, or when it was over. "We argued all the time," Alberto recalled, "and our fights had made us famous in our own world of artists and intellectuals." Bernardo Bertolucci, who became a friend of the couple, recalled that after one ugly argument between Alberto and Elsa, Alberto had to leave a restaurant during dinner and walk around the block until he cooled off. (At the same time, Bertolucci delighted in these evening conversations with his friends: he told his father, who begged him to go to college, "My university is having dinner every night with Elsa Morante, Alberto Moravia and Pier Paolo Pasolini.") Weaver recalled that Elsa would seize upon the smallest opportunity to blame her husband for something that was absolutely not his fault: if the restaurant they wanted to go to was closed, or a waiter had provided poor service, or a favorite dish was no longer on the menu.

Just as her mother had done to her husband, Elsa never hesitated to humiliate Alberto, and even to mock him as sexually impotent in front of others. Her aggression toward him seemed driven by a need to push buttons and see what came of it. In a dispute, when she felt she was right, which was nearly always, she refused to back down. And she always had to get the last word. As Tuck writes in *Woman of Rome*, Elsa was "always very outspoken, she had a mania for truth-telling, no matter how hurtful or aggressive, and she often made very provocative demands." Cesare Garboli once described the startling contrasts of his friend's personality: "Each time, our meetings were either a fight or a reconciliation. Elsa was a cannibal, waging war was her way of living; with her one had to attack or retreat, bite or be bitten."

She seemed to derive pleasure and energy from altercations. She was trying to goad her avoidant husband into anger. Alberto once said that cruelty can manifest in both tone of voice and in the words chosen to inflict harm; Elsa was cruel in both senses. As someone with "an almost pathological capacity for not taking offense," Alberto rarely reacted, but this was exactly the problem. Well aware that his apathy drove Elsa mad, he admitted that she always accused him of an "incurable detachment" that blocked him from reacting with emotion rather than intellect. Even in his book-length conversation with Elkann, this was a source of frustration: "Could you stop intellectualizing all your answers for a moment?" Elkann said at one point, seeming a bit exasperated.

In an interview, Tim Parks once commented on the Morante-Moravia dynamic, noting that Alberto was always "cool" to the relationship, someone "who would never commit himself entirely, and she was a passionate young woman . . . determined to be adored by him. So perhaps it was precisely the fact that he would never quite adore her that kept her trying to get herself adored by him, and then punishing him for not adoring her."

Weaver recalled that while staying at a borrowed apartment, he was eager to entertain friends. He found Elsa a difficult guest. Whenever he extended a dinner invitation, it was Elsa who set the time, and she would inform him of dietary restrictions that changed from one get-together to the next. (Her need for control extended to her professional dealings. After being hired by the Italian public radio station, RAI, in 1951, and given a weekly show to review films, her tenure was brief: she refused to budge under pressure by the station to give a particular film a positive review and was fired.)

Elsa also had what Weaver described as "a low boredom threshold." This would often cause her to react either with naughty, childlike glee, stirring up mischief with one of her cleverly imagined games, or by ignoring everyone. Weaver remembered that at one gathering at his apartment, Elsa discovered copies of a French art journal in a bookcase and spent the entire evening sitting in a corner on the floor, reading one issue after another and speaking to no one.

With Elsa, you never knew what you were in for. Her knack for truth-telling often upset those around her. Once, when her nephew Daniele came over to introduce his second wife, Elsa was alarmed to see that the woman did not shave her armpits, and took her to be a militant feminist. Things escalated, and an angry Elsa instructed her never to return to her home with hair under her arms. The wife never came back.

Elsa could also be wonderful company—a good listener, a great talker, and exceedingly kind. Daniele recalled of his aunt, "Alongside her written legacy there was her conversation, or even her living presence, as sharp and memorable as her writings." Those who met her, unaware they were in the presence of a great writer, "soon felt hopelessly charmed, whether compelled to go and read her writings or not." She had a dark sense of humor: Cesare Garboli once recalled that Elsa said to him, "I already know what I will do when I die. You will find a note in an envelope on which there will be written: '*torno subito*' ['I will be right back']." She was a great gift-giver and often paid for meals with friends at restaurants. She was loyal, magnetic, generous with her laughter, and someone whose companionship was "stimulating, exciting, even exhilarating in the most serious sense of the word." Daniele believed that Elsa "could have passed all her life without writing a single line, and yet remain forever in the memory of the people who had enjoyed her company." She also had a desperate desire to be loved, and sadly did not know that she was. Once, when a journalist friend said that he loved her, and that she was loved by many, she began to sob. "*Per tutta la vita non ho desiderato che questo,*" she said through tears: "In all my life I didn't desire anything else."

Along with her asperity and a temper that could frighten and alienate those who cared for her, Elsa possessed a nurturing side and served as an occasional literary mentor. She stepped in to help friends at unexpected moments and in surprising ways. One actor friend, Allen Midgette (who lived for a time in Italy and appeared in a few of Bertolucci's films), was so poor that he feared he might starve to death. He returned to his apartment one day to find that Elsa had thrown a piggy bank through his window. She was also highly sensitive to the slights and hurtful actions of others, such as Alberto's habit of absentmindedly leaving behind opened letters from her on the tables of hotels and restaurants. In a small act of revenge, she began to mark letters from him as "*Return to sender.*"

Anyone who knew her understood the ferocity of her integrity. Just as she could be generous and kind, and a delightful dinner companion, this formidable woman could turn prickly fast. If she felt that someone had said something stupid, she could not stop herself from eviscerating the person who offended her principles. She was quick to rebuke a friend who made a careless remark and would not tolerate nonsense. As Daniele recalled, "Even in a restaurant or other public venue she wouldn't refrain from interfering, straightforward and in a loud, angry voice, in the conversation of the nearby table if she overheard statements that she could suspect, say, of racism, of fascism, or simply of vulgarity."

As freely as Elsa expressed her strong emotions, for better or worse, she resisted kissing or hugging anyone. Talk was fine, no matter how heated, but touch was not. Even after Alberto returned from a long trip, she did not like to embrace him. When friends attempted to kiss her, she drew back, resulting in awkward interactions. To a close friend, she might extend a hand, but that was the extent of physical contact. Elsa was, however, an avid letter writer. She saw her close friend Pasolini nearly daily, and when she didn't, they kept up a warm correspondence in verse: once he sent her a calligram in the shape of a rose, and in return she wrote a poem in the shape of a cat. (By the end of her life, Elsa had amassed a correspondence of more than five thousand items, left in a state of disorder, but eventually organized, edited, and published by Daniele Morante in 2012.)

In her letters, Elsa made herself vulnerable, as in this 1953 letter to Luchino Visconti, claiming she was not *"una vera scrittrice"*: "Even if I did write a book, I'm not a real writer. Nowadays I'm telling everybody that I'm working all the time, and they do believe me. But that's not true. I say it just to avoid cocktails." However intimidating Elsa could be in person, her correspondence revealed much candor, admiration, and affection from friends—such as Italo Calvino, replying from Turin on March 2, 1950, to say that he loved receiving letters, "especially if they come from one of those very few people, like you, with whom I can *say something*":

Maybe you don't like hearing an author discuss one of his books with a kind of hostile detachment, you who tie yourself to the bitter end to the things you do, and who almost identify yourself with them. But you see, you have this gift of being able to unify the most disparate elements, always getting everything to work out, you have a very strong capacity for synthesizing things, a rare quality in a woman (rare? well, maybe synthesizing is the female gift par excellence). . . . You feel that the world is torn to pieces, that the things to keep hold of are very many and actually incompatible with each other, yet with your lucid and affectionate obstinacy you always make things turn out. For me, on the other hand, writing has always meant setting out in one direction, staking everything on one card, yet with the awareness that there are others, the awareness of risk and of not being able to exhaust all I have to say. For that reason my writing is always problematic.

I'll send you *Il Bianco Veliero* all the same. I want a dispassionate, detailed, rigorous verdict from you and I'll set great store by it.

Around the time she turned forty, Elsa toiled away on her second novel, *L'isola di Arturo* (*Arturo's Island*), while Alberto remained astonishingly productive. (By the end of his life, he had published many novels and short story collections, as well as plays, screenplays, translations, and more.) In 1953, he also helped launch a left-wing magazine, *Nuovi Argomenti* (New Arguments), which became one of Italy's most distinguished literary journals.

Elsa's sole "wifely" contribution to his work was to suggest the title for *La romana*, the novel that would bring Alberto international fame at the age of forty. He conceived it as a short story, finishing a draft four months later, then realized it should be a novel. He rewrote it twice and went over the manuscript a third time with detailed corrections before he was satisfied. Reflecting on the book in his *Paris Review* interview, he explained that he drew solely upon his experiences for constructing the psychology of his characters and every other aspect of his work, but "never in a documentary, a textbook, sense," he said. "No, I met a Roman woman called Adriana. Ten years afterward I wrote the novel for which she provided the first impulse. She has probably never read the book. I only saw her that once; I imagined everything, I invented everything."

From then on, he was on a roll fiction-wise, and an increasingly beloved literary figure in Italy. By 1957, Alberto had published eight books and won the Strega Prize for *I racconti*, a collection of his stories from 1927 to 1950. (In 1955, Gianni Franciolini directed a film adaptation.) Along with *La romana* came two novels in the same year: *L'amore coniugale* (*Conjugal Love*) and *Il conformista* (*The Conformist*), whose central character is so fearful of harboring sadistic and homosexual tendencies that he masks them by becoming a fascist police agent.

His 1954 novel, *Il disprezzo* (Contempt), chronicled a turbulent marriage, and it mirrored his own relationship, brimming with hostility. It was written at a time of extreme frustration with his wife. That year, Alberto took a lengthy trip with Elsa, starting in Egypt. He set off by ship before her, with the plan that she would join him after flying over from Italy. Arriving in Cairo, he sent Elsa a telegram asking her to bring his overcoat, a small request. But he committed a foolish error by addressing the telegram to "Elsa Moravia" without thinking. His wife brought the coat, but she was in a foul mood for the first few days over Alberto's offense. This cast a pall upon the rest of the journey, and as soon as the couple returned to Rome, Alberto told Elsa he would never travel with her again.

Later, Alberto said he regarded *Il disprezzo* as "one of my best novels, because it was at once profoundly felt and completely invented." Decades later, he confessed to Alain Elkann, "There were days when I wanted to kill her." Surely Elsa harbored the same impulse toward him, many times over. But her side of the story can only be pieced together in bits and pieces, through surviving diaries, interviews, essays, and correspondence. Alberto spoke freely and often about his writing and his life, but Elsa fiercely guarded her privacy. She stated explicitly that everything she had to say, and all that needed to be known about her was contained in her published work. She disliked being interviewed or photographed.

During distressing times of their marriage, Alberto couldn't bear to think of divorce—the sensible solution—because, as he put it in *Life of*

*Moravia*, "murder seemed easier than separation." Yet in his fiction, the analytical, aloof author was never one to spill from life directly onto the page for catharsis. He once described falling in love as "an existential catastrophe"—and something he had not experienced with Elsa. They were sexually incompatible. (Elsa alluded to this early on in her diary.) But he did love her and was never bored in the presence of such a passionate, volatile, fascinating woman. He spoke often and admiringly of Elsa's genius, no matter the state of their marriage. He took an unalloyed delight and pride in her work. Yet her behavior toward him was simply baffling at times: once, in a hotel room in Paris, Elsa suddenly began to moan and then passed out on the floor. Panicking, Alberto attempted to revive his wife with damp cloths, to no avail. She lay motionless. He frantically began calling doctors but had no luck reaching anyone on a Sunday. As he slumped on the bed, wondering what to do next, Elsa opened her eyes and started laughing. Like an opossum, she'd simply played dead.

Alberto claimed that as he became more detached from his marriage, he did not have a mistress, but "encounters" from time to time. Elsa had her own romantic preoccupations: for a time, she was besotted with the bisexual director and filmmaker Luchino Visconti, who had once had an affair with Coco Chanel, and who was engaged to an Austrian princess when he fell in love with a male photographer. The director Franco Zeffirelli had been a lover of Visconti as well. In the decades after World War II, Visconti—a longtime member of the Italian Communist party and one of the leading figures of neorealism—would achieve international fame and direct more than a dozen films, including adaptations of books by Dostoyevsky, Camus, and Mann.

Even Marlene Dietrich was said to be in love with him. Elsa supposedly had an affair with Visconti that began in 1955, while Alberto was traveling in America, but not everyone—including her friend Bertolucci—was convinced the relationship was consummated, or that it existed romantically beyond Elsa's imagination. She had close, somewhat maternal relationships with several gay men, especially the brilliant, controversial director and writer Pier Paolo Pasolini, whose murder in 1975, at the age of fifty-three, remains unsolved. His mutilated corpse was discovered on a deserted beach that was a favorite cruising spot. The autopsy revealed gruesome results. Among other savage acts, Pasolini had been beaten with a plank studded with nails, then run over by his own Alfa Romeo.

When Elsa knew Visconti, he was preoccupied with many creative projects, including staging Arthur Miller's *Death of a Salesman*, the first of Miller's plays to be performed in Italy. In any case, Elsa was spending a lot of time with Visconti, and she adopted his Milanese accent. He once sent her an owl in a cage as a gift. During this period she would come home late at night, sit at the foot of the bed, and excitedly recount the goings-on of the day to Alberto. He listened politely to her nightly reports, he said, like "an affectionate friend." (According to Alberto, he and Elsa had not had a physical relationship for years.) He had worked with Visconti years earlier, and described him as very handsome—suggesting a figure "in some great Renaissance portrait." After two years of this actual or one-sided affair, Elsa announced to Alberto that she was leaving him for Visconti. However, her grand plan was thwarted when her supposed lover failed to meet her. She expressed her grief loudly, and in a way that Alberto found over-the-top. "Besides being the writer of genius we know," he said, "Elsa was also a character with a considerable talent for acting and performance." When it seemed that she was leaving him for Visconti, the idea of her going away, he admitted, "grieved me very much." He described their union as a kind of existential symbiosis, something more than mere friendship—intense, despite being no longer sexual. Yet after she had been abandoned by Visconti, Alberto was unable to rejoice at her staying because living with her became almost unbearable. His 1952 story, *"Luna di miele, sole di fiele"* (translated literally as "Moon of Honey, Sun of Bile" and published in English as *Bitter Honeymoon*), is set on Anacapri, where

Alberto and Elsa traveled after their wedding. The story is a bleak portrait of a couple, Giacomo and Simona, just beginning to make a life together, with the groom pondering "the impossibility of love" and feeling anxious about his impotence. Surely Alberto was channeling his own emotions in writing, "He had a sensation of something like panic, when looking at her again he felt that his will to love was purely intellectual and did not involve his senses."

By then, Alberto and Elsa had achieved a comfortable middle-class life, and an apartment filled with paintings, elegant furnishings, and an extensive record collection. The introduction to Alberto's 1954 *Paris Review* interview features a wonderfully detailed description of via dell'Oca:

> On one side, extending unbroken from the Tiberside to Via Ripetta, sprawl the houses of working-class people: a line of narrow doorways with dark, dank little stairs, cramped windows, a string of tiny shops; the smells of candied fruit, repair shops, wines of the Castelli, engine exhaust; the cry of street urchins, the test-roar of a Guzzi, a caterwaul from a court.
>
> On the opposite side the buildings are taller, vaguely out of place, informed with the serene imperiousness of unchipped cornices and balconies overspilling with potted vines, tended creepers: homes of the well-to-do. It is here, on this side, that Alberto Moravia lives, in the only modern structure in the neighborhood, the building jutting like a jade and ivory dike into the surrounding red-gold.

Alberto's interviewers, Ben Johnson and Anna Maria de Dominicis, are greeted at the door by "a dark girl wearing the conventional black dress and white apron," with the distinguished author behind her in the entry hall, "checking the arrival of a case of wine." Alberto is described as tall and severe-looking: "the geometry of his face, its reflections, are cold, almost metallic; his voice is low, also metallic—one thinks, in each case, of gunmetal."

Meanwhile, Elsa was still a few years away from finishing *L'isola di Arturo*. In her fable-like narrative, set in the years leading up to World War II, Arturo Gerace recounts his growing-up years in a dilapidated pale pink two-story palazzo on the volcanic island of Procida, in the Bay of Naples. (She was said to have named her protagonist after Arthur Rimbaud, her favorite poet.) For a long stretch, Arturo's home represents security and safety. His existence is solitary but blissfully innocent, as he roams the island happy and free, diving into the sea "from the highest rocks," singing, and encountering "curious creatures" including a species he describes as being between a cat and a squirrel. Motherless, he recalls that a faded photograph of his deceased mother, taken when she was pregnant, is all he has left of "the object of fantastic adoration for my entire childhood." That she died as a teenager, giving birth to him, confirms for Arturo the local superstition that it was "forever fatal" for a woman to dwell in his cursed house, a rumor that gathers enough steam so that no woman would ever agree to be the family servant. In fact, the house is a former monastery known as Casa dei Guaglioni, or the Boys' House. "And so passed my solitary childhood," he recalls, "in the house denied to women." He remembers idolizing his "silent, brusque, touchy" father, Wilhelm, who regards women with contempt—and who, without explanation—stays away for most of the year, leaving his son to fend for himself. Arturo may as well have been an orphan.

He explains that did not attend school and had to educate himself, getting by with few items of clothing, no rules, no schedule, no regular meals. Arturo loves to read and feeds his appetite with hundreds of books in the house library, devouring tales of heroes both real and imagined. Freed from and abandoned by the world of adults and parental care, Arturo can make up the world as he goes along. His sole confidant and source of affection is his beloved dog, Immacolatella: "What a lot of fuss about a dog, you'll say. But when I was a boy, I'd no other friend, and you can't deny she was extraordinary. We'd invented a kind of deaf-and-dumb language between us: tail, eyes, movements, the pitch of her voice—all of them told me every thought of hers, and I understood." Immacolatella accompanies him everywhere, even on his rowboat—but he will lose her tragically too.

One day, when Wilhelm brings home a new wife, he tells his son, "This way, you'll have a new mother." At sixteen, the woman is just two years older than Arturo, and he is tormented by his complicated feelings for her. Meanwhile, Wilhelm, who treats his wife abusively and ignores her the rest of the time, is infatuated with a young male convict in the island prison. Thus, he sets a chain of events into motion that will wrench away his son's innocence, and ultimately ruin the notion of this island as a place of refuge, leaving Arturo with "an amorphous sadness, with no more feelings for anyone." And in the end, along comes the war, "imminent, inevitable." To leave Procida is to abandon his childhood idyll, but he has lost it already. He is ready to go, almost eager to become a soldier.

The heartbreak of *Arturo's Island* is in its exploration of a pure, innocent existence, removed from the complexities of adulthood—sex, betrayal, violence, abandonment—until everything that Arturo has so carefully constructed comes tumbling down. The heartbreak lies too in his unwillingness to relinquish the world he has fabricated for himself, filled with trust and hope, until he is forced from it. Reality is terrifying and cruel.

It is no coincidence that Arturo's youth unfolds in the same era in which Elsa grew up, or that her protagonist is a boy. *"Arturo, c'est moi!"* she once declared, having claimed that she wanted to be a boy and perhaps had been one in a previous life. She once explained in a rare interview that although Arturo lived on an island near Naples, "[the people] are not Neapolitan, they are very Sicilian on those islands," she said. "I have always been fascinated by the dark island people of the Mediterranean, and by writing about Arturo I could become one *moi-même*. And I've always wanted to be a boy, a boy like Arturo, who can hunt and fish and climb big rocks, and go about dressed badly, and have the dreams and illusions of a boy."

Elsa had always adored babies and children, and in later years spoke with regret about not having become a mother herself. Perhaps the only things she loved as much as children were caring for her cats and listening to music—particularly Mozart, whom she cited as her greatest influence. Yet as Tuck writes in *Woman of Rome*, "[I]t is difficult in retrospect to imagine how she would have pursued her career as a writer had she had children or, for that matter, difficult to imagine what sort of mother she might have been." She certainly lacked a good role model. Tuck posits that Elsa's lifelong interest in handsome young gay men arose from a sense of safety: there was a charge with no possibility of sex. But Tuck believes that the attraction "had more to do with her maternal instincts and her desire to have a son. . . . Elsa's love for these young men can be compared to the love that she might have felt for a child of her own."

At the same time, Elsa had always envied the freedom and power of men. They could be the heroes of their own lives. Girls, however, represented passivity and weakness, though perhaps it was self-loathing that made her ill at ease with her gender. Being associated with the diminutive label "woman writer" was repellent to Elsa too, and she refused to allow her work to be included in any anthology based on such a theme. And just as she could not stand being called by her married name, she was dismayed that most married women gave up their own surnames to be known only as "Mrs." or "the wife of" their husbands. How could they tolerate this elision of identity?

At times, Elsa seemed to harbor startling animosity toward her gender, both in life and in fiction. Some of her views were expressed through Wilhelm's contempt for women, an attitude that influences young Arturo: "They were ashamed of themselves," he says, "maybe because they were so ugly; and they went around like sad animals."

Further, he points out that families on Procida are "displeased" when a daughter is born: "They were small beings, who could never grow as tall as a man, and they spent their lives shut up in kitchens and other rooms: that explained their pallor. Bundled into aprons, skirts, and petticoats, in which they must always keep hidden, by law, their mysterious body, they appeared to me clumsy, almost shapeless figures."

Elsa often felt insecure and inadequate alongside Alberto, with his blithe and uncomplicated relationship to success. If he embraced happiness, Elsa's nature was almost to recoil from it. Yet at the same time she took great pride in herself, whether her physical appearance or her writing. Bold in every respect, she was one of the first women in Italy to wear trousers in public. However, she would never define herself as *un femminista*. As ever, she was full of contradictions, laid bare but never reconciled in her work.

Inhabiting boyhood through Arturo, Elsa stretched her imagination into other unexpected experiences. A lifelong cat lover, she directed the boy's devotion and affection toward a dog, and later admitted that she began to love dogs herself. She loved the sea but was terrified of it and unable to swim, yet she crafted glorious depictions of Arturo swimming in the Neapolitan sea. And in finding a way to "tell all the truth but tell it slant—" in the famed words of Emily Dickinson, through Arturo's worship of Wilhelm, and Wilhelm's secret infatuation with a young man, Elsa could explore her own tormented yearnings for gay men, notably her relationship with Visconti. As Stefania Lucamante, professor (emerita) of Italian studies at the Catholic University of America, notes in her essay anthology *Elsa Morante's Politics of Writing*, however much Elsa Morante has been criticized for her supposed misogyny, she was among the first authors in Italian literature "to openly address (and understand) the vexing situation of being homosexual in Italian society, homophobia, and the disturbance her characters [like Wilhelm] would bring to stifling societal norms."

When *L'isola di Arturo* was published in 1957, Elsa was the first woman to be awarded the Strega Prize, five years after her husband had won. Foreign rights were sold in France, Germany, Sweden, Norway, and Finland, and in 1959, Collins issued it in England with a beautiful watercolor illustration on the cover. This was a very good time for Elsa, workwise: in 1958, a collection of her poetry, *Alibi*, was published by Longanesi Editions. Three poems were addressed to her cats.

In the United States, Blanche Knopf wrote to a colleague, "I have just bought the one great book in Italy that by all accounts is worth having." She paid fifteen hundred dollars for the US rights to the novel. Unlike the difficulties she'd experienced with the American edition of her previous novel, this time, Elsa felt good about the deal. She had met (and liked) Blanche in Rome and was honored to land at such a distinguished publishing house. The two began to exchange warm, affectionate letters, and Blanche started taking Italian lessons. Although there were some issues with the translation, the women remained friendly, and Elsa was pleased to be closely involved with various decisions. *Arturo's Island* was published in the United States on August 17, 1959, the day before Elsa's forty-seventh birthday, translated by the writer and film critic Isabel Quigly. The biographer and Flaubert scholar Francis Steegmuller, who would marry the novelist Shirley Hazzard four years later, contributed a blurb: "The most beautiful novel I've read in years." (In 2019, *Arturo's Island* was reissued by Liveright, with a new translation by Ann Goldstein.)

The reviews were enthusiastic. In the *New York Times Book Review*, Frederic Morton wrote, "Miss Morante possesses the Italian gift of distilling universality out of the primitive. But she also has a fine feminine instinct for the singing detail." (The use of "feminine" to describe her instinct could not have pleased Elsa.) "The combination enables her to create a poetic, princely savage of a hero," Morton noted, "half freebooter, half Huckleberry Finn. She catches the echo and iridescence of a tragedy from which lucky old Huck was spared: growing up." Despite writing a favorable review, the critic chose to open it in an unfortunate way: "In 1951 Elsa Morante—in private life, Mrs. Alberto Moravia—made her American debut as a novelist with 'The House of Liars.'" She was still very much Elsa Morante in her private life, of course, and never anything but.

Two days later, in a review in the weekday *New York Times*, Gilbert Millstein praised *Arturo's Island* as "sublime," adding, "I also want the book to be as widely read as is possible for a fine contemporary novel. I am not being excessive." He waited until the penultimate line to mention that Miss Morante "quite incidentally, is the wife of Alberto Moravia."

About a year and a half earlier, having expressed to Blanche Knopf her desire to visit the United States, Elsa finally arrived in New York City in September 1959 for a monthlong trip. During her time there, she met Bill Morrow, a tall, handsome twenty-three-year-old painter from Madisonville, Kentucky. A former model, blue-eyed and blond, he had a wide social circle of friends and both men and women seemed to fall in love with him. Like Visconti, he was someone whom everybody was drawn to. In fact, he was so good-looking that Alberto once said he had never quite grasped male homosexual love until meeting Bill Morrow. In Rome, Bernardo Bertolucci asked a friend to tell him about the young man whom everyone was talking about "as if he were Jesus Christ."

Bill and Elsa fell into an intense love affair. He had been the one to pursue her, and he was the New York souvenir Elsa brought back to Rome. She rented an apartment for them on via del Babuino, and he spent his days painting while she worked on her next novel, *Senza i comforti della religione* (Without the Comfort of Religion). Communication between them was challenging, as Bill didn't know much Italian, and Elsa was not a confident English speaker. She used impassioned hand gestures to make meaning when the words would not come, or would stop herself with a "how do you say . . . ?" or toss in a French word to fill the gaps in her English. Yet Elsa was happy, perhaps happier than she had ever been, and full of life. In 1960, during a stay in New York, she wrote to her dear friend Pier Paolo Pasolini, "This is not *a* city, but *the* city, it is the universe, the firmament, the viscera of the earth. You would love it!"

Despite her love for Bill, she understood he was troubled, and fretted over him in a maternal way. He was an epileptic, prone to seizures. He drank to excess and was addicted to Seconal. And he had been hospitalized at least once following a suicide attempt. Still, he worked steadily toward a show of his brightly colored paintings in 1961 at the Galerie Lambert in Paris, and another the following year at the Nuova Pesta gallery in Rome. By this time, Alberto and Elsa were married in name only. While Elsa found love with Bill, Alberto moved on with the writer Dacia Maraini, with whom he would remain for the next two decades (until she ended the relationship). "I fell in love in the only way I am capable of: very slowly, beginning almost with indifference and ending with passion," recalled Alberto. As he and Elsa led separate lives, they discovered they got along much better that way—to the extent that they took two trips together, one to Iran in 1958, and a journey to India in 1960, accompanied by Pasolini. Both trips reminded Alberto why he had vowed never to travel with his wife. In Iran, Elsa refused to leave her postcards with the hotel desk clerk, convinced he would steal the postage money without mailing the cards. When Alberto and Elsa went to the post office to buy stamps, Elsa became angry when the postal worker only spoke Farsi and blamed Alberto. In India, she berated him for not being more patient when a number of beggars surrounded him. She returned to their hotel in a rage, began packing her bags, and calmed down only after Alberto and Pasolini pleaded with her to stay.

Relations between Alberto and Elsa were cordial enough for him to write something for *Vernissage*, Bill's exhibit in Paris. Alberto loved painting as an art form, ranking it just below literature and above cinema, and once saying that it was the art he understood and loved best. He praised Bill's paintings for the Paris show, writing that they were "so immediate, so pure, so calm and limpid" and ending his piece with a prescient line: "Thus, once again, art will have been paid for by life."

In 1962, a month after his show in Rome, Bill went to New York for a brief trip. He planned on returning to Italy to settle in Rome with Elsa as a permanent resident, but never made it back. On a windy day in April, believed to be hallucinating on LSD, Bill jumped from a Manhattan skyscraper.

At fifty, Elsa felt that there was no joy ahead, no future. Shocked and devastated by the loss of Bill, she was no longer able to write. She dropped *Senza i comforti della religione* (Without the Comfort of Religion) and never worked on it again. Alberto said that in the aftermath of Bill's death, "Elsa had a great sense of the tragic. . . . [S]he staged a great mourning scene no less sincere than the grief displayed in southern Italy by bereaved widows and mothers." In 1964, Elsa wrote in her diary: "Two years since April 30. And I continue to live as if I were still alive. At certain moments, I forget the horror. Some bit of consolation arrives, as if I had found you in something else. But then the pain returns unexpectedly." Also, her mother died in a nursing home in 1963, at the age of eighty-three. Although Elsa had rarely visited Irma and was once chastised by a nun at the clinic for wearing trousers, she organized an elaborate funeral for her mother.

Now Elsa referred to writing only in the past tense, convinced that life was over. She was finished, used up. "What has happened and where have you been and have you been writing?" Blanche Knopf wrote in the spring 1963. Elsa did not respond. Knopf wrote again in early 1965, upset at the lack of response and mentioning that the author was overdue to write a new book. Still no reply. Elsa had not been in touch with her Italian publisher, or with her agent, for quite some time. (Although Einaudi published a collection of twelve stories by Elsa in 1963, they were written years earlier.) In yet another letter, Knopf tried again, writing to say that she had heard Elsa was finishing a novel: "It has been too long since I have heard anything from you so I long to have an answer to this. I hope you are well and having a lovely time and getting on fast with this new book."

Slowly, Elsa found her way back to living, beyond mere survival. She began to travel a bit, alone or with a friend, with no itinerary or plan: "I stop where I like and for however long I like," she wrote in her diary. She went to visit her brother Aldo for Christmas in Mexico City. After Pasolini enlisted her to select music for the soundtrack of his new film, *The Gospel According to St. Matthew*, she found that her involvement in the project kept her focused and occupied. She finally moved out of the apartment she had rented for Bill and herself, and went back to the via dell'Oca flat. Elsa immersed herself in home redecoration, making the place her own with new furniture, new wallpaper, and Bill's paintings. She hated television and did not own one until 1969, when she bought a set just to watch the moon landing. She never turned it on again. The previous year, she managed to publish another poetry collection, *Il mondo salvato dai ragazzini e altri poemi*.

Meanwhile, Alberto's stature had grown: he was president of PEN International from 1959 to 1962, and had published a few more novels—including the iconic *La Noia* (*Boredom*), which won the Viareggio Prize and was adapted for film. He appeared to lead a charmed life. And he had become enough of a literary celebrity that the *New York Times* covered his world tour in May 1964, including a stop in New York to give a lecture at the Metropolitan Museum of Art, where he won "great applause" from the audience of 750 people. The article also mentioned that his typewriter had been stolen in Vienna, which was a bit of a problem since he had been sharing it with Dacia. Like Elsa, Dacia was an afternoon writer, but she wrote daily, with a strict routine. Alberto would put in his few hours at the typewriter, then hand it off to Dacia to do her work while he took his afternoon stroll. Having given no physical description of Alberto, the *Times* reporter, Harry Gilroy, kept a keen eye on Dacia: "As [Moravia] talked, Miss Maraini came along, 27 years old, a blonde with blue-gray eyes, dressed in a brown leather coat and red skirt, pretty and graceful. She announced that before leaving Rome she had finished another novel. She has been writing since 19."

Alberto and Elsa, after more than twenty years together, would always have a profound bond. As Alberto said in *Life of Moravia*, "About Elsa there would be many things to say; I'd never finish." He added generously that "she believed, and she was right to believe, that she was a great writer."

Both must have been relieved that there was no stormy finish to their union. It simply stopped. There was no divorce; Elsa was Catholic. (After the relationship ended, someone remarked to Alberto, "Pity. Morante-Moravia had such a good sound.") He went off to live with Dacia in Lungotevere della Vittoria, while Elsa stayed at via dell'Oca, but Alberto made sure that Elsa was financially secure. Rather than sending her "the usual bourgeois monthly allowance," he said, he opened a bank account in her name, with a checkbook of her own, so she would have full control and autonomy over the money. If Elsa had not met Bill, and if Alberto had not fallen in love with Dacia, they might have remained together, however unhappily. But as they happened to drift off in different directions, Alberto said, the marriage collapsed on its own. He recalled flying to Africa with Dacia, gazing out the window of the plane, and suddenly feeling "a sense of absolute physical liberation. As if I had rid myself of something heavy, like a plaster cast." Even so, for many years afterward, he admitted he "felt intermittently a horrible sensation of being abandoned." Regardless of the circumstances around the cessation of a relationship, and no matter the nature of the relationship, he believed that every ending was a kind of death.

In the early 1970s, Elsa worked on a new novel, *La storia* (*History*), set in Rome and its outskirts between 1941 and 1947, and divided into nine chronological sections by year. She had a very specific agenda for this book. It was intended to reach everyone—not just the intellectuals, the cognoscenti, but the poor and uneducated. Her epigraph conveys this desire in a borrowed line from the Peruvian poet César Vallejo: "*Por el analfabeto a quien escribo*" ("To the illiterate for whom I write"). Einaudi published the novel in 1974, and in the interest of accessibility,

Elsa pushed for a paperback release, rather than the traditional hardcover, and she set the bargain price of two thousand lire. She accepted a five percent royalty on sales, rather than the customary ten percent in Italy. She also selected the grim cover image by Robert Capa, depicting a young man lying dead on a pile of rubble. The picture was accompanied by a provocative caption: "A scandal that has lasted ten thousand years."

This sprawling novel, with its doomed characters and depictions of wartime atrocities, may have seemed like the least likely candidate for a wildly popular read. And because of its failure to align with the political left, or any particular movement—and its vision deemed too pessimistic—the novel was polarizing and controversial. (The weekly magazine *La Fiera Letteraria*, meaning "Literary Fair," even devoted two issues to analyzing whether *La storia* was a masterpiece.) Yet several thousand copies of the novel were flying off booksellers' shelves each week, and within a year it had sold eight hundred thousand copies. (*La storia* would be adapted into a film by the director Luigi Comencini in 1986.) Elsa's agent wrote a letter to Knopf saying that they no longer knew who was buying the book, "since there appear to be copies in every Italian household by now." Some critics regarded it as one of the great novels of the twentieth century, on a par with the works of Joyce, Kafka, and Proust, among others. Knopf published the American edition in 1977, with a translation by William Weaver, and foreign rights were sold in several other countries. Although the novel would perform poorly in the United States, it was a huge hit in France and reprinted three times by Gallimard. Best of all, Elsa fulfilled her wish to reach people from all walks of life. "For the first time since anyone can remember, people in railroad compartments and espresso bars discuss a book—the Morante novel—rather than the soccer championship or latest scandal," raved Paul Hofmann, a Rome correspondent for the *New York Times*. Calling the novel "a literary sensation" and "the most successful Italian book since Giuseppe Tomasi di Lampedusa's *The Leopard*, Hofmann noted that the author was the estranged wife of Alberto Moravia and that she had been living as a recluse during the writing of *La storia*. Describing her previous books as "more praised than read," Hofmann went on, "Miss Morante has for years been cultivating obscurity. She does not belong to any coterie of intellectuals and does not sign manifestos or publicly back inflammatory causes. Now, apparently to her immense dislike, she suddenly finds herself a celebrity, 'La Morante.'"

William Weaver, who was living in Tuscany while he worked on the translation, adored and admired his friend but admitted she was "a pain in the neck." Decades later, he described his experience to the *Paris Review*:

> Every now and then she would call me up in the morning. I had told her once that I worked from the time I got up until about ten-thirty, and then I would have a cup of coffee, and then I would work again until lunchtime. She would always phone at ten-thirty, thinking that that was my break. The reason I took the break was that I didn't want to think about translation for half an hour or so before I went back to it. But she would call and start asking questions. She said, Now on page three hundred and fifty-nine when I use the word so-and-so, how will you translate that? And I said, Elsa, I'm on page one hundred and twenty-three. I've got no idea! That didn't stop her, and she started calling me almost daily at ten-thirty, ruining my morning. Finally I sat down and wrote her a long letter: Dear Elsa, I'm giving up the job. I think you better find somebody else. I don't think that this is working. I made a copy for the publisher and another for my agent, and I sealed them all in airmail envelopes on a table in the entrance hall, from which the mail went out in the morning. It wasn't going to go out until the next day. Just then Elsa called and said, I'm calling to say this is the last time I'm going to call you because I realize that this is not helping you. She had read my mind. I thought I'd torn up all the letters, but I apparently saved

a carbon for myself, and years later when a student of mine was going through my papers he said, Bill, here's this weird letter to Elsa Morante. I'd completely forgotten about it. She was by far the hardest person I worked with.

Elsa described her novel as "an act of accusation and a prayer." Whereas in previous stories, she had spun the lives of ordinary characters into lyrical and fantastic tales in which reality played an intrusive role, now war was the subject, ineluctable, with powerless working-class people fighting to survive the horrors and chaos of war and its aftermath. The novel opens in 1941, with a teenage German soldier named Gunther wandering the streets of Rome, in search of a brothel. He gets drunk and stumbles down the street, running into a widowed, epileptic, half-Jewish teacher, Ida, weighed down with her shopping bags. Under the guise of offering to help, Gunther ends up in her home, "raping her with rage as if he wanted to murder her." On his way to the African front a few days later, he's killed in an Allied air attack. Ida is pregnant. She's left to raise the baby, Giuseppe, who is also epileptic, along with raising her troubled older son, Nino, who will flirt with fascism and later join the Communist-led resistance. Even after the war ends, tragedy upon tragedy is yet to come. Ida too is swallowed up by madness and almost unbearable grief. Salvation is nowhere.

In her introduction to an American edition of *History* for members of the First Edition Society of Pennsylvania, Elsa explained her intentions in writing it: "With the present book, I who was born at a time of certain horror (in our 20th century), I wanted to leave a documented testimony of my direct experience of the Second World War, exposing it as an extreme and bloody example of the total body of history through time. Here is History for you. Just the way it is and just the way we contributed to make it."

For some critics, *History* is Elsa's masterpiece, her towering achievement. Others have never come around to this messy novel, with its mix of reportage, philosophical asides, didactic storytelling ("History is a history of fascisms, more or less disguised . . ."), passages of poetry, jeremiad of atrocities, and elements of magical realism in the form of human-canine communication: a talking dog. ("Often presented as the one Morante novel everyone should read, *History* has neither the charm nor the dazzling imaginative richness of the others," Tim Parks wrote in the *New York Review of Books* in 2009.) The book reads like a bunch of narratives loosely stitched together, punctuated by a polemical take on historical events. Additionally, each temporally marked section of the novel opens with a few pages of italicized factual summaries of the year's corresponding developments: *"Revolutionary movements begin among the peoples of the colonies. Clashes with the British police in Calcutta and in Cairo, with a high number of victims among the demonstrators"*; *"In China, battles between the Red Army and the Kuomintang continue."* These summaries are not really framing devices, however. Writing in *Harper's Magazine* in 2009, Robert Boyers, a professor of English at Skidmore College and editor of the literary journal *Salmagundi*, noted that these prefaces "do not, except in rare instances, directly relate to anything that follows in the respective chapters. Considered as framing devices, they are fragmentary and transparently inadequate. They cannot possibly tell us what to make of the abundant narrative materials assembled in the various chapters, where the focus is relentlessly intimate. Morante's humble yet gargantuan task is to look closely at the experience of living in a time of crisis, to take us inside the thoughts and feelings of ordinary people. What there is of theory in any of this is minimal and clearly irrelevant in shaping the impressions we derive as readers who are privy to these lives."

In a piece entitled "Melancholic and Magic History" in the April 28, 1977, issue of the *New York Review of Books*, Stephen Spender praised Weaver's translation for the American edition and wrote that "to try to extract a message or lesson from Elsa Morante's book is to follow too literally the clue hinted at in the title. The story that she has to tell stands marvelously on its own." He praised her further, writing, "She is a storyteller who spellbinds the reader. Like Flaubert she seems a great processional artist who can cover an enormous canvas, introducing, as the plot develops, new characters who are fixed and made convincing in a few swift strokes, and who are caught up in the sweep of the whole narrative."

Natalia Ginzburg once mentioned how much she admired her friend's confident use of the third-person voice in the novel—the narrator, who is Morante herself, serves as both storyteller and witness to the horrific events that unfold—because in her own work, Ginzburg felt unable to "climb up on mountains and see everything from above." When *La storia* first came out, she had given the novel an excellent review in *Corriere della sera*, proclaiming it "the most beautiful novel of this century." Inexplicably, Elsa reacted negatively to the piece, insisting that Ginzburg's review was *too* enthusiastic, almost aggressively so. As ever, Elsa was tough to please.

Writing in the *New York Times* on April 24, 1977, the critic Robert Alter gave the novel a negative review. He noted that although *History* offers "a good many arresting moments" and "manages to carry out wonderful forays into the uncanny, moving from bleak earthbound things to metaphysical vistas," the novel fails as a whole. Alter was put off by, among other things, the author's inability to resist "a pathetic overload of detail and commentary." Further, he wrote that "Morante's compassion . . . frequently spills over into pathetic excess, and her tough realism breaks down into a tediously proliferated series of disasters rigged by the novelist against her own creation." Nonetheless, the *Times* ran an excerpt from *History* (a passage chronicling the final days of the German occupation of Rome), and the novel was selected as a recommended read, along with novels by Joan Didion, Donald Barthelme, John Cheever, and others.

The most damning review came from a most unlikely source: her dear friend Pasolini, who wrote what can only be described as a hit job for the magazine *Tempo Illustrato*. This was her first novel in nearly a decade, but Pasolini showed no mercy. He praised the sheer ambition of *History*—the title alone, claiming history as a constructed narrative, revealed its monumental aims. Yet his piece brimmed with hostility and condescension. He criticized as implausible everything the characters did and said, mocking their "unrecognizable" dialects. Dividing the novel into three discrete sections for analysis, he claimed that the last two were "nothing more than a mass of haphazard thrown together information." He also ridiculed Elsa for the "mannerism" of her prose, though if anything she avoided the heightened language (or overheated, as some critics charged) of her previous novels. The cruelest aspect of the review was his attack on her political agenda, which he claimed lacked credibility. Pasolini also felt that the author had made use of suffering, poverty, and deprivation in false and exploitative ways.

Either he had given up on his friendship with Elsa or he was attempting to kill it. The two had grown apart in the last few years, but it must have been impossible for her to contain her hurt at this betrayal, or to comprehend the viciousness, on every level, of her friend's review. After the piece appeared, Elsa never spoke to Pasolini again, and he was murdered the following year.

She began working almost immediately on what would be her fourth and final novel, *Aracoeli*. She was reading Dante, Proust, and Baudelaire, among others, as she wrote. This period coincided with Elsa's descent into isolation, in which she rejected some longtime friends, stopped seeing many acquaintances, and made no more attempts at romantic love. That part of her life was dead. After sending the completed manuscript of *Aracoeli* to a typist, she began suffering from leg pain that left her bedridden for months. (How much of this pain was psychosomatic is unclear.) Now in her sixties, Elsa was depressed by what she saw as the ugly decay of her aging body. She felt a persistent desire to disappear, and she was quicker to rage. She gave up on beauty, let her hair go white, and dressed like an old lady. Her friend Carlo Cecchi was startled one day to run into a haggard Elsa on the street, walking with a cane.

Named for the Basilica of Santa Maria in Aracoeli ("Altar of Heaven") in Rome, the chilling story has no chapter breaks, no respite. The forty-three-year-old homosexual narrator, Manuel, an ugly, self-hating, recovering drug addict, chronicles his lonely and painful quest to visit the Andalusian birthplace of his late mother, Aracoeli, a former peasant girl who married his father, Eugenio, a handsome Italian naval officer, over the objections of his bourgeois parents. Manuel confesses that his mind has been conditioned to accept "irreparable rejection," and that "if I look in the direction of my future, I see only a twisted track along which my usual self, always alone and older all the time, continues to drag himself back and forth, like a drunken commuter. Until an enormous crash comes, and all traffic ceases." He has never been abroad. Life toggles between small rooms in Milan: the little furnished one where he struggles to pay the rent, and the "little publishing firm" consisting of "two office rooms complemented by a dark, windowless toilet" where Manuel spends his days reading and translating texts under consideration from aspiring authors ("the majority of them elderly") and writing up reports. It's a dreary job he likens to swallowing glue.

*Aracoeli* was published in 1982, with an American edition from Random House two years later, translated by William Weaver. It contains familiar elements from the author's previous novels: flashbacks, dreams, class tensions, familial secrets, innocence lost, scandalous love, psychic wounds, and the pessimism of *History* taken to new heights—or depths, rather. We are tossed once again into the land of the incomprehensible and inconsolable. Reviewing the American edition on January 13, 1985, in the *New York Times*, the critic and translator Raymond Rosenthal described the experience of reading *Aracoeli*: "Most of the time one feels cornered, as one does when an importunate acquaintance tells a tale of woe that deserves pity but utterly fails to arouse either real interest or sympathy."

Manuel is a ghost-chaser. He reveals that thirty-seven years have passed since Aracoeli was buried in the Verano cemetery in Rome, his native city, but he is headed to Spain because "after so many years of oblivious separation," he is going to look for her. At times, "especially in spells of extreme loneliness—a desperate pulse starts to throb in the living, and it drives them to seek their dead not only in time but also in space." He recalls that in the Second World War, "during an air raid on the city the Verano cemetery had been devastated by bombs: many graves had been uncovered, tombs demolished, cypresses uprooted." Manuel believes that his mother fled her own grave, "in fear, bloodstained, in the same rumpled nightgown she was wearing when I visited her for the last time." He has idealized memories of her love only from the first few years of his life, when she nursed him, and he adored her intensely, and was the center of her world. But he is displaced after she gives birth to his younger sister, who dies soon after. When Aracoeli reemerges from her depression and grief, she is a different woman, self-absorbed, wild, and unrecognizable. She becomes highly sexualized and turns into a nymphomaniac, rejecting her son in favor of reckless and random encounters—then dies from a brain tumor. "Not since Celine has there been so violent a protest against life's conditions," wrote Rosenthal, "such outrage at the thought of death, so relentless an assault on the bare physical facts of human existence; but without Celine's saving satiric humor and his lyrical poignancy." In *Woman of Rome*, Lily Tuck admits that the first time she read *Aracoeli*, she found it "almost pointlessly disturbing and shocking." Upon rereading, "I have also grown to admire it—perhaps because it is so dark and resists any attempts to classify it." In this sense, *Aracoeli* is not unlike the author herself, who defied all attempts to be classified in any fixed way, or aligned with a particular ideology, and who was brave enough, as Tuck points out, to have "knowingly sacrificed clarity and logic in order to express her vision of a chaotic world."

When Manuel confesses, "Of all the possible blessings people hunger for, the only one I ever wanted was: 'to be loved,'" his yearning is reminiscent of the sadness Elsa had expressed many times at feeling unloved. "Even stray animals seek, more than food, caresses, spoiled, even they, by the mother who licked them as cubs day and night," Manuel says. It is surely no coincidence that he sets off on his Andalusian journey right around the date of Pasolini's murder in 1975. Like Elsa, Manuel is nearsighted, a sign of frailty and a source of anxiety and shame. The disgust he feels about his deteriorating body corresponds directly with Elsa's sadness over her physical decline, the self-loathing magnified in old age. There was not much left to live for. Indeed, as Tuck writes, by the end of the novel "one is left with the terrifying awareness that nothing matters any longer for the protagonist or, perhaps, for the writer as well. . . . Only death remains."

Less than six months after *Aracoeli* was published, on April 6, 1983, Elsa tried to kill herself. After swallowing some sleeping pills, she closed all the windows of her apartment and turned on the gas. Her maid of more than three decades, Lucia, saved her just in time. An unconscious Elsa was rushed to Rome's San Giacomo Hospital. (It shut down in 2008 after nearly seven hundred years of continuous operation.) Alberto came to see her right away. While she was being treated, doctors discovered a buildup of fluid in her brain; the pressure could cause brain damage or prove fatal. The surgery required draining the trapped fluid, and despite the risks, Alberto and Elsa's sister, Maria, believed an operation at a local clinic was the right decision. Elsa survived, but as a shadow of her former self. She was a shocking sight to those who visited her afterward, and her recovery at the clinic was uneven and slow. She was comatose at first, and after that went in and out of periods of lucidity. Elsa spent most of her time in bed. When she was up to it, she read the copy of Dante's *Inferno* in her lap, and sometimes she would be taken outside in her wheelchair to sit in the garden. Lucia slept in the same room each night, never leaving her side, and Alberto was a good friend to his estranged wife during this time, visiting her often. After rallying briefly in mid-1984—working with a physical therapist and learning to walk a few steps again—Elsa hoped to return home by Christmas and perhaps even write again. (She had some good news: *Aracoeli* was awarded the prestigious Prix Médicis Etranger in France.) In the clinic, Elsa befriended a young Libyan boy with cancer in the room next to hers, teaching him Italian and giving him a copy of *Peter Pan*. "You are the only light in this dismal place," she told him.

In January 1985, after being rushed into emergency surgery for a perforated ulcer, Elsa suffered peritonitis. She had to be catheterized, and after that she was in extreme pain and discomfort, left nearly catatonic or asleep much of the time. She was alive but not living, and her condition did not improve over the next several months. On November 25, Elsa had a heart attack and died in her bed.

"I still feel the tremendous loss of Elsa Morante," Natalia Ginzburg said in an interview with *Salmagundi* in the fall of 1992. "[Her death] was not only a personal loss to her friends, but a great loss to the world. She was, I believe, the greatest writer of our time. I don't know how much her work is valued in [the United States], but here while she had great success she was also rejected by a number of people. And this rejection caused her much suffering."

One of the contemporary Italian writers most influenced by Elsa Morante is the pseudonymous author Elena Ferrante, who achieved international fame with her Neapolitan novels. (Her name alone displays the influence: Elsa/Elena, Morante/Ferrante.) Ferrante once said that as a teenager, she was captivated by *House of Liars*: "There I discovered what literature can be," she said in an interview with *Vogue*. "That novel multiplied my ambitions, but it also weighed on me, paralyzing me." In 2014, asked by the *New York Times* where she saw herself in the Italian literary tradition, Ferrante replied: "I've always been more interested in storytelling than in writing. Even today, Italy has a weak narrative tradition. Beautiful, magnificent, very carefully crafted pages abound, but not the flow of storytelling that despite its density manages to sweep you away. A bewitching example is Elsa Morante. I try to learn from her books, but I find them unsurpassable."

Loved, hated, neglected, and admired, Elsa Morante was a writer to be reckoned with. After her death, Italy's leading newspapers wrote lengthy obituaries devoted to her and her work. (Many erroneously cited her birth year as 1918, but she was seventy-three when she died.) The funeral was packed. A crowd of mourners waited outside in the cold to pay tribute as her plain wooden coffin, laden with wreaths, passed by in the procession. Alberto also attended the mass in the church of Santa Maria del Popolo.

A few months after Elsa died, Alberto caused a stir by marrying Carmen Llera, a young Spanish woman. "The grand old man of Italian literature, Alberto Moravia, 78, married a 32-year-old publishing executive in a brief ceremony at the Rome City Hall Monday," UPI reported on January 27, 1986. "'Moravia is different because no one can write as well as he does,' Carmen Llera said of her new husband, whom she had lived with for three years. The couple declined to kiss for photographers and television cameramen and left almost immediately after the ceremony—Moravia going back to work on his novel and Llera off to the publishing house where she runs the press office."

On September 26, 1990, Alberto died in his apartment. He was hailed as Italy's most widely read author, his works translated into some thirty languages and selling millions of copies around the world. President Francesco Cossiga praised Alberto as a "biting but also highly sensitive narrator of Italian society in the 20th century: its contradictions, bewilderments and anxious search for values."

Elsa was not, and never would be, a writer for everyone, but her reputation remains secure. In recent years, new editions of her novels have been published, including the reissue of *Lies and Sorcery*, translated by Jenny McPhee. As the critic Robert Boyers notes in his introduction to the 2009 edition of *Aracoeli* (which he describes as "unbearably poignant"), Elsa asked her readers, particularly in her final two works, to "absorb complex shocks of feeling." She refused to offer a comfortable reading experience. He adds: "These are not novels for the faint of heart."

Alberto spoke movingly in his memoir about how Elsa's death affected him, saying that although it was not caused by criminal violence, like the fate of Pasolini, it was "a horrible death, undeserved, unjust, and decidedly unlucky."

In her 1959 interview with the *New York Times*, Elsa—the most famous female writer in Italy at the time—was asked whether she and Alberto had influenced each other's writing. She stiffened. "No," she said. "No. He has an identity. I have an identity. *Básta*." The interview stopped there. She had nothing more to say.

# ELAINE DUNDY
## and Kenneth Tynan

"Life was perfect, perfect, perfect."

The Dud Avocado made me laugh, scream and guffaw (which, incidentally, is a great name for a law firm)," Groucho Marx wrote in a fan letter to the author. "If this was actually your life, I don't know how the hell you got through it." Gore Vidal praised the debut novel as "one of the funniest books I have ever read," and said it should have been subtitled "Daisy Miller's Revenge."

The author was a thirty-seven-year-old American woman named Elaine Dundy. Her novel, published by Victor Gollancz in England in the winter of 1958, chronicles the boozy, comedic, virginity-losing misadventures of recent college graduate Sally Jay Gorce—beautiful, exuberant, privileged, stylish, and irresponsible—who lands in Paris in the late 1950s, ready to conquer all. (Her surname came from a character in James Thurber's *Men, Women and Dogs*.) The protagonist swerves from cafés and nightclubs to society parties and the beds of handsome young men. "We were looking for a mood," says Sally Jay, "and were hell-bent on living." She's a not-so-innocent abroad, impulsive and free as only the young can be: "Frequently, walking down the streets in Paris alone, I've suddenly come upon myself in a store window grinning foolishly away at the thought that no one in the world knew where I was at just that moment." One critic called the novel "light as a champagne bubble," praising the charm of Sally Jay's "innocent zest for life." When E. P. Dutton issued the American edition, the publisher took out a large ad in the *New York Times*, accompanied by blurbs, charming illustrations, and snappy copy: "Sally Jay is the captivating, off-beat heroine. Held together by safety pins, led by her 'questing profile,' she whirls from the Dives of the Left Bank to the Ritz, in love with Paris and with love itself."

Elaine Dundy—née Brimberg—was born in 1921 to a Jewish cloth-ing manufacturer, Samuel Brimberg, and his wife, Florence, in Man-hattan. Along with her parents and two sisters, Shirley (b. 1919) and Betty (b. 1924), Elaine lived for her first eight years in a large, sunny apartment on Central Park West, in the same building that would later be home to luminaries such as Robert De Niro, Paul Simon, and Sting. One had only to eavesdrop on Elaine's bedtime prayers to get a sense of the family's prosperity. Decades later, she could still remember her earnest recitation:

"God Bless Mother, and Daddy," I began, and went on with, "God bless Shirley and Betty (my sisters), Mademoiselle (my French governess), Anna (Betty's German Fräulein)." Then came the three Marys: "And Mary the cook (Polish; dank black hair), Mary the waitress (Irish; fiery red hair), Mary the cleaner (nation-ality unknown; hair hidden under a bandanna)." Then: "Jerry (our chauffeur, Irish; whom I loved unconditionally)." There were also a chambermaid and a laundress too vaguely noted to be entered into my supplications. On I trudged, with: "Grandma, Grandpa, all my aunts, all my uncles and all my cousins." Then came a continually changing rota of best friends to be blessed—or allowed to slip into oblivion—after which, thinking the job well done, I asked Him to bless me too.

It was all very Eloise at the Plaza. The Brimbergs were part of the "Jewish new rich," as Dundy called them, who in the 1920s increasingly occupied the neighborhood, especially along the park. Elaine, Shirley, and Betty went to the Ethical Culture School, just a few blocks up, and the girls were "togged by Tots Toggery," Fifth Avenue's most expen-sive children's store. They were herded into the playgrounds of Central Park by their nannies and governesses. The girls fed peanuts to pigeons, went roller-skating, played hopscotch, and "skipped rope and bounced balls to a combination of numbers and nonsense rhymes." They loved going to the Sheep Meadow, which at the time had actual sheep, and the sisters delighted in feeding them bread. (In 1867, the park's architects, Frederick Law Olmsted and Calvert Vaux, added two hundred Southdown sheep on fifteen acres, where the wooly creatures remained until 1934.) In the spring, the girls searched for four-leaf clovers and wove clover blossoms into makeshift jewelry that wilted and died hours later. They loved going to the merry-go-round in the park, and Elaine recalled that "once I caught the gold ring and had so many free rides that when I got off I was sick and dizzy and threw up."

Decades later, Elaine shared her childhood reminiscences in her breezily titled autobiography, *Life Itself!* The madcap spirit and breezy voice of *Dud Avocado* shine through in every line of her book. At first glance, her childhood seems almost absurdly idyllic, too good to be true. There were trips to the family's summer home in New Jersey, with her parents and their friends, horseback riding, swimming, and playing tennis and croquet on the lawn. Back in the city, seven-year-old Elaine practiced gymnastics for hours on the Oriental rug in the living room: "In my self-propelling mania, in my need to keep turning myself upside-down, [the carpet] was my friend, my helper, my support." She loved going into her parents' bedroom, spraying herself with her mother's expensive perfumes, putting on her jewelry, and dressing up in Florence's dreamy evening gowns, "all embroidered beads and floating chiffon and so skillfully sewn." The precocious girl also read, drew, practiced her French, and daydreamed. Life was filled with "safe, rich, carefree days."

Then everything changed: just before her eighth birthday party at the Brimbergs' house in New Jersey, Elaine was struck by a car. That may not have been the worst part. At the hospital, where her wounds were dressed and the gash on her forehead stitched up, she was grateful for the kind doctors and nurses who made her feel brave. But when Florence showed up, wearing a nightgown and her hair unkempt, she frightened her daughter with her "wild, disordered appearance" and hysterical crying. Even though Elaine was the victim of a car accident, she felt ashamed for having caused trouble for her family. There were no hugs of joy and relief from her mother, and her father blamed her for crossing the road. After being discharged from the hospital, Elaine had an allergic reaction to the tetanus shots, got a high fever, and was forced to isolate in a room at home, away from her family, as she recovered.

There was deeper trauma to come. A few months later, on the evening of October 29, 1929, Elaine was playing in the living room when her father came home. Without speaking to her, he dropped his newspapers to the floor and collapsed in loud sobs. She rushed over to jump in his lap, but he pushed her away. She tried again. He slapped her hard, over and over, and held her down while screaming at her. When Shirley tried to intervene, he slapped her too. The girls retreated in terror, frantically stuffing their pillowcases with essential possessions and intending to run away. Just as they reached the elevator, Sam grabbed them and began hitting them. The stock market had suffered a colossal crash that day, wiping out entire fortunes and provoking economic collapse on what would be known as Black Tuesday. The Great Depression had begun. "The mighty fortress that was our wealth had crumbled as if made of cardboard," she later wrote, "wreaking havoc on every member of the household." The faulty wiring of the family dynamic was now fully exposed.

The Brimbergs fled the city to Great Neck, Long Island, but just three years later, Sam reversed his fortunes and managed a remarkable comeback. He became the president of a steel company, and in 1935 the family moved back to Manhattan. This time, success felt even sweeter: they lived on Park Avenue. But the return to solvency, luxury, and comfort did little to heal their dysfunction. For the children, it was a harrowing existence.

Although Elaine was happy at school, her home life felt like "a prison where my father was the warden, we sisters the inmates, and my mother the snitch." The girls were close, bonded by trauma and unable to find safety with their mother. Florence was too scared of her husband to stand up for her daughters and did her best to stay on his good side. The girls had to protect themselves and each other. Evenings in the Brimberg home were predictably awful: Sam would drink, work himself into a "towering rage," and lash out at his daughters. Elaine was perceptive enough to realize that he was not a monster out of control. He was completely in control, which was what made him so frightening. When he wasn't yelling at her or demeaning his children in other ways, Sam often retreated in stony silence. He never referred to Elaine by her name, addressing her with "you," or "she" when Elaine was in the same room.

At home, he was a violent bully. To the world beyond 1185 Park Avenue, Sam Brimberg was a different man. The successful Polish immigrant was admired and well liked. He was a devoted husband and father. Both he and Florence were prominent members of Jewish society. In their wide circle of friends were David and Gertrude Nemerov, who owned a Fifth Avenue department store and whose son, Howard, would become a famous poet. Their daughter would become a famous photographer, known by her married name: Diane Arbus. The Brimbergs were generous philanthropists, and much in demand for dinner parties and important social events. Sam was one of the founders of the Albert Einstein College of Medicine at Yeshiva University, a benefactor of the Jewish Guild for the Blind, and more. He was known to be a good man.

Elaine, who said she never overcame "my real terror of Daddy," could not help envying the genuinely happy childhood her mother had enjoyed, with a father, Heyman, who adored his children. Elaine's grandfather was a Latvian immigrant who arrived in America with no money and little English. A brilliant engineer, he became a millionaire thanks to a single invention—a pioneering self-threading screw known as the Parker-Kalon screw, used in the engine for Charles Lindbergh's *Spirit of St. Louis* and even in a major restoration of the Statue of Liberty. Florence, who was cultured, pretty, and well read, proved enterprising, too. After graduation from college in New York, she founded her own nursery school, which was among the first in the city. She left it only to marry Sam, who became a millionaire at thirty-five. Elaine loved her mother, but could never quite forgive her silence around Sam's cruelty. Even when Florence, at the age of ninety-one, wrote a letter of explanation and apology to her daughter, she seemed to justify her husband's abuse as the result of his difficult childhood in Warsaw and the pressures of his business. (Florence died in 1996, just a few months before her hundredth birthday.)

In her teens, Elaine fantasized about killing her father by poisoning his food. She recalled a "significant" incident that occurred when she was seventeen years old: after an argument escalated between them, Elaine grabbed a knife and taunted her father, asking him if he wanted to kill her. He charged toward her. She raced down fourteen flights of stairs onto Park Avenue, with her father pursuing her until he gave up and turned back. Hours later, when she returned home, she threatened to tell her school what happened. Her mother's response was shockingly callous: "Oh, please don't, Elaine. It would embarrass me."

No expertise in psychiatry is required to understand how Elaine was damaged by her father's abuse, the deleterious effects on her self-esteem, and how that fraught relationship would shape her relationships with men. (Alcohol was her primary coping mechanism.) As she reflected on her childhood decades later to a reporter, she said that "wealth, luxury and opportunity [were] counterbalanced by fear, unhappiness and repression."

Her sisters had a tough time, too. Shirley, who became a leading experimental filmmaker—the *New Yorker* called her "one of the prime inventors of creative cinematic nonfiction"—fell into drug addiction and other troubles. "She was wounded by [our father] in a way that would last for the rest of her life," Elaine wrote, "and lead her to seek more and more dangerous ways of rebelling against him."

Elaine's years on Park Avenue weren't entirely grim. She had a wonderfully rich imagination, fantasized about movie stars, and was a passionate theatergoer—as a teenager, she attended Broadway matinees by herself. After seeing Ethel Merman in her Broadway debut, in the musical *Girl Crazy*, she was stagestruck. Elaine idolized Noël Coward and once got his autograph at the stage door. Orson Welles was another idol. (One day she would know him as a dear friend.) In her teenage years Elaine started drinking alcohol and smoking cigarettes, both of which liberated her from a depressing life at home. She went to night-clubs to see jazz and blues performers with her first boyfriend, Gil, and had the thrilling experience of seeing Billie Holiday onstage at a club in Harlem. She also fell in love with comedies such as *Bringing Up Baby* and *His Girl Friday*, consuming as many films as she could, and she was enamored of screwball heroines: "I will never forget my utter relief when I first came upon these characters. I knew at once I would have to be like them because I could not be like anyone else."

Elaine enjoyed writing fan letters to celebrities and was always de-lighted when she got a response. At the age of fifteen, she decided to write a letter to King Edward VIII, c/o Buckingham Palace, to express her sincere condolences for the loss of his father and to congratulate him on becoming king.

She graduated with honors from Sweet Briar College in 1943 hav-ing no idea what to do with her life—except for losing her virginity, which she did that fall, describing the experience as "painless and even slightly pleasant." Her next boyfriend was a former high school class-mate, Terence, known as Terry, whose father was the Pulitzer Prize–winning playwright Max Anderson. Elaine got a taste of what an ideal adult life might look like.

Spending time with Terry offered proximity to well-known actors, writers, and artists by way of his father. This excited Elaine. She met Kurt Weill and his wife, Lenya, as well as Ingrid Bergman, who was starring in one of Max's plays, and she loved hearing Max "talk shop" and share the latest theater gossip. One weekend, he changed Elaine's life by asking if she wanted to audition for a new play, saying that she looked just right for one of the lead roles. Although Elaine was too afraid to accept the kind offer, something clicked: she knew what she wanted to pursue and decided she needed proper training. She would eventually ask her father for money to pay for acting school, which he did. It was unfortunate that her relationship with Terry had no future, as he knew Max adored her and would be disappointed not to welcome her into the family. "You're too ambitious for me," Terry told her. "It wouldn't work." His apprehension was less about her ambitions as an actress than her ambitions for him as a writer. She believed in his talent, encouraged him, and was angry at the rejection. "Why was I supposed to feel guilty for trying to help Terry become a writer?" she recalled. "But good wives were not supposed to be naggers and pushers. . . . I would be one of those terrible, emasculating wives who drive men mad."

For Elaine, acting school was a great consolation after the breakup. She loved the camaraderie among her fellow aspiring actors (and new group of friends), and found that acting was everything to her—vocation and therapy, a safe place to exchange "my old, injured, irrational self for new ones that worked better. It was my solace and my excitement." Best of all, her British acting teacher gave her the gift of a new identity. After mentioning that the name Elaine Brimberg didn't suit her, he suggested another: Elaine Dundee. It was perfect. All she did was change "Dundee" to "Dundy" to lose the association with the famous Scottish marmalade.

By the age of twenty-seven, Elaine was not yet a star, but she was a working actress. After auditioning for a part in *Yerma* by Federico García Lorca at the Cherry Lane Theatre in Greenwich Village, she scored her first New York job. She appeared alongside a twenty-six-year-old actress named Bea Arthur, who encouraged her to apply to the Dramatic Workshop Repertory Theatre. Elaine took her advice, got accepted, and had the pleasure of working with a young actor named Bernie Schwartz—who became known as Tony Curtis—and she was attracted to the handsome, charismatic Harry Belafonte.

In 1949, Elaine left to pursue other jobs, including plays, radio work, and TV commercials. The gigs were steady, and her dream had come true, but not at the level (or income) she had expected. She also hated living at home, which her father had insisted upon. Through a college friend, she heard there were many opportunities for American actors in Paris. Elaine got a passport, negotiated a monthly allowance from her father, and off she went.

She fell in love with the city upon arrival, and made new friends quickly, including a nineteen-year-old from California, Judy Sheftel, who would become Judy Feiffer—wife of the cartoonist Jules and a lifelong friend to Elaine. When she wasn't working, wandering around the city, or hanging out in cafés, Elaine drank a lot and picked up and discarded lovers. ("In Paris you got over liaisons in record time," she recalled.) Having inherited her mother's love of beautiful clothing, she was happy to learn about sample sales in Paris. One of her great finds was a glamorous, off-the-shoulder orange-and-brown silk Schiaparelli dress that Judy convinced her to buy. "Wore it to a party given by a contessa and knocked 'em dead," she reported in a letter to her mother. "Only trouble—I can't walk in it."

It wasn't long before Elaine found acting work, mostly doing voice-over jobs for French films being dubbed into English. She fell into the same trap she had experienced in New York—working and earning money, but waiting to be discovered. "I had a wonderful time though my career was almost invisible," she recalled. When would her big break come? She'd lived in Paris for a year and was feeling impatient. After a few visits to London, she decided to move there and was able to stay at the flat of an English friend in Dorset Square. They spent their nights at a packed basement club called the Buckstone Club, behind the Haymarket Theatre. It had become a popular hangout for actors, especially "all the young lions on their way up." Because there was no sign outside, the club was exclusively for those in the know. Playwrights such as Harold Pinter and John Osborne were regulars, as were Claire

Bloom, Vanessa Redgrave, Maggie Smith, and Richard Burton. "Every young actor playing in every West End theatre and the Old Vic went down those stairs," Elaine recalled. It was a fun, rowdy place to eat, drink, and gossip.

One day Elaine walked into the Buckstone for lunch with her ex-boyfriend Peter, who spotted a tall, slender young man in a booth, holding a cigarette and holding court. After Peter made an introduction, the man invited Elaine to squeeze into the booth and join the group of rapt listeners. She was struck by his ability to seduce his audience with confidence and charm, even as she noticed what she later called his "violent" stammer. He had the elegant hands of a concert pianist. He wore a double-breasted camel hair jacket, plum trousers, yellow socks, and black shoes. On his wrist was a Mickey Mouse watch. His name was Ken. A few months later, he would marry her.

A recent graduate of the University of Oxford, Kenneth Tynan stood apart from his classmates with his outré style, including a woman's raincoat, bottle-green suit, purple doeskin suit, gold satin shirt, cape lined in red satin, and an array of bow ties. (The novelist Elizabeth Jane Howard, who had a brief affair with him years later, once aptly described him as "a creature of self-constructed layers." She also noted "an air of indolence about him, but this was underlaid by a sharp and perceptive intelligence. He looked much of the time as though he were waiting for something to amuse or excite him at any moment.") One classmate recalled him as tall, beautiful, and slightly androgynous, "with pale yellow locks, Beardsley cheekbones, fashionable stammer, plum-colored suit, lavender tie, and ruby signet-ring." As an undergraduate he was an overachiever, handling his academic work with ease—all while exploring ambitions that included, among other things, directing, producing, playwriting, and acting in a production of *Medea* in which he played the chorus wearing pink tights. He took part in school debates and served as editor of the weekly newspaper *Cherwell*, which was banned after Ken sent out a lengthy questionnaire about sex to female undergraduates. He was the drama critic for the *Isis*, a student publication launched in 1892 by the fabulously named Montague Horatio Mostyn Turtle Pigott. The budding critic was not immune to hyperbole: in a review of *Othello*, Ken raved, "I have seen a public event of enormous constellated magnitude and radiance."

Ken had chosen Magdalen College, as he later told a reporter for the *Guardian*, "because I wanted to read English literature and the professor of English at the college was C. S. Lewis, who was a terrific influence in my life and I think the greatest English literary critic of this century, and one of the best writers of English prose who ever lived. I think that he is a Johnsonian figure and I absolutely worship him." Ken sought a father figure and Lewis was happy to oblige. Their relationship went well beyond academic discourse. "I took all my private problems to him," Ken admitted in the same interview. "He was enormously helpful." Ken was engaged at the age of eighteen to a fellow student, "and on the eve of the marriage, she suddenly deserted me and went off with an Irish peer and I was shattered and very suicidal." Decades later, he confessed, "I was so wounded by that, I was determined nobody would ever, ever walk out on me again. And they never did. I am totally dependent upon the affection of women. I was determined from then on to be so fucking charming that any girl that I really wanted was going to stay."

For consolation he turned to Lewis, who reminded Ken of having endured air raids in Birmingham during the war, pointing out that several homes on Ken's street were leveled. (A land mine, dropped from a plane by parachute, missed the Tynan house by inches.) "You have been living on borrowed time already for about seven years," Lewis said. "So, for God's sake, don't talk about suicide now." Ken could always find cheer in being the center of attention, and on his twenty-first birthday in the spring of 1948, he hired a riverboat in London to sail along the Thames and invited more than two hundred guests to celebrate.

Ken thoroughly enjoyed his time at Oxford, which he believed led to all his career fortune afterward. He put it plainly in a "deathbed interview" in 1979 with a young American journalist, Ann Louise Bardach, which was published in the *Guardian* more than twenty years later, in 2001:

> The thing about Oxford is that it is a breeding ground of privilege, and Cambridge is too. And it's no accident. The people who were at Oxford at the same time as I was are the group of undergraduates that now control the means of communication in England. They edit all the magazines. They are all the leading journalists. They are in control of every level of the TV. They are, as I call it, the Oxford octopus. They are also the cabinet ministers on both sides, Tory and Labour. All people that I went to Oxford with. So, if I want to pull a string, I just pick up a telephone. The old-boy network works like that. Everybody, of any import, in the law, the professions generally, was at Oxford with me.

In October 1950, shortly before meeting Elaine at the Buckstone, Ken had published a buzzed-about collection of theater criticism and profiles, *He That Plays the King* (the phrase taken from *Hamlet*). The book was irreverent, deeply personal, wickedly mean, and a love letter to what the author termed "heroic acting." There was a preface by Orson Welles, who admired Ken's "capacity for violent opinion, for knowing how to cheer and not being afraid to hiss." The *Sunday Times* theater critic Harold Hobson, who helped launch Ken's career and would become his professional rival over the next decade, received a galley copy of *He That Plays the King* from Ken's publisher and wrote a kind letter to the author, noting that the evocation of acting was the most difficult aspect of criticism, "and in this you are an absolute master." Hobson added that although he did not always agree with Ken's assessments, "your book seems to be the most dazzling thing written upon theatre during my lifetime." A year after publishing it, Ken would write in a letter, "I still like parts of it; and the rest is, at worst, <u>characteristically</u> bad."

As he alternately charmed and terrorized the theater world, Ken knew how to command attention. The man famed for his provocations would shock viewers in 1965 when he became the first person to utter the word "fuck" on television, during a late-night program in which he discussed the topic of censorship with Mary McCarthy. The expletive resulted in a formal apology from the BBC and an angry letter to the Queen from a morality campaigner, insisting that Tynan "ought to have his bottom smacked." For reasons that will soon become clear, the phrase was apt.

Here was the brilliant young critic on Laurence Olivier in *Henry IV, Part Two*:

> This Shallow is a crapulous, paltering scarecrow of a man, withered up like the slough of a snake; but he has quick commiserating eyes and the kind of delight in dispensing food and drink that one associates with a favourite aunt. He pecks at the lines, nibbles at them like a parrot biting on a nut; for all his age, he darts here and there nimbly enough, even skittishly; forgetting nothing, not even the pleasure of Falstaff's page, "that little tiny thief."

Ken was besotted with great actors. When he panned a performance, however, he showed no mercy: one Broadway actress was described as "shaking her voice at us like a tiny fist"; Sir Ralph Richardson in *Timon of Athens* was derided for his performance at the Old Vic for having employed "a mode of speech that democratically regards all syllables as equal." Ken often provoked rage in the objects of his contempt. Not that he cared. "I will not accept and will fight against your almost psychopathic desire to denigrate me and my work," the actor and director Sam Wanamaker struck back following a blistering review of his stage adaptation of Zola's *Thérèse Raquin*, in which Ken noted that the show's three stars seemed to be acting in three different international cities—and that Wanamaker's performance in particular was marked by "nasal expostulations and enormous, anguished shrugs."

Whether operating in vicious-takedown mode or as rhapsodizing cheerleader, Ken entertained his readers, never left them bored, and went on to influence many writers. He once said that the mark of a good critic was telling his readers what was happening in the theater of the day, and the mark of the great critic was telling them what was not happening in that theater. As the playwright and critic Jack Richardson later wrote of Ken, "[His] influence as a critic lay in his willingness to take an actively partisan role as a critic. It gave his writing a lively urgency that made theatre reviewing seem something more crucial to society than wine-tasting." Richardson praised Ken as "the most intelligent and effective drama critic writing in English."

Luckily for Ken's readers, British theater was undergoing an exciting renaissance in the 1950s, and he was there to capture it all. Among his admirers was Michael Billington, the *Guardian*'s chief drama critic from 1971 to 2019, who praised his "combination of a voluptuous prose style with a crusading moral fervour," noting that Ken's prose "clicks into place with the satisfying resonance of billiard balls struck by a perfectly aimed cue." (Billington also called *He That Plays the King* "the best writing on acting since Hazlitt.") And Benedict Nightingale, the longtime drama critic for the *New Statesman* and for the *Times*, once confessed, "I don't think I've ever penned a review without thinking of Tynan, envying his dancing prose and realizing how much finer a piece he would have produced." The journalist, critic, and author John Heilpern was another Tynan fan: "[W]hen I was a novice reporter in the mid-60's, I saw Tynan sweep rakishly into the building as if he owned the place, which he did in a way. Always dandyish, he was wearing a white suit on a rainy day, and to my young, wide eyes it was like glimpsing royalty. I remember—I'm slightly embarrassed to admit—that I immediately called home to tell my parents excitedly: 'I just saw Ken Tynan, and he's wearing a white suit!'"

In a 2001 piece, James Wolcott expressed admiration for the enduring pleasure of Ken's prose, with its "float-like-a-butterfly, sting-like-a-bee style." (He also mentioned Ken's "conversational cobra-strikes.") Susannah Clapp, the current theater critic of the *Observer* (Ken's professional home for nearly ten years), wrote a tribute to him in 2016 for the newspaper's 225th anniversary. "It has long been received wisdom that the most famous of my predecessors was a dazzling advocate and gadfly," she wrote. "Asked to look through the archive of arts pieces, I decided to put his reputation to the test. It survived." She added: "Fervour and precision; pungency and political commitment. Above all, it is his range—of subjects and emotions—that knocks me out. It has long been evident that when Tynan talked about 'high-definition performance' he was evoking himself." Further, she noted his power in "[making] it seem that dramatic criticism was the natural prism through which to look at the whole of life" and "showing that the theatre could send you back to daily life with enhanced eyes."

Ken charmed nearly everyone he encountered and knew it. Upon meeting Elaine, they were "mutually magnetized." When she asked her ex-boyfriend Peter about Ken's background, Peter said that Ken was a "wonder boy" critic, director, and actor whose new book had caused quite a stir. After *He That Plays the King* came up in yet another conversation, Elaine decided to pick up a copy. She loved it and saw it as a good excuse to chat with Ken again. He invited her on a first date lunch the next day at the Buckstone, and afterward a double feature: *It's a Gift* with W. C. Fields, and *A Day at the Races* with the Marx Brothers. They drank champagne, smoked, and talked for hours. Elaine wore her beloved Schiaparelli dress. Things got interesting when Ken made a sudden, and no doubt drunken, declaration: "I am the illegitimate son of the late Sir Peter Peacock. I have an annual income. I'm twenty-three and I will either die or kill myself when I reach thirty because by then I will have said everything I have to say. Will you marry me?"

He had a most unusual childhood. For half of each week, his father was Sir Peter Peacock, a prominent businessman and politician in the northwestern town of Warrington, in Cheshire, where he lived with his second wife, Maria, and five children. (His first wife, Maria's sister, died in 1890.) He was well liked around town, and in 1913 became the town mayor. For his patriotism in the war effort, encouraging local men to enlist, Sir Peacock received a knighthood in 1918. An oil portrait of him is part of the Warrington Museum & Art Gallery collection and still hangs in the town hall. He is shown as a pillar of society, a regal figure in a fur-lined cape and a large medallion bearing the town crest.

From Thursday to Sunday of each week, he had another life. Eighty-one miles south, in Birmingham, he was Peter Tynan. He lived there with his partner, Letitia Rose Tynan (known as Rose), and he traveled back and forth between the two households by train or chauffeur-driven car. Back in Warrington, Maria—or, following her husband's knighthood, Lady Peacock—refused to grant him a divorce. His response was to forsake his civic duties, his title, and more to assume the humble alias "Peter Tynan" and avoid scandal. He even had two ration cards during the war.

On the morning of April 2, 1927, Rose gave birth to their son, Kenneth Peacock Tynan, in Birmingham. Peter was fifty-five; Rose was thirty-eight. Ken had a doting mother who fed his love of theater by taking him to plays. Of his relationship with his father, Ken recalled, "We got on not badly, but not closely. He wanted me to be a lawyer, so he was pleased when I was successful in school debating societies." His pronounced stammer delayed his speech until the age of three, and he would grapple with his stammer for the rest of his life. But he was a prodigious reader and loved writing early on. Ken kept a diary from the age of six, recording detailed descriptions of his mother's cooking, accounts of favorite pantomimes, his father's practical jokes, and more. He was a bedwetter, insecure, and desperate to be liked by his peers. He loved going to movies, especially American ones, and wrote down his impressions afterward in his diary. He also "reviewed" the plays he attended. After seeing John Gielgud in a production of J. M. Barrie's *Dear Brutus*, Ken rated the actor 96 points out of 100.

Ken later claimed that at the age of nine, he had demanded, and received, a hundred books for Christmas. Certainly his parents recognized their son's deep intelligence and curiosity, and encouraged him to pursue his interests. He bought plenty of books, magazines, and records with the money they gave him, and at one point purchased a monocle for himself. As a child, he was an avid and confident letter writer, such as in this rather prescient gem to the editor of *Film Weekly*, mailed a few months before Ken's eleventh birthday in 1938:

> If it is actually true that Warner Brothers intend to put Humphrey Bogart in a series of "B" pictures, they will be making the greatest mistake of their lives. His gangster in <u>Dead End</u>, the "D.A." in <u>Marked Woman</u> and the producer in <u>Stand-In</u> were great pieces of acting, and show Bogart to be a grand character actor who needs real recognition.
>
> K. Tynan

Although his emotional and intellectual needs were largely met, he dreamed of life far beyond the Midlands, which was ordinary and working class. Describing Birmingham as "the ugliest city in the world, that cemetery without walls," Ken knew his destiny was elsewhere. "His was a very adult mentality," one of his classmates later recalled, "and one that wanted to make an impact." Academically gifted, Ken attended a local boys' public school, King Edward's, named for founder King Edward VI in 1552. Famous alumni included Edward Burne-Jones and J.R.R. Tolkien. Ken won twelve major school prizes and was an extracurricular all-star too, serving as editor of the literary magazine, secretary to the debate society and literary society, and a member of the cricket team. He acted in school plays ("I should be brilliant," he declared ahead of his performance as Shylock) and dabbled in politics.

When the headmaster invited the boys to hold a mock election, Ken signed on as the Independent candidate—advocating a repeal of the laws governing homosexuality and abortion, using a debate to praise the joys of masturbation, and posting a provocative manifesto on the school bulletin board. After the headmaster demanded that he remove his inflammatory statement, Ken refused and resigned as a candidate.

The young cinephile saw *Citizen Kane* five times—all within the first week it opened in Birmingham—and managed to correspond with Orson Welles, whom he worshiped. Ken was also a devoted theatergoer, left awestruck by the performances of a favorite actor, Donald Wolfit, in productions of *King Lear*, *Macbeth*, *A Midsummer Night's Dream*, and *Twelfth Night*. As a teenager, he gave this astute take on *Hamlet* in a letter to a friend: "He suffers from splenetic fits of melancholy, as when he insults Ophelia and browbeats Gertrude; then he is the jerky neurotic once more. Each actor will create a new Hamlet; and if you can see the play without noticing inconsistency between what he says and the way he says it, then the new creation is a triumph."

By the age of twelve, Ken had become a persistent autograph collector, writing letters to public figures with requests for their signatures, helpfully including a stamped addressed envelope, signing off "Your faithful fan," and following up to grumble if they failed to respond: "This is the third time I have written to you, and on each of the previous occasions, I have been sent a photo with a PRINT of your autograph on it." Winston Churchill obliged the first time around. Ken also collected signatures from Lady Astor, Joseph Kennedy, Neville Chamberlain, H. G. Wells, and various actors and musicians.

Initially he was not so persuasive, however, in begging his parents for permission to travel alone to London to see a close friend: "They say I have no right to go against their wishes at sixteen," Ken complained to his friend in a letter. "My mother has threatened (quite seriously) to disinherit me if I go." He did convince her and made the most of his trip, seeing nearly two dozen plays and writing up his reviews.

It is astonishing that Ken supposedly had no clue about his father's double life until the day he died in July 1948. Rose conveyed the sad news and summoned her son home to Birmingham. While he was waiting at the train station, he was startled to see a large photograph of his father in the newspaper, accompanied by an obituary with an incongruous headline about a man named "Sir Peter Peacock" dying at the age of seventy-six.

Decades later, in his wide-ranging interview with Ann Louise Bardach in 1979, Ken recounted the awkward conversation with his mother in which he learned the truth about his father. Despite a cavalier retelling of the encounter, Ken had cut off contact with Rose and refused to forgive her. (Although he blamed her for concealing the truth, it's possible that Ken knew much earlier and had suppressed it.) In 1958, Rose was discovered by the police wandering the streets and clutching a suitcase with the words "I don't know where I'm going, but I'm going to those who love me." After suffering from dementia, she died in a mental institution. "I could have postponed her death at the expense of my own absorption in self-advancement," he later wrote. "I chose not to." In any case, his anecdote in the interview with Bardach presented a portrait of equanimity upon hearing the news of his father's dual life: "I embraced her and commiserated, and I said, 'This is a picture of dad. Explain.' She burst into tears and said, 'Well, we weren't married and we thought that you would be ashamed of us.' I said, 'On the contrary, it's the most romantic thing I ever heard—[that] he should run away from his past and give up everything for love. It's fantastic!'"

He said that he regretted not having known the secret in his father's lifetime, "because he was quite an important man, he was knighted and he moved in quite important political circles. But he took my mother's name, which was Tynan, when he came to live with her in Birmingham. He was known to the neighbours as Peter Tynan. I am, I suppose, Kenneth Peacock, really."

Indeed he was. Ken may not have known the reason for his pavonian middle name, but he lived up to it through his preening vanity, dazzling verbal plumage, and flamboyant style of dress. He was a natural-born showoff, proud of his tail feathers.

By the time Elaine came along, in 1950, Ken was a legend in his own mind, and on his way to actual renown thanks to the sensation caused by his book. He was brash and "mind-bogglingly erudite," but there was a vulnerability to him too. Elaine found his stammer endearing. She recalled Ken as a beautiful young man, with his "fair English-pink complexion, high cheekbones dramatically dominating the outline of his elongated face. His forehead was high and bony, his pale beige-blond hair curved back from his brow like a wing, and his large well-shaped mouth gave him an attractive equine look." His boldness and brilliance as a writer added to the allure: "I admired Ken's talent to the point of worship," Elaine recalled. He was scheduled to direct an adaptation of Jean Cocteau's *Intimate Relations*, a job from which he would be fired after the actress Fay Compton demanded his ouster. It was a humiliating setback, especially for someone with directorial aspirations, but a year later he was hired to direct a television play of Jean-Jacques Bernard's *Martine*, starring a young Claire Bloom, and what he considered an "amputated version" of *Titus Andronicus*. Elaine loved everything about Ken, including his trademark style of smoking: holding a cigarette between the third and fourth fingers of his right hand. He explained the affectation by saying that it allowed him to write and smoke at the same time, but told others that he smoked like this to avoid nicotine stains.

Ken and Elaine's relationship moved fast. They saw each other daily, and within a few weeks she moved into his flat at 19 Upper Berkeley Street in Marylebone. "Life was perfect, perfect, perfect," Elaine recalled of those days of "undomesticated bliss." Her sole "home virtue" was making bacon, eggs, fried bread, and tea for Ken. His household contribution was to set traps for mice at night, then throw them out the window the next morning. Soon acting had slipped to second place in her mind. "I had gained the love of an extraordinary man," she recalled. "And, finally, I had been discovered. Not by world acclaim, as planned, but by a lover: a soon-to-be husband." When they married on January 25, 1951, all the London newspapers printed pictures of the couple on the front page. Elaine bought her wedding dress at the luxury department store Harvey Nichols. She sent a wire to her parents: "Have married Englishman. Letter follows."

Ken called his new wife "Skippy"—he said it suited her—and soon she called him "Skippy" too. "I was madly in love with him and stepped happily into the Wonderland of his fame," Elaine later wrote. She loved being with "an insider with gilt-edged connections and with whom further bright discoveries would be made together." Ken was unquestionably the star of the couple, but Elaine still had some ambition left in her, and she worked fairly steadily, albeit in minor, unmemorable roles. At thirty, she was a working actress without a career. "Always I played cameos, never leads," she recalled. Yet she was thrilled for the opportunity to work with Orson Welles on a radio series, and on a BBC production of Edna Ferber's *Dinner at Eight*.

By the end of 1951, Ken's book had gained more attention in literary and theater circles, and he achieved international fame. In May, he also had his first (and final) professional stint as an actor, appearing as the player king in Alec Guiness's production of *Hamlet* at the New Theatre. After a scathing review of his performance by the *Evening Standard*—the critic had an ax to grind—Ken responded a few days later with a letter to the editor ("I am a quite good enough critic to know that my performance in Hamlet was not 'quite dreadful': it is, in fact, only slightly less than mediocre"). Ken was unflappable. After all, his comings and goings were recorded in celebrity gossip columns, and he was in demand both socially and professionally. He and Elaine were given the best tables at the best restaurants, and invitations to parties from celebrities they had never met. In 1952, Ken took over as drama critic for the *Evening Standard*, writing a weekly column. He was twenty-four years old.

The newspaper promoted its brilliant new critic ("the voice and spirit of youth") at newsstands throughout London: "He has delighted theatregoers and infuriated those producers who have come under his lash." The attention was a lot of pressure for Ken, but his newfound power had perks, too. The socializing was relentless: "John G., whom I'd never met, asked me suddenly to supper, and we talked until three," Ken reported in a letter to Cecil Beaton. (The "G" was for Gielgud.) He and Elaine loved collecting famous people as friends. There were always shows to see, extravagant dinners to enjoy, cigarettes to smoke, and pre- and post-theater drinks to consume. She had begun to experience blackouts, as she recalled in her memoir, but was having too much fun to do anything about them.

Sometimes she felt like a spectator in her own life, amazed by the array of extraordinary people they spent time with—Humphrey Bogart, Gene Kelly, Tennessee Williams ("Tenn"), Richard Burton, John Huston, Graham Greene, James Thurber, and others. The golden couple began spending about six weeks in Spain every summer, watching the bullfights with Hemingway. Ken described bullfighting as "a logical extension of all the impulses my temperament holds—love of grace and valour, of poise and pride; and beyond these, the capacity to be exhilarated by mastery of technique." (In 1955, he would publish *Bull Fever*, an examination and appreciation of the sport he found so thrilling, and dedicate the book to Elaine.)

Ken and Elaine were desired everywhere. "We attended the best theatrical parties, dined at the best tables in Sardi's and 21, met the choicest stars and playwrights and drama critics, saw the best plays and were feted in penthouses by the wealthiest host and hostesses assiduously courting that starry world," Elaine recalled of a visit to New York. Their popularity was such that one year, for a surprise birthday party in honor of the director Mike Nichols, Richard Avedon flew Ken and Elaine from London to New York. When they arrived, he had them nailed into large crates and carried, gift-wrapped, into a Chinese restaurant he had rented out. Nichols opened the crates with chisel and "out we burst, human presents," Ken recalled years later in his diary.

Elaine was proud of how important her husband was—the life of the party, cynosure of every social gathering. She loved how some people feared him and everyone was drawn to him. She liked to say that in addition to having a genius in her maternal grandfather, "I had a genius in my own bed."

In 1952, Ken and Elaine moved to 29 Hyde Park Gardens—a "smart, warm, huge new flat, overlooking the park," as Ken gushed in a letter to Beaton. For Elaine, it was an exciting time to be in the city: "London was in the midst of a renaissance for artists," she recalled. "In literature and playwriting the Angry Young Men were making their splash and new young actors like Richard Burton, Peter O'Toole, Albert Finney, and Peter Finch were coming into their own. London was an orderly place where it was safe to take risks. Optimism was the rule of the day and I was there."

That spring, they welcomed their first and only child. Elaine was certain she had conceived "in a berth on a night train from Madrid to Barcelona." They named their daughter Tracy, after Katharine Hepburn's blueblood character in *The Philadelphia Story*, their favorite film, and asked Hepburn to be Tracy's godmother. (Cecil Beaton was also a godparent.) Elaine knew that as a wife and mother, she was obliged to handle all the domestic chores, including preparing meals and keeping the house reasonably tidy, but she had no interest in those tasks. (One could hardly blame her. A decade after writing *The Feminine Mystique*, Betty Friedan wrote in a *New York Times* piece, "Locked as we all were then in that mystique, which kept us passive and apart, and kept us even from seeing our real problems and possibilities, I, like other women, thought there was something wrong with me because I didn't have an orgasm waxing the kitchen floor.") Elaine was left equally deflated by having to decorate the new family home, and the thought of shopping for furniture, carpets, and curtains was more than she could bear. Drinking helped.

She was a faithful assistant to her husband as he worked on his columns amid various book projects, magazine pieces, and a play adaptation. To his readers, Ken made writing seem effortless, each line gliding across the page, but he fretted over every word and punctuation mark. Before each deadline, after having breakfast and reading the morning newspapers, Ken would lock himself away in his study like a mad scientist in the laboratory, sitting at his desk in a bathrobe or silk dressing gown, hunched over his typewriter, often staying up through the night to produce his work—always neatly typed, single-spaced. He smoked nonstop, but claimed he could not write otherwise. "His reviews were seductive, alluring, appealing, erudite, outrageous, and funny, funny, funny," Elaine later wrote. "These pieces changed one's mood." Ken kept a quotation posted above his writing desk: "Rouse tempers, goad and lacerate, raise whirlwinds." The quote was his own. He adored the sacred gods of theater, but his reviews took down those gods when the occasion called for it. He once wrote a cruel review about Orson Welles, friend and personal hero, for what he deemed a subpar performance in *Othello* ("huge shrug")—a review that Ken's editor, Charles Curran, described as a "successful operation without an anesthetic." The brilliance of his prose was accompanied by a not insignificant amount of self-regard. As the *New Yorker* writer John Lahr (who edited *The Diaries of Kenneth Tynan*) wryly observed of Ken, he was "his own greatest invention, and he loved his Maker."

While he worked, Ken smoked cigarette after cigarette and drank booze through the night. "When I opened the door of his study," Elaine recalled, "the smoke, as if from a nuclear blast, shot out to engulf me." She took care of him from a safe distance, heating up corned beef hash or cans of soup for her husband ("served on demand") and tiptoeing around the house to avoid disturbing him. Once his column copy was ready, Ken would reemerge from his study: "At that moment he always looked very strange; rather insane," Elaine recalled—then "fall into bed like a log, plunging instantly to sleep." She would swing into action, copy in hand, and her frantic routine was always the same. She dressed quickly, grabbed a manila envelope, hopped into a taxi, and, serving as messenger, delivered the copy to the newspaper herself. Later she would settle on a more efficient method, giving the envelope to a taxi driver and having him hand it off to Charles Curran. In an era before photocopies, faxes, or email, it must have been stressful to watch Ken's final draft go off unaccompanied in a taxi each week. And he usually pushed his luck right up to the last minute of a deadline, resulting in pleading phone calls from Curran—not to him, but to Elaine: "Mrs. Tynan, you *must* see that he gets his copy in on time!" Mrs. Tynan did her best.

When Ken was fired from the *Standard* over a dispute with his editors, Elaine tried to point out the silver lining: journalism had stopped him from doing the work he really wanted to pursue, including writing a memoir on his Oxford days, producing a play he'd adapted from *Cold Comfort Farm*, the Stella Gibbons novel, and the book he wanted to write on bullfighting. (He once claimed that he saw "more nobility, more grace, more passion and more exhilaration in the Spanish bullrings" than on the English stage.)

Ken would hear none of it. He pressured Elaine to take the blame for the nasty, threatening letter he had written to his editor in a fit of rage, which cost him his job. "I had pledged myself to support him in every way," she later recalled. "I did not type out his poems, or copy by hand his masterpieces, like Vivienne Eliot or Sonya Tolstoy or other wives did for their great writer-husbands. Nor did I wash and iron his shirts or work as a secretary to earn the money we needed for him to go on with his art. So this was the least I could do."

Maybe it was the second least thing she could do. A few months earlier, she walked into the flat to overhear Ken on the phone, clearly talking with a mistress. He hung up the phone, confessed to cheating, and promised to end things immediately with the woman, a married acquaintance of theirs. Elaine neither forgave him nor forgot, but simply chose to carry on. Even then, she must have had a presentiment of worse things to come.

Between caring for a one-year-old daughter and accommodating her husband's needs, Elaine began to lose her sense of self. "Ken *was* my self-esteem," she recalled. "No illusion was more crucial to my belief system, even to my stability, than that Ken remain the sun around which I revolved." Apart from what belonged to him, nothing was all hers. Even the paper she used for writing to Ken's editors, begging for his job back, was Ken's stationery, at Ken's desk, in Ken's study. She had carefully organized it for him, giving him a metal file cabinet and creating neat files with his correspondence, contracts, and more. Elaine had no paper, no desk, no study. There was no "room of one's own," neither physical nor psychological. She made herself small and unassuming for Ken, and on the rare occasions when she booked a television acting job, she never talked about it with her husband—and he never asked. Ken was her source of both safety and danger. She never knew which would come when, refuge or attack, but it was all she had.

No matter how badly Ken behaved, Elaine tried hard to please him and served as his tireless advocate. Seeing how depressed he was after losing his job, Elaine sent a copy of *He That Plays the King* to the publisher of the *Observer*, knowing that it showed off Ken's brilliance at its best. The publisher wrote Ken a kind letter in response, offering him freelance work. In 1954, still in his twenties, Ken became the head theater reviewer at the *Observer* and established himself as the decade's leading drama critic in Britain. He owed his good fortune entirely to Elaine's moxie, yet he never thanked her. Apart from a stint with the *New Yorker* from 1958 to 1960, when the Tynans moved to New York, Ken would remain with the newspaper until 1963. By then, his marriage was dead.

Almost from the start of their relationship, there were problems in the bedroom. As Elaine would later learn, beating a woman was a form of foreplay to Ken, an urge he suppressed early in their marriage. Although he revealed that he had dabbled in sadomasochistic sex at Oxford, he downplayed his interest and claimed he was done with it. His spanking and caning days were a schoolboy's explorations, nothing more.

BUT JUST THREE YEARS INTO THEIR MARRIAGE, KEN ADMITTED TO Elaine that their sex life bored him. He gave her books to read about sadomasochism, along with pornographic photos, which left her uncomfortable rather than aroused. She was willing to do anything to boost her troubled marriage, but their initial S&M session did not end well. "To cane a woman on her bare buttocks, to hurt and humiliate her, was what gave him his greatest sexual satisfaction," Elaine recalled. It made her furious, yet she felt unable to voice her outrage. This was not sex for intimacy or pleasure, but an excuse for Ken, with his wife's reluctant consent, to engage in acts of domination and cruelty. (He caned her once for having an affair with Kingsley Amis, "one stroke for each letter of his name.") Ken would later admit in his journals that for the masochist, physical pain was not a source of pleasure. Instead, "the apprehension, the preparation, the threat, the exposure, the humiliation—*these* are thrilling, and so is the warmth afterwards, and the sight of the marks; but the impact of cane on bottom is no fun at all."

Over time, Elaine realized that Ken's bottom smacking was an obsession, and that it was abusive, not some naughty fetish. He kept a collection of headmaster's canes and spanking-themed magazines, and in his diaries, Ken self-identified as a "spanking addict." Years later, he was determined to produce, write, and direct a film with "an erotic and anally sadistic theme," as he wrote in his diaries, but it was perpetually in limbo and never made. And six years into his second marriage, he would indulge in an intoxicating affair with an out-of-work actress who shared his sexual preferences. (He claimed to have put her across his knee one afternoon and spanked her in Regent's Park.) In February 1973, well into a second marriage at that point, Ken recorded in his diary:

> Since last November I have been seeing (and spanking) a fellow spanking addict, a girl called Nicole. Her fantasy—dormant until I met her—is precisely to be bent over with knickers taken down to be spanked, caned, or otherwise punished, preferably with the buttocks parted to disclose the anus. She also enjoys exposing and spanking me. Meeting only for intensive and exhausting sexual purposes, we have delighted each other for months.

Their encounters were not always delightful. As James Wolcott noted in the *London Review of Books*, writing about Ken's diaries, one of the weekend getaways with Nicole turned into "a slapstick fiasco after she administers a vodka enema (his bright idea), which shoots through his anal canal like Prussic acid, turning his bottom into a scalding volcano."

But that would be life post-Elaine, and it was years off. For now, Elaine was his wife, and she had no choice but to deal with Ken's demands. Although she submitted to several S&M sessions, her capitulation felt humiliating. She later described feeling like "an accomplice collaborating at her own ruin." In return, Ken ridiculed Elaine, accusing her of being puritanical and bad in bed. He later blamed her in his diaries, claiming that his wife had "taunted and threatened and blackmailed" him over his "filthy desires," causing him to hate himself. *She* had wounded *him*. In Ken's mind, turning reality on its head, he was the victim—displaying classic behavior of an abuser. It's no wonder Elaine, caught in a cycle of abuse, kept trying to please her husband to preserve the relationship at all costs. He only resented her more. "Ken, the Tot of Destiny, had turned into the Marquis de Sade," she recalled, "and I in response had become a virago."

It didn't take long for Elaine to realize that her husband had more in common with her father than she could have guessed. He was a bully with a frightening temper, and violent toward women. He was also a master manipulator. Sometimes when he did not get his way—whether indulging his penchant for flagellomania, or some other demand—he would stand on the ledge of their living room window and threaten to jump. Elaine knew two things for sure: he would never leap to his death, and she was obliged to "rescue" him every time. "I knew that he might slip and fall," she recalled. "And that his blood would be on my hands."

With stormy fights, booze, infidelity, jealousy, rage, and spite in the marital mix, their union easily reached train-wreck status. Yet the couple had an amazing capacity to put up a united front in public, and there was a kind of genuine love between them. "We gave each other a tremendous feeling of specialness, uniqueness, even glamour," Ken once said of the marriage. "We looked on each other with the absolute certainty that nobody quite like us had ever existed." They were charming, self-absorbed, and adept at entertaining their high-powered friends—a constant rotation of famous directors, writers, actors, and other members of London's cultural elite. But as parents, Ken and Elaine were disastrous. In an interview decades later, Tracy was understanding and generous in her perspective, if not entirely forgiving: "My parents were flawed people who both had flawed upbringings themselves," she said. "They did the best they could. They simply didn't have the skills to make it work." She described their socializing as "obsessive."

One notable instance of their shortcomings took place on Tracy's twenty-first birthday in 1973. She was a student at Sussex University, studying social anthropology. Ken decided to take over the Young Vic for a grand party, but he invited more of his friends to the theater than hers: the two hundred starry guests included Liza Minnelli, Peter Sellers, Lauren Bacall, and Maggie Smith, along with a performance by a comedian who told cringeworthy jokes about Jews and Black people. Ken was gutted to learn that Princess Margaret would be out of town on the date of the party and considered postponing the event. It was all about Ken: a celebration hosted by and in honor of him. The costs spiraled out of control. "This would be a testament to his ability to attract A-list celebrities into his life," Tracy noted. Compiling and tracking the guest list consumed him over a period of months. He chain-smoked and drank gin and ginger ale as he agonized over every detail of the party, with no regard for what his daughter might have wanted for her milestone birthday. The entire night proved so mortifying that Tracy snorted cocaine to get through it, and enjoyed a rare if inappropriate father-daughter bonding moment when she and Ken took turns doing cocaine using a rolled up five-pound note and one of his credit cards. He claimed it was his first time trying the drug, and that they ought to keep it a secret.

Ken had another special gift for Tracy. A few days before the lavish party, he arranged a surprise film screening at a private club in Mayfair for twenty guests, including Tracy's new boyfriend and his parents. The selection? Sammy Davis Jr.'s "personal copy" of the 1972 pornographic film *Deep Throat*. As if the situation couldn't get more bizarre, the showbiz man himself made a cameo to introduce the movie, saying he hoped everyone would have a good time. Tracy—sexually inexperienced, traumatized, and baffled by the cinematic ordeal arranged by her own father—took Valium to fall asleep that night.

The year before had not been much better, when Ken composed a poem for Tracy's birthday that began:

> *Twenty*
> *Is plenty*
> *For most girls, who then*
> *Cease to be people*
> *And live through their men.*

In Elaine's autobiography, her recollections of motherhood conjure a close relationship with her daughter ("Tracy was, daily, a most profound illumination and revelation"). She portrays herself as an imperfect but loving mother. Tracy's 2016 memoir, *Wear and Tear: The Threads of*

*My Life*, tells a very different story of a childhood marked by sadness, neglect, and poor self-esteem. The cover of the book features a black-and-white photograph of the dashing Tynans in the living room of their Mount Street flat, both dressed in faux-leopard-skin pants, sitting on a chaise longue, gazing into each other's eyes. Behind them is an oversized reproduction of Hieronymus Bosch's *Garden of Earthly Delights*, which Elaine called a "conversation piece" but had always frightened Tracy.

She recalls living with "my often irritable, unpredictable mother" and "my nervous, chain-smoking father who was forever struggling to meet deadlines," and in whose company she spent little time alone. If her father wasn't home writing and smoking, he was out eating, drinking, theater-going, party-going, or cheating on his wife. Neither he nor Elaine were present for Tracy's sixth birthday. Instead, they were off in Spain, drinking and watching the bullfights. Their daughter was left to spend the day with her au pair, one in a series of women along the way who raised her. Upon her return, Elaine's birthday gift to her daughter was a box containing two pairs of frilly underwear, yellow and orange. (Tracy had hoped for a doll or stuffed animal instead.) "I wanted parents who weren't always going away or going out," she later wrote. Her almost criminally negligent parents were not "present" even when they were around, and she felt deprived of the emotional safety that every child craves. She and her mother seldom hugged, so on the rare occasions when her mother embraced her, the encounters were awkward. There were no sit-down family meals and Elaine did not cook. Tracy was left to eat meals alone or with an au pair. Most days, when she woke up for school, her parents were still sleeping. They were rarely home when she returned.

Late one night, she woke up to hear her parents screaming. It was not an unusual event in the Tynan home, but this time Tracy was startled by the sight of her mother standing in her doorway yelling, "Your father's trying to kill me!" Eventually Tracy fell asleep again, and the next day her parents proceeded as if nothing had happened.

There were similar scenes to come, with drunken screaming matches, plates smashing, and ashtrays hurled. Each parent seemed to draw energy from provoking fury in the other, and both were oblivious to the deleterious effects on their daughter. They were far too consumed by the important people in their orbit, such as "Larry" Olivier, Vivien Leigh, Marlene Dietrich, Cecil Beaton, Kingsley Amis, and John Osborne. (Dietrich was more of a frenemy to Elaine. She recalled that Dietrich once offered to babysit for her, but Elaine had a cynical response. As she later told a journalist: "Dietrich had been monopolizing my husband . . . perhaps she thought babysitting our new baby would mollify me.")

In the spring of 1956, Ken championed Osborne's first play, *Look Back in Anger*, calling it "the best young play of its decade," and Jimmy Porter "the completest young pup in our literature since Hamlet." He made it *the* play to see and heralded an exciting era in British theater—a less insular one, removed from polite society and marked by realism and attention to the working class. (Audiences supposedly gasped upon seeing an ironing board on a London stage.) He may as well have been describing his own marriage when he wrote: "Mr Osborne's picture of a certain kind of modern marriage is hilariously accurate; he shows us two attractive young animals engaged in competitive martyrdom, each with its teeth sunk deep in the other's neck, and each reluctant to break the clinch for fear of bleeding to death."

Both Elaine and Ken were extremely status conscious, and to Tracy, their endless infatuation with celebrity seemed "more like an addiction, a need to fill some bottomless hole in their psyches." Ken and Elaine collected famous people like trophies. They jumped at a chance to host a dinner party for Marilyn Monroe and Arthur Miller, even hiring a caterer for the occasion, and were deflated when a "hysterical" (according to her husband) Monroe canceled an hour before guests were set to arrive.

Their privileged world seemed normal to their daughter, who knew little about what a healthy version of family life might look like. Elaine's friend "Jimmy" Baldwin came to the flat one day and taught Tracy the twist. And it was no big deal for Tracy to find herself in a stretch limousine with Richard Avedon, who photographed Elaine for the book jacket of her second novel, or with Mary Martin after seeing the Broadway production of *Peter Pan* with Elaine. (Tracy vomited on Mary Martin's lap in the car.)

One night, Tracy heard her parents fighting and snuck down the hallway to discover her father on the ledge of the bedroom window, in his underwear, threatening to jump. Her mother, naked and smoking, taunted Ken in response: *"Why the fuck don't you?"* This episode left Tracy transfixed, as if witnessing a proverbial train wreck. It was uncomfortable, but she couldn't look away. "I realized for the first time my own fascination with my parents' behavior," she later wrote. "Watching them was like watching a horror movie, scary but riveting." Sitting quietly in the corner at her parents' parties—eavesdropping, observing the antics of the beautiful people around her—became a habit of hers: "I felt like I was watching a play, with the grown-ups as the stars." She didn't know who many of them were. But she knew they were important.

Lonely and shy, Tracy found a sense of control by being a "good girl" in contrast to the chaos around her. She felt oddly responsible for her mother and often blamed herself for bad parental behavior. "I've been thinking," Elaine announced one day to nine-year-old Tracy, "it would be nice if you curtsied when you were introduced to people." Baffled by her mother's request, but wary of causing trouble, Tracy did whatever would please her mother. "She was a reasonable child," Elaine wrote in her memoir. "And most things she wanted we were able to supply."

Again, Tracy had a radically different view of her childhood. "Most of the time I was scared and confused and felt I was in a movie with lots of crazy people," she later wrote. "I believed I was supposed to play the normal one, particularly since there was no other role available." She was indeed a reasonable child, forced into parenting her parents. When she needed reassurance, there was nowhere to turn for safety. And the bizarre scenes at home weren't limited to the crockery-smashing rows between Elaine and Ken. Both were plenty "crazy" on their own. While watching TV with her au pair one night, Tracy was startled to hear a loud "Fuck!" erupt from her mother. An inebriated Elaine appeared before them—naked yet again and unsteady on her feet—as she attempted, and failed, to pour champagne into a glass. "Don't you think you ought to put some clothes on, Mrs. Tynan?" said the nanny gently. "Aren't you getting cold?" Elaine stumbled off to her bedroom.

The tumult of the Tynan marriage was not lost on outsiders. As Orson Welles once remarked, "They were obviously having a terrible time together, the nature of which we weren't interested in looking into." The writer and journalist Sally Belfrage, a frequent party guest of the Tynans and Elaine's close friend, recalled: "[I would] arrive at the door of the Mount Street apartment where the locks had usually been changed by one or other of the Tynans . . . ring the bell, sounds of screams and smashing crockery and tiny Tracy opening the door, trying to find out which lock was working. Ken shouting, 'I'll kill you, you bitch.' Smash, smash, a whimper from the au pair, and Tracy, poised and calm, saying, 'Hello, how nice to see you. Come in. Can I take your coat?' And taking one into the living room, and pouring drinks and sitting down, looking very interested." She described the couple's hectic social life:

> Meet Elaine in the late morning at the French Club or the Colony, drinking, drinking, drinking, picking up people and discarding them. They would go back to Mount Street late in the afternoon and then go out to dinner with Ken until 3 or 4 in the morning. It would take me about a week to rest up. But Ken and Elaine were at it again the next day. There was this frenzied feverish activity all the time, and there was never any pause to allow anyone to think or reflect what it was about. The essential thing was to keep moving in as many crowds of amusing people as possible.

Elaine's close friend Judy Feiffer was shocked to witness the uglier side of Elaine and Ken's tempestuous marriage. She recalled that Elaine showed up at her apartment one night, her dress covered in spaghetti. "Ken and I disagreed about a play," Elaine said, by way of explanation. Judy said that her friend wore the stains "like a badge of honor. It was as though she wanted me to see the proof of what he'd done to her."

The marriage had gone in one direction, downhill, since 1951. Less than four years into it, while Tracy was still a toddler, Elaine had a revelation at the grocery store as she hesitated before buying a large jar of peanut butter. It occurred to her that she might be single again soon, and the larger size would go to waste. She bought a small jar instead.

As it turned out, the Tynans' marriage would drag on for years, with all its savagery, loathing, and spite. In the summer of 1957, Ken turned thirty. He went to Spain with a new mistress, an actress named Carol Saroyan, and as they lay in the dark, she suddenly said, "Someone burly came in." Ken shot up in bed, and sure enough, a large man had appeared in their hotel room. "I'm sorry," he said, "but I'm Mr. Sullivan representing Mrs. Tynan." (He happened to be a private detective.) That was the end of that. Ken phoned Elaine, apologized profusely, and offered to fly home the following day. "And so I went back to seven more years of the inferno with Elaine," Ken later recorded in his diary. Before leaving for Valencia to meet Carol, whom he valued for her "sexual compatibility," Ken had left desperate notes for Elaine all over their flat: "My life turns on you only my love," "I have nothing to do any more without you my darling," "Please do not leave me today." It was as if she were the one flying off to cheat on him—although she was having an affair with Cyril Connolly at the time. Upon his return, Elaine demanded a divorce. Ken begged for another chance, talked her out of it, and they returned to what was for them a state of normalcy: together again, but on the verge of divorce.

Their turbulent marriage endured out of mutual devotion, guilt, familiarity, and a compulsive need to continue performing the role of "happy couple" for their wide social circle. The frequent separations, accusations, and affairs were never-ending, and neither party was blameless. Even as Ken lashed out at Elaine for her affairs, he was always having a dramatic fling of his own—such as with the Chinese actress Tsai Chin, who was stunned that Elaine often showed up at her flat when Ken was there, and she would watch in disbelief as the two of them would launch into one of their vicious arguments right in front of her.

Perhaps the beginning of the end of the Tynan union can be traced to 1958, the year Elaine published *The Dud Avocado*. Ken would make her pay for that.

The year got off to an exhilarating start. On January 12, her novel came out to rave reviews: "As delightful and delicate an examination of how it is to be twenty and in love in Paris as I've read," declared John Metcalfe in the *Sunday Times*. John Davenport in the *Observer* called *The Dud Avocado* a "champagne cocktail," writing that "one falls for Sally Jay from the first sentence." Elaine's protagonist seemed to charm everyone. (That fall, another beloved heroine, Holly Golightly, would make her debut in Truman Capote's novella, *Breakfast at Tiffany's*.) *The Dud Avocado* promptly hit the top of bestseller lists in Britain and went into a second printing. It is telling, and quite sad, that for Elaine, what proved most gratifying was being able to justify her existence to Ken.

In late July, E. P. Dutton published the American edition, and laudatory reviews appeared in the *New York Times* on consecutive days. *Time* magazine ran a positive review ("caustically funny"), accompanied by a brief profile of the "brown-eyed, lissome" author. ("[Her husband] contributed the title and some advice: 'Take out all the exclamation points.' His wife took out most of them.") For Elaine, the critical acclaim in the United States was especially meaningful, because fourteen American publishers had rejected her novel before Victor Gollancz bought it in England. He had published authors such as George Orwell and Daphne du Maurier, and more recently, Kingsley Amis's *Lucky Jim*. At first, Gollancz told Elaine that his offer to accept *The Dud Avocado* was contingent upon publishing under her married name. She refused.

Writing in the Sunday *Book Review*, the critic Martin Levin—noting in the second paragraph that Dundy was "the wife of Kenneth Tynan"—praised her novel as "a Baedeker of neo-bohemia, setting down with pungent realism the sights, sounds, and overpowering aromas of what Jack Kerouac has called the Subterraneans (Paris branch)." He also mentioned that upon its initial publication in England, *The Dud Avocado* "exploded in Bloomsbury like a case of overheated Coca-Cola: the jacket is scrawled with handy testimonials to its 'exquisite gaiety.'"

In a subsequent piece, Orville Prescott, the main book reviewer for the *Times* for nearly twenty-five years, cited his fatigue over the endless stream of writing about Americans in Paris (Hemingway, Fitzgerald, et al.). He noted that "the gayest and most cheerful I have ever read is *The Dud Avocado*":

> Unlike the morose and maudlin young women who pursue their men so glumly in several recent French novels about youth and love and Paris, Sally Jay Gorce is not corrupt. She is only enthusiastically in love with life. And life, as Sally Jay sees it, means men and love affairs.

As much as he adored the novel and admired Dundy's talent, Prescott couldn't help ending his review by noting of the author, "She is the wife of the English drama critic Kenneth Tynan and lives in London."

Each fresh round of praise for Elaine rankled Ken more. Ever the devoted wife, she began going out of her way to avoid injury to Ken's ego: at parties, she would scoot people out of earshot once they started complimenting her novel—all to protect Ken's feelings. But much to his annoyance, the praise kept coming. "I was so pleased to read Elaine's notices," John Osborne wrote in a letter to Ken. "Please give her my love and congratulations." Worse, Ken's friends teased him about Elaine's success: "Poor old sod. Here you are, slogging away week after week to stay where you are, then along comes your wife and does it in one."

Indeed, she had achieved both popular and critical acclaim, along with the admiration of those she called the Big Personalities. Terry Southern took to calling her "Miss Smarts." Gore Vidal, whom she adored, became a close friend and confidante around this time, and they had sex once. Around this time, Penguin acquired the paperback rights to *Dud Avocado*, and there was intense competition to acquire the film rights. Foreign translation rights were sold in Dutch, German, and more. Elaine was photographed for an excerpt in the UK edition of *Harper's Bazaar*.

Ken felt emasculated and betrayed. "You weren't a writer when I married you!" he yelled one night as he threw a copy of her book out the bedroom window. Becoming a writer was a saving grace for Elaine, who had grown weary of the couple's endless socializing and felt a "gray everydayness, a monotony" that depressed her. Writing a novel was like creating her ideal acting role, and she savored the freedom of it. She also found a reason to get out of bed. With Sally Jay Gorce arriving in her mind "fully formed," Elaine felt energized and knew she was onto something—but she had no confidence that her manuscript would find a publisher, much less in multiple countries, nor that it would be met with immediate success. She was touched when her friend Ernest Hemingway praised the book, telling her, "I like the way your characters all speak differently." (He lamented that his own characters sounded the same.) "Larry" Olivier joked to Elaine that since her book seemed to be making a lot of money, they could elope and she would support them. And the much-treasured fan letter from Groucho Marx arrived on September 20, 1959. It read in full:

Dear Mrs Tynan,

I don't make a practice of writing to married women especially if the husband is a dramatic critic, but I had to tell someone (and it might as well be you since you're the author) how much I enjoyed *The Dud Avocado*. It made me laugh, scream and guffaw (which, incidentally, is a great name for a law firm).

If this was actually your life, I don't know how the hell you got through it.

> Sincerely,
> Groucho Marx.

Ken couldn't take it any longer. One day he confronted Elaine, warning that if she ever dared to write another book, he would divorce her. "That did it," Elaine later recalled. "Early next morning I sat down and started a new novel." It was the beginning of what would become *The Old Man and Me*, published in 1964 and inspired by her romance with Cyril Connolly.

Although he had probably blocked it from his mind, Ken was the one who had encouraged his wife to write a novel in the first place. Just as Elaine hit a new low over her "invisible" acting career—"I worked regularly and steadily, but the parts were *nothing*"—Ken said he believed in her talent as a writer and that she should simply go for it. Now that she had stopped calling her agent, what did she have to lose? After reading the manuscript, he declared it would become a "colossal bestseller." Elaine was relieved. "I believed him," she later wrote. "No one could predict how a play or novel would be received by the public like Ken could."

He even came up with the title. One evening, over dinner with their friend Sandy Wilson—an Oxford friend of Ken's whose hit musical *The Boy Friend* gave nineteen-year-old Julie Andrews her Broadway debut—Elaine complimented Sandy's thriving avocado plant and expressed her frustration at being unable to do the same. "What you have is a dud avocado," he replied, prompting Ken to mention that the phrase would make a great book title. (Gollancz disagreed at first, insisting it sounded like a cookbook.) The fruit was referenced within the novel, when Sally Jay is likened to an avocado by a would-be suitor: "A hard center with the tender meat all wrapped up in a shiny casing. So green—so eternally green . . . And I will tell you something really extraordinary. Do you know that you can take the stones of these luscious fruits, put them in water—just plain water, mind you . . . and in three months up comes a sturdy little plant full of green leaves? This is their sturdy little souls bursting into bloom."

KEN HAD NOT MADE THE WRITING PROCESS EASY FOR HIS WIFE. WHEREAS he had his study as a refuge for creative work, Elaine wrote each day "slowly but steadily" on the living room sofa with a typewriter propped up on her knees. Her back hurt. She resisted the urge to drink, forcing herself to stay sober before sitting down to write. Discipline took a lot out of her. She began turning down Ken's invitations to openings so she could keep the time to herself, which embarrassed and angered him: "What's worse for a married critic than not having his wife—probably one of the reasons he married in the first place—accompany him to the theatre?" she later wrote. With rare exceptions, Elaine wouldn't budge. Her selfishness was necessary for the work. In response, Ken developed "a deadening coldness," she recalled. "I tried to match it, but was never able to." Even so, she knew that Ken could also be "kind and loving and generous and fun and charming, suddenly piercing my heart by doing things such as taking dancing lessons because he knew I loved to dance."

Elaine had come close to filing for divorce just after signing her book contract with Gollancz, but she had a change of heart after Ken begged her to reconsider. He said that she was the center of his world and threatened to kill himself. (This push-pull would become a pattern, always ending in reconciliation.) Somehow Ken knew exactly how to seduce his wife anew, whether bad-mouthing his mistresses to her, insisting they gave him no pleasure, or surprising her with a custom red-leather-bound copy of *The Dud Avocado*, edged in gold, with an inscription that read, *"From the Critic to the Author."* All was forgiven.

Not long after the book's publication, Elaine met an attractive Englishman, Mark Culme-Seymour, at a party. She liked that he was neither a writer nor an actor. In the mood to be "wicked," Elaine flirted with Mark, he flirted back, and they slid easily into a "perfectly normal, perfectly conventional yet exciting" affair, one she felt she deserved after the suffering she had endured in her marriage, and being made to feel ashamed of her success by her husband. She had no trouble compartmentalizing her affair. "I was able to blend it into my life," she recalled. "I was feeling my oats, feeling I'd earned the right to do anything I felt like. I was changing from a pre-*Dud* reflector to a post-*Dud* generator."

In the fall of 1958, the Tynans set off for New York. Both Ken and Elaine must have hoped that the change of scenery would shake up their marriage for the better. Ken was invited by William Shawn, the editor of the *New Yorker*, to step in as drama critic after the death of Wolcott Gibbs. He was offered a two-year contract, so the couple sublet their Mount Street flat and rented a furnished apartment on the Upper East Side of Manhattan. (Tracy attended school at Brearley.) Because Ken preferred working in the bedroom, on the nights he was on deadline for his *New Yorker* pieces, Elaine had to sleep on the couch.

As always, the parties were nonstop, providing an easy, booze-soaked distraction from their ongoing battles. The fights were vicious as ever. One day, in the midst of a screaming-and-throwing-things match in the living room, "when we saw that the maid was trying to get in to clean the room, without missing a beat we moved into the bedroom she had just finished putting in order." Unfortunately for Ken, at every party they went to, nearly everyone Elaine met had read her book and said they loved it. Gore Vidal hosted their first New York party, and unlike Elaine, he enjoyed the full support of his younger companion, Howard, who tended to all domestic duties, including household finances and cooking: "Gore does the writing," Howard explained, "and I do all the rest." Elsewhere, the Tynans mingled with writers such as Norman Mailer, William Styron, Isak Dinesen, and Philip Roth, and socialites such as Gloria Vanderbilt. They went to W. H. Auden's fiftieth birthday at his apartment on St. Mark's Place, where they met the poet Marianne Moore and enjoyed champagne from a bathtub filled with bottles on ice.

All the while, Elaine dealt with her "toxic fury" at Ken by stewing in private and drinking more. The following year, in 1959, she came across an ad in the *New York Times* with a provocative headline: "Are You an Alcoholic?" There were about twenty questions, used by Johns Hopkins University Hospital to determine the extent of a patient's alcohol addiction. According to this test, answering yes to three or more questions meant you were "definitely" an alcoholic. Elaine answered yes to half of them.

The Tynans decided to spend that summer apart, with Elaine and Tracy (and their nanny) on Martha's Vineyard, and Ken in Europe. But craziness made a comeback when Ken sent an urgent and pleading letter from Berlin. Without his wife, he could not write, could not live. "You are the only proof I have that I exist," he wrote. "I am in love with you in the same way that the earth revolves around the sun. If I don't see you within a few weeks, I shall take to my bed and have one of those wasting diseases people died of in Victorian novels." After much agonizing, Elaine decided not to join him—and later she used his words in a novel.

By the time they reunited in England in the summer of 1960, the couple settled upon an open marriage. This arrangement essentially meant business as usual, but "keeping our private lives and private thoughts closed from each other," Elaine recalled. Easier said than done. One night, the Scottish poet George MacBeth banged on the front door, demanding to see Elaine. He pressed the doorbell for two hours, until the police showed up, while Elaine and Ken had an epic screaming match and Tracy put her pillow over her head to block out the altercation. Not long after, Ken walked into the flat one afternoon and discovered his wife in the kitchen with MacBeth, who wore nothing but a necktie. Ken grabbed the poet's clothing and threw it out the window into the building's courtyard, which meant that Elaine's lover had to sheepishly borrow one of Ken's raincoats before leaving. For months the clothes remained outside, rained on and ruined.

After witnessing hundreds of her parents' rows, Tracy must have wondered what on earth kept them together. "They deemed this the solution to their compulsive infidelity," she later wrote, but "it never succeeded in quenching the jealousy, anger, and resentment that animated their interdependency." Elaine admitted as much: "The Band Aid solution was to stay under the same roof, but as far away from each other as possible." One or the other kept making threats to leave (especially Elaine, who yearned for a quickie Mexican divorce), but neither bothered to do anything about it. There was heart-tugging and foot-dragging on both sides. But Elaine started to build a life of her own and an identity disconnected from her husband. She spent time with what she called her "new non-Kenelaine friends," including various theater types and the writers Emma Tennant and Francis Wyndham—all of whom "proved to be a strong centrifugal force in spinning me away from Ken."

Elaine kept writing, too. An idea for a comedic play, *My Place*, began percolating in her mind, and after she finished a draft, she was honored when the producer of *Oliver!* held a reading of the play on the same West End stage where the musical was being performed. She then made a number of revisions and sent a draft to Gore Vidal, whose play *The Best Man* premiered on Broadway in 1960 and was nominated for a number of Tony Awards. She never showed a draft to Ken.

Elaine loved immersing herself in *My Place* and other creative projects. Things weren't going so well for Ken, however. He had resumed his position as the *Observer*'s drama critic, but a book of his collected writings, *Curtains*, received a "very bitchy, personal and intemperate attack" from the "literary serial killer" Mary McCarthy. The headline ("Curtains for Tynan") said it all, and Ken was as devastated as McCarthy might have hoped for. His mother died in the winter of 1961, leaving him steeped in self-pity: "You have family, parents, sisters," he complained to Elaine. "I have none. Now I'm really an orphan." And a television series he was producing began to fall apart. So did Ken. He became addicted to Dexamyl (a widely abused amphetamine, discontinued in 1982) and kept up his usual daily intake of booze and a few packs of cigarettes. After producing an incomprehensible *Observer* piece that he barely remembered writing, Ken knew it was time to see a psychiatrist. To the meticulous prose stylist, writing nonsense was a shameful nadir. He also knew it was time to move out of the Mount Street flat, so he rented a place in Knightsbridge and fell into a new affair with the painter Brenda Bury. Her 1963 portrait of Ken is in the National Portrait Gallery. (Bury later said that while sitting for the painting, her subject was "looking round for a way to escape.")

Meanwhile, Elaine was thrilled when *My Place* opened in a pre–West End tour in January 1962, but the reviews were mixed and it turned out to be a valuable learning experience rather than a theatrical hit. She was proud to have written a play, and disappointed that it had been, in her view, poorly directed. "I went back to my novel," she recalled, "where I could have more control." She also began to take control of her situation with Ken. Both felt trapped in the endgame of their marriage and now she was ready to do something about it. The outcome would prove crazier and uglier than she could have imagined.

That fall, Elaine put an end to the couple's talking-about-talking-about-divorce cycle and served Ken with actual divorce papers. "The strain of my unsettled relations with him was taking its toll," she later wrote. "I was restless, irritable, disdainful and bitchy." It was hardly surprising that Ken refused to give his consent, but Elaine did not expect more ledge-standing from him, both in the physical and psychological sense. Although she still felt confident that he would never leap to his death, he once again succeeded at emotional blackmail. The usual begging for mercy and second chances started up again, and a distressed Ken insisted that Elaine speak with his psychiatrist to hear from an expert just how badly the patient was suffering as a result of Elaine's decision. From Ken's perspective, she was endangering his life by filing for divorce. His therapist agreed that Ken was suicidal and said so when he met with Elaine, but she refused to withdraw—not at first, anyway. Again Ken wore her down. She put the divorce on hold.

Even as Elaine was determined to extricate herself from the marriage, Ken continued to make her life miserable. She was foolish to imagine that by separating from her husband and filing divorce papers, he was no longer her problem. And she still came running when he called, even as far as Spain, hating herself for caving in. When she began an affair with a Scottish laird named Peter Combe, Ken was furious—never mind his numerous infidelities or his current girlfriend. He demanded to know where Elaine had been spending her nights and accused her of abandoning him. After receiving an anguished, over-the-top letter from Ken with "pages of professions of love followed by pages of accusations mixed in with threats to kill himself," she turned to her friend Orson Welles for help, asking him to speak with Ken. Welles reported back to Elaine with some simple advice: "You'd better divorce him because he's destroying you." Ken was either still in love with her, or he regarded her as a possession he would not relinquish—perhaps both. At one point, determined to reconcile, he insisted on a meeting with Elaine and her Scottish paramour to talk things over. Who was the lunatic: Ken for requesting such a meeting, or Elaine for acquiescing? She wanted him to suffer, and to pine for her, and at the same time she pitied him. She even agreed, as a final favor, to accompany Ken to a bullfight in Spain. That night in her hotel room, Elaine took a sleeping pill and went to bed. Not long after, Ken came knocking at the door. He was leaving early the next morning and wanted to say goodbye. Too tired to argue, Elaine let him in. Ken assaulted her, "leaving me unconscious on the bathroom floor with two black eyes and a broken nose."

Welles and his wife, Paola, helped Elaine and ensured she received medical treatment. Although her wounds healed in a short period of time, the psychological damage lingered, made worse by Ken's refusal to acknowledge his behavior when he showed up on her doorstep one day, despite a restraining order against him:

On the whole he downplayed what he'd done—no apology, only an off-hand mention that his shrink had dismissed it, merely saying it was clear that he'd kill me or I'd kill him if we stayed together. He was neither ashamed nor sorry for what he'd done. Nor did he seem embarrassed that I'd told people about it. There was always part of him that gloried in his reputation as a lady-killer, the sinful, depraved Don Juan. The mad, bad, dangerous-to-know sadist.

As she settled into a new flat at 31 Devonshire Place Mews in Marylebone, Elaine began seeing a psychiatrist. "Forced to look at how loony my life was," she later wrote, "I fell into a deep depression." Ken kept phoning her. "Everything without me was a void of loneliness and masturbation," she recalled. (Even Tracy knew then that "there was no cure for my parents' marriage.") Once, when Ken coaxed Elaine into visiting him at the Mount Street flat, she saw the familiar schoolmaster's cane and wondered "how long it had been there, whom it had been used on, whom he intended to use it on." She knew that Ken was in poor health, suffering from coughing fits that sometimes lasted through the night, yet he still kept up the boozing, smoking, and Dexamyl. All this despite having an affair with the woman who would become his second wife, and despite having been hired as the dramaturg (literary manager) of the newly formed National Theatre—his dream job, though he earned about £46 a week. He was invited to join the theater by Sir Laurence Olivier, who was appointed artistic director and hired Ken away from his criticism post at the *Observer*.

With the exception of the ongoing marital strife, Elaine was thriving: she was invited to guest-edit an issue of *Queen* magazine themed "the war between the sexes," and enjoyed collaborating with well-known writers and poets on various features. She got freelance journalism assignments from *Esquire*, *New York*, *Cosmopolitan*, and other publications. A Manchester newspaper asked her to cover an international literary conference in Salzburg. And *The Old Man and Me* came out as a response to the wave of work by so-called Angry Young Men, with a tough, ambitious, and scheming protagonist. (She was not "likable" and "feminine" in the way that Sally Jay had been.) Elaine knew she would ruffle certain critical feathers with her Angry Young Woman, but couldn't help wondering, "Where were full-length portraits of what I called a Girl With a Plan, whose vices and passions were explored and exploited by their authors with the same intensity as those of the men?"

The novel was praised by, among others, Doris Lessing, Edmund Wilson, and Dawn Powell, who called it "a terrific job—fierce, gamey, vixenish—as if it was bled not written . . . [d]efinitely demonic, exquisitely carved, deadly murderous comedy." Elaine was introduced to Powell by Gore Vidal, who said, "Here are the two funniest women writers around." As Elaine later recalled, "We just looked at each other. What are you going to say? It was a real conversation stopper."

Miles Davis, an acquaintance of Elaine's, read the book. Aside from a comment about her use of slang, he didn't offer his opinion. The novel received mixed reviews, yet the negative ones did not shake her hard-won confidence. "I tore them up and flushed them down the toilet," she recalled. "I'd become a writer." One day she had lunch in Hollywood with George Cukor, who would win the Academy Award for Best Director in 1965 for *My Fair Lady*. Unprompted, he raved about *The Old Man and Me* and later expressed his desire to direct an adaptation. After that deal fell through, Elaine got excited when Cary Grant said he wanted to make the film, and again when David Niven said he was eager to do it. Nothing ever came of those conversations, and Elaine gave up. Her novel was not a commercial success, anyway—in the United States, Dutton ended up remaindering the book and Elaine feared she would be marked as "a small circle writer's writer." When she received a letter from one of her great literary idols, P. G. Wodehouse, offering effusive praise and urging her to write a third novel, her faith was restored.

On May 12, 1964, Tracy received a call on her birthday just before bedtime at her boarding school in Devon. Maybe her mother was phoning to wish her a happy birthday? Elaine had often gotten the date wrong. As it turned out, the timing was mere coincidence. "Hi, darling," she said. "I'm in Mexico. I've just divorced your father." Having threatened Ken with a divorce on many occasions, now she had really done it. After thirteen years, the cycle of rows and reconciliations was over. The split later made the news in *Time* magazine, various gossip columns, and the wires: UPI announced the news with the headline "Wife Divorces Kenneth Tynan." Tracy felt numb after her mother phoned. "I thought about my birthday and wondered why my mother had forgotten to wish me a happy one," she later wrote. "Maybe she meant the divorce to be my birthday gift." Her father, at least, had sent a card.

Both parents would handle the details of their divorce clumsily with Tracy. Elaine had decamped to New York to get as much physical distance as possible from Ken, while he stayed in the Mount Street flat. Tracy returned home from spring break to discover that a beautiful woman had moved in with her father. Nothing was explained. Thinking about the impact of his behavior on others wasn't in his wheelhouse. "There was a deep insecurity in my father," Tracy recalled. "He was a very complicated person, generous and selfish by turns. He had a way of saying or doing things that he thought would reassure me but often had the opposite effect."

Ken made no attempt to ensure that Tracy felt comfortable around his new companion, Kathleen Halton. She wondered whether Kathleen was there to replace her. Attempts at bonding were awkward and unsuccessful. Apart from a shared love of cats, there was little to say. "She wasn't old enough to be my mother," Tracy later recalled, "but she was too old to be my sister or a friend. Should I shake hands or hug her? Was I meant to call her Kathleen, or Mother, or what?" Still, over the next few years, as she divided her time between her parents' homes in London and New York, Tracy liked being with her father, "because I preferred being away from my mother as she sank deeper and deeper into depression," she recalled. "By the time I was fourteen, she had added pills to her alcohol consumption." It wasn't unusual for Elaine to pop open a bottle of champagne at ten o'clock in the morning.

Kathleen was an Oxford University graduate, twenty-eight years old, the daughter of a Canadian war correspondent, and still married when her affair with Ken began. She was an aspiring journalist. After agonizing over her infidelity and returning to her husband, Oliver, she decided to end her marriage around the same time that Ken and Elaine's divorce was finalized. (Ken also had a brief affair with the actress, dancer, and singer Rita Moreno before committing to Kathleen.) Ken once described Kathleen as the "Rolls-Royce" of women, whatever that meant. Tracy recalled her as "a trophy wife, but with brains."

Meanwhile, in 1963, Elaine, now forty-two, had settled into a duplex rental in the West Village after her friend, the director Sidney Lumet, invited her to take over his lease. Her friends in the city included Rosemary Harris, Mike Nichols, Renata Adler, and Claire Bloom. Elaine was relieved that the "long dance of death" of her marriage was over, and she had no trouble occupying herself with new dalliances and boyfriends, and as always, lots of parties. Yet even after having an ocean between them and "what should have been the decent burial of our marriage," Ken—still with Kathleen—kept up contact. He tried inviting himself to her parties (she refused), called her on occasion, and wrote love letters addressed to "Elaine Tynan." She would waver but would not break. "I understood that it was Ken's manipulative genius ever to pour oil on troubled water and then light it," Elaine later wrote, and that any non-Tracy-related communication with him would be "supping with the devil."

Now that she was in the city, Elaine began spending summers with Tracy in Westhampton, on the east end of Long Island. Tracy loved spending her days at the beach but dreaded the evenings alone with her mother. At night, Elaine was drunk and out of control. "In the middle of my life I had lost my way," she recalled. She would often ramble incoherently about how much she hated Ken, and how he was still in love with her. "I didn't want to know the details of their sordid obsessions with each other," Tracy wrote in her memoir. She recalled one particularly frightening incident when she decided to cook hamburgers for her and Elaine. Feeling proud of the care she'd put into the dinner, she set out the plates and presented them to her mother. "Not enough pepper!" shrieked a drunk Elaine, who then poured a whole container of peppercorns onto the plates and ruined the meal. But it got worse: "She picked up a large carving knife," Tracy recalled, "and started waving it around, yelling, 'I'll show you how to prepare food.'" Tracy ran into her room and barricaded the door. Her mother ordered her to come out, but Tracy curled up on her bed, terrified and silent, until finally Elaine gave up. Later that night, Elaine offered a slurred apology outside Tracy's room, but she refused to open the door.

Tracy called a friend in East Hampton and invited herself over, but she was too ashamed to talk about Elaine's behavior. Her friend's house proved a welcome refuge for the next two weeks. Being the daughter of a raging alcoholic meant keeping secrets, like it or not. "By this time," she recalled, "I had learned how to stuff unpleasant feelings down into the deepest reaches of my body and psyche."

Over the next few years, Tracy saw her mother's condition deteriorate, perhaps in no small part owing to Ken's marriage to Kathleen in 1967, when Tracy was fifteen. After Elaine moved into the same high-rise building where her good friend Tennessee Williams lived, near Central Park, Tracy would overhear them chatting on the phone about their pill routines. (Tennessee's bedside table was piled high with vials, bottles, and hypodermic needles.) Elaine was being pulled lower and lower by booze, drugs, and depression. Recently she had fallen down a flight of stairs, drunk, and sprained her back. She doubled her dosage of Ritalin to get high and took the barbiturate Seconal to fall asleep. Even she could acknowledge that she was coping with her problems pharmaceutically.

On New Year's Day, Tracy came home in the morning to find her mother passed out and surrounded by empty pill containers, empty vodka bottles, and the stench of cigarette butts. "I shrugged, walked to my room, and crawled into bed," she recalled. It was just another binge. Still, she worried about her mother, especially because the notion of identifying "rock-bottom" seemed impossible to fathom. "My life was episodic," Elaine later recalled. "There was no through thread holding it together. I couldn't even thread the needle."

A few months later, in 1968, alarmed by the grip of her addiction, Elaine checked herself into the Austen Riggs Center, a psychiatric treatment hospital in the Berkshires. Tracy was relieved. "I would no longer be responsible for her," she wrote in her memoir. "I had a nagging concern that eventually, one of her vodka-and-pill cocktails would end up being fatal. At the time, I had no idea that my mother's self-destructive behavior was a cry for help, but I did sense that she longed for someone to save her. And when I was with her, I felt that the someone was meant to be me. It made me extremely uncomfortable, and sometimes I found myself wishing she would die so I wouldn't have to deal with her anymore. The minute I felt this, I would be racked with guilt."

Upon learning from her mother that James Taylor was a fellow inpatient at the time, Tracy, a big fan, was eager to visit. But she was too late: he'd been discharged before she arrived. In any case, she was glad to see her mother sober and well. Initially, Elaine suffered from "a paralyzing depression accompanied by panic attacks." She stayed at Austen Riggs for the next year and continued with the program as an outpatient for several more.

Elaine published a third novel, *The Injured Party*, in 1974, and heard through a friend that Ken was enraged by it and had gone around telling everyone that he was not the sexual sadist portrayed in the book. When it came out, she moved back to London, and in 1976, just as she was beginning to regard herself as a solid Austen Riggs graduate, ready to stand on her own, she suffered a relapse after downing several tablets of Heminevrin, a strong painkiller used to treat acute alcohol withdrawal. It was the same drug that killed Keith Moon, drummer for the Who, at the age of thirty-two in 1978. Elaine woke up in a hospital emergency room, "staring at a priest saying the last rites of the Catholic Church over me." Her mother came to visit and flew her back to New York. "There was nowhere to go but up," recalled Elaine. "But when?" She stayed at her mother's apartment before moving to the Stanhope Hotel, and drew up her will.

At Mount Sinai Hospital, Elaine received a series of electroshock treatments that she believed saved her life. She was able to socialize again, including going to George Plimpton's fiftieth birthday party in 1977, and she took on journalism assignments. Although she would never write another novel, she did manage to write nonfiction, including *Finch, Bloody Finch: A Biography of Peter Finch* (published by Holt, Rinehart & Winston in 1980), and *Ferriday, Louisiana* (Dutton, 1991), a quirky history of a town that claimed to have produced more famous people per square mile than any other small town in America.

The most notable of Elaine's late-life works was an unexpected (even to her) biography: *Elvis and Gladys*, recounting Presley's formative years and the intense relationship with his adoring, domineering mother. "Prior to 1977," she explained, "I didn't know that Elvis was alive until he died." Once she knew, she was obsessed. In her early sixties, tethered to no one, Elaine was having the time of her life. She spent more than five months living at a Ramada Inn in Tupelo, Mississippi (Presley's birthplace), with various side trips to Memphis and elsewhere—befriending locals, researching and interviewing, educating herself on all things Presley, and collecting as many rich stories as she could. As someone who admitted she had only ever known celebrities, spending meaningful time with "real" people was surprisingly fun.

Determined to get everything right in her book, she hired a genealogist for her project, who discovered that Presley's great-great-great-grandmother through her maternal line was a Native American Cherokee named Mourning Dove. Elaine also took a provocative stance against the conventional media portrayal of Presley, telling a reporter: "He was such a cultural explosion, such a wild sexual force, the only way they could deal with it was to present him as dumb." She also became a big fan of Presley's music. In an interview, she assessed his gifts with brilliant precision: "To produce what Elvis produced in his voice, i.e., biological aptitude, can be measured and broken down into sense of pitch, timing, harmony, rhythm, and tonal memory, interval discrimination, mode (or chord) discrimination, melodic sequences, and musical imagery, and these are governed by the structure of the vocal cavities, the lips, teeth, tongue, soft palate, jaw muscles, and the thickness in length of the vocal cords. It helps if you had a mother who loves you, grew up in a small town, and was a determined dreamer. Otherwise, it can only be explained by saying he was a prodigy, probably learned it all before he came out of the womb."

Published by Macmillan in 1985 and reissued in 2004 by the University Press of Mississippi, *Elvis and Gladys* was hailed by *Kirkus Reviews* as "thoughtful and truth-telling," "Elvis's most literate life story yet," and "the most fine-grained Elvis bio ever." The gossip columnist Liz Smith praised the book, saying it was perfect for "any Elvis lover who wants to know more about what made Presley the man he was and the mama's boy he became."

As Elaine was working her way toward sobriety and a fulfilling creative life, Ken was struggling. He was no longer feared and revered. After a frustrating tenure at the National Theatre, he was pushed out by the new director, Peter Hall, in 1973, leaving him wounded and bitter. His avant-garde erotic revue, *Oh! Calcutta!,* had been a massive success—the title is a dirty pun in French, as he loved to point out—yet he earned only a fraction of what he should have because of a poorly arranged contract and his own financial mismanagement. He fancied himself a stage or film director but failed to convince others of his potential. His health declined, and he was consumed by self-loathing and regret. He had lived beyond his means for far too long, and with mounting debts no longer had the budget to enjoy the bon vivant lifestyle of the Elaine era. Money was tight. The notoriety he'd sought, and won, for so long had faded, though many of his celebrity friendships endured. (He described his social circle as "upper-bohemian showbusiness.")

In 1976, Ken was suffering from emphysema, which came as no surprise after decades of heavy smoking. He moved to Santa Monica, calling himself "a climatic émigré." Tracy, now living in Los Angeles and working as a successful costume designer, was not pleased about her father's proximity. (She married the film director Jim McBride and had two children.) Tracy wrote in her memoir that the father-daughter relationship remained "contentious and complicated," and that she did not feel integrated into his new family. Kathleen was neither mother nor friend, and Tracy found that they were "polite but guarded with each other."

Ken and Kathleen tried to make a splash in Hollywood. She wrote a well-received novel and adapted it into the film *Agatha* (based on the eleven-day disappearance of Agatha Christie in 1926), starring Vanessa Redgrave, Timothy Dalton, and Dustin Hoffman. It was a success, but for Kathleen rather than Ken. William Shawn came to the rescue by paying him generously to write a series of *New Yorker* profiles of contemporary luminaries such as Johnny Carson, Mel Brooks, and others. The pieces were collected in Ken's much-acclaimed book *Show People* and remain some of his best work.

Even as Ken's health declined from what he called "my bloody chest disease"—a wakeup call if there ever was one—Ken refused to give up his beloved Dunhills, or even cut back on his habit. He continued smoking up to forty cigarettes a day. Although married to Kathleen and living with their two young children, Roxana and Matthew, he was unhappy as ever. He carried on his long-running affair with Nicole, and meticulously recorded their sexual escapades in his diary entries. He had terrible rows with his wife. Ken admitted to a reporter that "the mistress and the wife hate each other." Rather than relinquish the mistress, he complained: "That's what has caused a lot of grief in my life in the last six years, because I have tried to divide my life between them, and it hasn't worked out."

Despite the precarious state of their marriage, Kathleen stood by Ken, tolerating his relationship with Nicole. He had lost neither his wicked wit nor his charm, and just as he had done with Elaine, he managed to hook Kathleen into a maddening cycle of wooing and rejection. In her absence, he lamented, "I am Saturn without its rings, a planet of leaden melancholy." Elaine knew this kind of language all too well.

Ken and Kathleen were still emotionally attached to one another, and more importantly, they were getting invitations to great parties—socializing with guests such as Paul Newman, Billy Wilder, and Bianca Jagger. Although Elaine had been with Ken at his peak, and by his side for all the glory, Kathleen witnessed Ken at his nadir—not just from failing health, but depression, writer's block, and self-pity. "I have no active professional identity at all—a sepulchral prospect on which to wake up every morning," Ken wrote in his diary at the age of forty-seven. "Were I to commit suicide, I would merely be killing someone who had already—to many intents and purposes—ceased to exist." Worse, he felt his state of mind had taken a toll on his notorious libido: "Sex in such a context seems as trivial as reading comics in a cancer ward."

Like Elaine, Kathleen was disturbed by her husband's obsession with sadomasochism. By the late 1970s, the glamorous blonde had embarked on affairs of her own. Ken privately recorded the names of her alleged lovers in his diary, including Warren Beatty, Gay Talese, Bernardo Bertolucci, and "others unadmitted." Meanwhile, he supplemented his affair with Nicole by seeing prostitutes. As a journalist and fiction writer, Kathleen found that her talent was both encouraged and dismissed by Ken, just as he had done to Elaine. She too was relegated to the living room to write—hunched over a small table to work on her screenplay. It proved bittersweet that her 1987 biography, *The Life of Kenneth Tynan*, was the high point of her career. (She also edited a volume of Ken's letters.) "It was such a weird thing, to write about your husband," she admitted. "I was a passionate sleuth, torn between being the outsider and insider." The *New York Times Book Review* praised the book for being "almost frighteningly judicious." Kathleen died of cancer on January 10, 1995, at the age of fifty-seven.

By 1979, Ken was dependent on his wife more than ever. He required an oxygen tank day and night, could no longer drive, and struggled to walk even a block. To help him breathe better, he was often hospitalized to have a tube inserted in his trachea, with close calls in the ER at other times. He asked Tracy to purchase a book for him, and when she discovered at the bookshop that it was a suicide manual, she refused to buy it. "He sulked like a child denied a new toy," she wrote in her memoir.

Ken may have given up on living, but only death could make him forsake his cigarettes. At home, visitors were alarmed to see that even while hitched to his oxygen tank, Ken smoked and smoked. He took pills to wake up and pills to sleep, and, like his first wife, drank Chandon Blanc de Noirs during the day. He also loved eating bars of Toblerone, his favorite chocolate. The dying man still knew how to find pleasure where he could.

Although Elaine cut off contact with Ken twenty-five years earlier to save herself, the long stretch of time and distance enabled her to take a kinder, gentler view of their marriage. How exciting life had been alongside her husband, as he influenced postwar theater and vivified the best parties in London and New York. Ken was the toast of the town, no matter which town he was in. Elaine believed no one could predict quite like Ken how a play would be received, and that his passion, intelligence, and wit were nearly unrivaled. As bad as their marriage had been—narcissistic cruelty, drunken rages, and so on—he was, in the end, the love of her life. "Well, we did bad things to each other," she once reflected. "Now, some three decades later, I look back in gratitude at him: I look back in wonder."

In 1980, as Ken was rapidly deteriorating in a hospital in California,

Elaine happened to call Tracy one day to ask how he was doing. "He's lonely," her daughter said. As Elaine recalled in her memoir, "The end found me at last doing the right thing." She sent a copy of her Peter Finch biography to Tracy, who said that Ken had asked to read it, and enclosed a kind letter to her former husband. She let him know that he would find "echoes of him" in everything she wrote or would ever write. She fondly recalled a trip they'd taken to Paris, where they had the great pleasure of hearing Edith Piaf sing "Non, je ne regrette rien." But Elaine's letter was a gesture of thanks, not forgiveness. With great affection, Ken replied on May 20, 1980:

Dear Elaine,

I read the book in hospital in one long munch. It wasn't until I'd finished that I realized what an enormous amount of research you'd done, and how lightly you carried it off. I might give you an argument about Finch being "a very great actor"; but apart from that, I have nothing but congratulations.

I liked your letter, too. It was very nice to feel, after so many years, that something like a normal relationship was being resumed. I know what you mean about Paris and always will.

Love and thanks for everything.

HE DIED TWO MONTHS LATER, AT FIFTY-THREE. HELPING HER STEP-mother plan a memorial service in Beverly Hills, Tracy was stunned by the invitation list: "It read like the Who's Who of Hollywood and included everyone from Johnny Carson to Orson Welles." Kathleen pressured Tracy to make follow-up calls to the invitees, which involved phoning legends such as Gene Kelly, whom she'd met once at the age of five. Still, she recalled, "The outpouring of letters and tributes both overwhelmed and moved me." At the service, Tracy could not help feeling proud of the "celebrity turnout," knowing how much it would have pleased her father: Warren Beatty, his sister Shirley MacLaine, Swifty

Lazar, Joan Didion, and many others came to pay tribute. Elaine did not attend. The subsequent fall memorial in London, at St. Paul's in Covent Garden, was another "star-studded event," Tracy recalled, with guests including Tom Stoppard, Albert Finney, and Princess Margaret. And decades after her father's death, Tracy noted in her memoir that "not a month goes by when I don't see him quoted in a magazine or newspaper. He may be dead, but his words live on." (Sort of. All his books are out of print.)

Against all odds and then some, Elaine outlived Ken by nearly thirty years. She moved to Los Angeles to be near Tracy and her family—very much against Tracy's wishes—and continued to battle addictions off and on, as well as macular degeneration in her final years. On May 1, 2008, during a ten-day meditation retreat, Tracy received a call on her cell phone: her mother died of a heart attack. After fifty-six difficult years with Elaine, whose behavior had so often infuriated and frightened her, Tracy could not help feeling relief. Talking with a Buddhist guide at the retreat, she blurted out: "I don't know if I believe in reincarnation or whatever, but please reassure me that my mother's not coming back." Elaine was laid to rest at the Westwood Village Memorial Park in Los Angeles, where Marilyn Monroe, Billy Wilder, Truman Capote, Rodney Dangerfield, Walter Matthau, and Dean Martin were also buried. ("A celebrity hound to the last," Tracy wrote of her mother.) Elaine's life was filled with fascinating characters, remarkable friendships, adventure, glamour, and literary success. In 2007, at the age of eighty-five, Elaine gave a final interview in which she reflected on her wild life. "I don't know where it all went," she said. "But I'm still going strong. I think I could be described as persistent."

# ELIZABETH JANE HOWARD
## and Kingsley Amis

"I really couldn't write very much when I was married to him because I had a very large household to keep up and Kingsley wasn't one to boil an egg, if you know what I mean."

The first time Kingsley Amis kissed Elizabeth Jane Howard, she felt as if she could fly. He was a married man. She was not his wife. They had known each other for one day.

It was love, as they say, at first sight. In 1962, Howard, known as Jane, had been appointed director of a literary festival in Cheltenham. She was the author of three novels and a story collection and known for her TV and radio appearances in the UK. Although now a major annual fall event in the Cotswolds, at the time the festival was obscure and poorly attended. Jane's position was prestigious but unpaid. Among her tasks was organizing a symposium on "Sex and Literature," to be chaired by an editor from the *Sunday Telegraph* (one of the festival's sponsors). Jane had invited Joseph Heller, Carson McCullers, and Romain Gary to take part. Without consulting her, someone from the *Telegraph* had also invited the author Kingsley Amis to join them. "I thought he would be an 'Angry Young Man' who would think the whole thing was silly," she later recalled. Jane phoned the assistant editor (and her cousin), Peregrine Worsthorne, to complain, but he refused to revoke the invitation.

After the event, Jane felt that the panel had been disappointing, "stilted and uncertain," owing to the moderator's inability to generate a lively conversation and an odd lack of levity. (This seems rather surprising, given the topic and participants.) Yet she was pleased that the festival as a whole, under her direction, was the first to make a profit. She also enjoyed getting to know McCullers, who was in a wheelchair and required a nurse. Jane recalled McCullers clutching a glass of bourbon "at an experienced tilt." She was in awe of this small, frail woman, whom she later described as "a decadent waif, vulnerable but at the same time full of presence."

Amis, a forty-year-old father of three, had come to Cheltenham with his wife, Hilary, known as Hilly. As a gracious gesture, Jane invited the couple to stay with her at the house she had rented. After the panel event ended, they went out for a late dinner and returned home. Kingsley wanted to stay up and drink. His wife went to bed. Jane, charming, beautiful, and "posh," felt obliged to join him. She ended up talking with him all night long about work, marriage, and more. They kissed as his wife lay sleeping upstairs. "If I ring you up, will you see me in London?" he asked. Of course she would.

The next morning, Hilly and Kingsley left after breakfast. Jane decided she was already in love with him. The timing was perfect: she was just ending her second marriage, one she had managed to endure "by pretending it wasn't there." That week Kingsley set off for Majorca with his family and Jane went on holiday to the South of France. When she returned to London, they met at a pub in Leicester Square. They had not ordered drinks before Kingsley mentioned that he had booked a room at a hotel. Would she join him? Or should he cancel the reservation? They spent the night together.

Jane understood it was "wrong" to have an affair with a married man, and it was also stupid. Having done it many times before, she chided herself for letting history repeat. "Surely I'd learned enough about what that was like to know it deflected me from writing and made me miserable." Still, Jane could not deny that she felt "violently" attracted to Kingsley.

Now she would have to endure the constant fear of getting caught, the unbearable passivity of waiting for the phone to ring, and the terrible knowledge of her culpability in dismantling a marriage. Yet she was deliriously happy. She rationalized her behavior with the knowledge that Kingsley's relationship with Hilly was in deep trouble anyway (which it was), and that the marriage had endured extramarital affairs by both spouses (also true). An acquaintance of Hilly and Kingsley observed that they "seemed to have no verbal or sexual inhibitions at all." Kingsley insisted that he was determined to preserve his home life, however unhappy, for the sake of his children, Philip, Martin, and Sally.

From the start of the affair, Jane made compromises. She devoured three of Kingsley's novels, as well as his poetry, while he read nothing of her work and expressed little interest in it. She tried not to mind. (As she noted, decades later, "people in early love are generally hell-bent on finding the best in each other.") When she summoned the nerve to show him a magazine feature she'd written about her grandfathers, he said, "That's a dear little piece." Nearly a year later, after finally reading her 1959 novel *The Sea Change*, Kingsley praised it in his own way. "That's a very good novel indeed," he said. "I am so relieved. I was afraid you wouldn't be any good."

It was hard being the mistress. Kingsley told Jane bluntly that he planned to stay in Majorca with his family for the year, and that he would return to England only a few times. "I shouldn't see much of you," he said. Yet he refused to relinquish his mistress or his wife, and told Jane that they must be "discreet," adding: "If it came out, I will blacken you—I want you to know that." When they met in London, the couple would encounter friends such as Violet Powell (wife of Anthony) and the novelist V. S. Pritchett. Each time, Jane recalled, she and Kingsley had to perform an awkward "jolly old pals" conversation for the sake of appearances. Eventually, they arranged to go out only after dark. (They once checked into a Barcelona hotel as "Mr. and Mrs. Friend.") Between trysts, they sent love letters. Just a few months after meeting Jane, Kingsley wrote: "I feel very good about you and me. You're gorgeous." And in a letter the following year: "You get more beautiful all the time. I can't stop thinking about you. Every other woman I see reminds me of you—to her disadvantage." He signed off, "Kisses from your loving Hunter"—a signature he used regularly to conceal his identity, in case the letters were found. (Sometimes he signed off with variations such as "Generalissimo Hunter" or "Lord Hunter," or with his middle name, William.) He vented about the nettlesome baggage that was his wife. "I rang [Hilly] up and was hung up on," he wrote, expressing his annoyance about a "drunken-abusive-humorous-jeering call" he received from her at two o'clock in the morning. He craved Jane's body when they were apart. "Dearest dove," began one missive:

> I miss your mouth and your breath and your skin and your hair and your smell and your left eyelid and your right breast and right collarbone and right armpit and the back of your neck. And all your other things. And your voice. And eyes. And hands and everything. I've never missed anyone like this before. . . . Even thinking of things remotely connected with you makes me react physically—remind me to tell you how.

Jane's letters often conveyed anxiety, vulnerability, and self-doubt. She worried that she had revealed too much of herself, that she was too needy and sentimental. She also encouraged Kingsley to drink less. Gradually, as Jane became more trusting, she sought to deepen their relationship: "Perhaps you might enjoy *more* of your life through me," she wrote. "I mean collect aspects, add more bits to it. I know sometimes now when you're frightened: not of me of course, but of life generally and of your life, in particular. I think I could change some of that, at least, for you." Elsewhere, she confided: "My whole body feels different: breasts so sharp with feeling it hurts to put on a brassiere. Perhaps people in love shouldn't wear clothes."

"You're on the edge of my thoughts all the time," he wrote to her, "and when you move right into the middle of them, I beam to myself." He composed poems for Jane. He praised her for being "sexually fantastic (i.e. suitable to male fantasies)." He said that she was a good person. He told her that he enjoyed life more because of her, and that he liked women "more than I did through being your lover." He confessed that writing letters was difficult when all he really wanted to do was have sex with her. "I love you a lot," he wrote, "but very much in this distressingly carnal way." He was honored by her trust in him, and wholly embraced whatever aspects of herself she considered inadequacies. "I want to repeat what I said about never rejecting you," he wrote. "That won't and couldn't happen . . . I know you need gentle handling, but I *like* handling you gently." He was unfailingly tender, reassuring, optimistic, generous, and affectionate: "You delight me from top to toe." And: "I love everything about you, especially everything."

Some of Kingsley's friends were surprised that he had fallen in love with Jane. They found her imperious and mannered. One friend joked that "a duchess makes a thrilling screw. But I wouldn't have thought that it'd last. Still, there are other thrills, doubtless; indeed K. speaks very highly of them." Part of Jane's appeal was surely her "poshness," which must have felt like a coup for Kingsley. That she was a writer made her even more desirable, as Philip Larkin noted: "Another Ted-Sylvia team?" Kingsley could talk freely about his work with her and feel inspired and understood.

Soon the couple rented a flat for the "enormous sum" of fifteen pounds a week. Jane was not officially divorced from her second husband, and Kingsley had not extricated himself from Hilly. Gone were the days of praising his wife's virtues, as he had done in a 1947 letter to Philip Larkin: "The great thing about Hilly," he wrote, "is that when I don't want to talk to her, she doesn't mind; or at least she doesn't complain, which is the same thing for our sort."

Kingsley had lost his virginity as a freshman at St. John's College, Oxford, and enjoyed an active sex life ever since. In 1946, he had seduced Hilly Bardwell, who had given up her art course at the Ruskin School of Art and was getting by as an art model instead. The wayward daughter of a Ministry of Agriculture official, she was a good listener with a lovely temperament. He was five-foot-ten and handsome, but a bad dresser, with a bad haircut, and teeth "all over the place and yellow and snarly." He was seven years older, his university time interrupted for three years by army service. Seventeen-year-old Hilly recalled being "absolutely dippy" about Kingsley, who was selfish, funny, clever, and oddly vulnerable—after their dates, he was afraid to walk home alone at night.

Hilly got pregnant just before Kingsley's final exams. He wanted her to have an abortion, but decided to marry her instead. "As regards the impending marriage," he confided in a letter to Philip Larkin, "it's hard not to look upon it as a *faute de mieux*, though this feeling is decreasing slightly."

Philip, named for Larkin, was born in 1948, Martin was born a year later, and Sally in January 1954—the same year, and the same month, in which Kingsley's brilliantly funny novel *Lucky Jim* was published. The author was thirty-two. Along came money and fame, as well as the Somerset Maugham Award for fiction. In a letter to a friend, P. G. Wodehouse expressed annoyance at the book's success, complaining about a recent review in the *Spectator* by Kingsley, "saying how bad my stuff was." Noting the irony of the *New York Times* praising *Lucky Jim* as "funny in something approaching the Wodehouse vein," he added, "I should imagine he is one of these clever young men whom I dislike so much. They very seldom amount to anything in the long run."

BEFORE HIS BREAKTHROUGH FIRST NOVEL, KINGSLEY TAUGHT LITERA-ture at University College of Swansea in Wales. He was so poor that he would return empty beer bottles to the local pub to collect the deposits, and for a time, he and Hilly lived with her parents. To earn extra income, Hilly worked at night in the café of a local cinema, bringing home leftovers for dinner. But in 1951 she had been fortunate enough to buy a house for the family after receiving an inheritance from her mother. Kingsley had grown up lower-middle class, with "no social advantages at all," as he once said in an interview. Born in a grim suburb of London in 1922, he was an only child in a family "frightened of toppling into the working class." He had no sense of managing or saving money and maintained a lifelong indifference to it.

Kingsley's relationship with Jane was hardly his first experience with infidelity. (Martin once described him as "a man who used to *live* for adultery.") Taking to heart the old adage "Do what you love," Kingsley had cheated on Hilly since the birth of Philip, working his way through most of the women in their social circle and beyond. Once, after being issued an ultimatum by his wife, Kingsley confided to Larkin, "Trouble is it's so hard to give all that up, habit of years and all that, and such bloody good fun too." Hilly had enjoyed her fair share of retaliatory sex, although she was far more discreet than her husband.

It wasn't long before Hilly knew of her husband's affair with Jane. Whereas after getting caught with previous dalliances, Kingsley expressed contrition to his wife, this time was different. Jane had affected him profoundly and he knew his marriage was in jeopardy. Even Hilly had to admit, "I don't think I've ever seen anybody as beautiful as Elizabeth Jane Howard." The children began wondering about their absent father. One day their nanny said to Martin, "You know your father's got a fancy woman in London." He was too young to process what this meant. He just wanted his father back.

By her own admission, Hilly was drinking too much and popping pills to cope. As she later recalled, Kingsley was stunned by Hilly's rage and her unwillingness to accept life on his terms. "My alternative was to sit it out until the big passion [with Jane] burnt out a bit and just have him as a visitor, have him call round and not break off relations," she said. "You know, so he had two homes."

She had discovered one of Jane's letters in his jacket pocket and promptly sent the evidence to a lawyer. On a previously planned trip to Italy and Yugoslavia with Kingsley, they fought constantly about Jane. But Hilly enjoyed what must have been a satisfying means of revenge: an impulsive act of bodily graffiti. After Kingsley fell asleep on the beach one day, she wrote in lipstick on his back: "1 FAT ENGLISHMAN I FUCK ANYTHING." Then she snapped a photograph.

By 1963, the marriage was over. Hilly walked out on him, but of course he was already long gone. By then, Kingsley was also a literary star, both as a novelist and a celebrated critic. Now it was up to him to explain to Philip, Martin, and Sally why he was living with another woman. He had apparently forgotten that he once told his sons, "Never doubt that I love your mother. Never doubt that we will always be together." Hilly was in an awful state and often had trouble getting out of bed in the morning. She took in lodgers for extra money. Once, after she overdosed on sleeping pills, which she claimed was accidental, she was rushed to the hospital. Hours later, an infuriated Kingsley showed up at her bedside and screamed at her.

He was vaguely aware of the impact his behavior had on those around him, but displayed no empathy for Hilly's suffering. As for the children, by spending lavishly on gifts to appease them, Kingsley hoped they would forgive him and accept Jane as an alternate maternal figure. This was magical thinking. At one point, during an awkward "heart-to-heart" talk about how marriages can unravel, a lachrymose Philip said to Kingsley: "You're a *cunt*."

As Martin later said, their parents' divorce yielded "a terrible numbness and incredulity, and with it a kind of childish stoicism. It was my first conviction that life was going to be tough." But he had to admit, upon meeting Jane, that she made a powerful first impression: she was "tall, calm, fine-boned, and with the queenly bearing of the fashion model she once was." (She had modeled for *Vogue* in the late 1940s.) Once Kingsley settled into his new life with Jane, his letters to Hilly were thoughtful ("How are you for money?"), and he typically signed off with "love," or "heaps of love." He took care of Hilly financially and even bought a house for her. The letters were brief, expressing interest in her latest endeavors, offering reports of the children ("Mart is still lazy but we're working on him") and making arrangements for where the kids would spend the holidays. Hilly promised to "try harder" to get over Kingsley, though she admitted that she didn't know whether she would. A few years after their divorce, she opened a successful fish-and-chip shop called Lucky Jim's. "Anyway," she wrote in one letter, "thanks my darling for all you do for me all the time." The old nastiness was gone.

Jane, meanwhile, was cautious as she navigated her new role as step-mother. Although kind and warm toward the children, she did not force a relationship with them. "I decided that all I could do to begin with was to feed them well, and regularly, and to be in every other practical way as reliable as I could manage," she recalled. Jane's relationship with Hilly, such as it was, could not transcend enmity on both sides. Kingsley proved useless in managing the transition and its ongoing turmoil: "He simply wanted everybody to settle down," Jane recalled, "so that he could write his books in peace and enjoy himself when he wasn't working." He dealt with family strife as he did with any other unpleasant matter—by retreating and drinking, writing, ignoring the trouble, blocking out unpleasantness, pretending as if nothing was amiss. Denial did wonders for his productivity and sense of well-being. In his 1966 novel, *The Anti-Death League*, one character says, rather tellingly: "I've never been particularly keen on having to think about things, and on things that make you think about things."

Kingsley's own avoidance of "things" left Jane in the unenviable position of "the irritating killjoy, the tiresome prig," someone who attempted to impose order, structure, and discipline in the household. He was useless in that regard. Jane worried about how the predictable rhythms of domestic life would affect her husband in the long term. For certain writers, she knew, a comfortable marriage was "beside the point: they crave the frenzied ecstasy, the obsession."

Her relationship with Kingsley was a stabilizing force, at least for him. Both were ambitious writers, but only one could achieve success. The other was expected to lend unconditional support and forsake all personal desires. If Jane could not tolerate in herself the ruthlessness often required in fully realizing one's talent, Kingsley did not give it a second thought. He pursued his vocation in a headlong way, with no regard to the fallout on those closest to him. Even though he had been seduced by a sexy novelist, what he really needed, day to day, was an attentive housewife and caregiver. Theirs was a hierarchical relationship in which Kingsley was always on top, rather than the equal partnership Jane hoped for. He was encouraging and supportive about her work, but only to a point. Her autonomy was tolerated so long as it did not interfere with her husband's needs, which it almost always did. Any effort to speak up fell on deaf ears, but Jane could convince herself that she felt content in her marriage if she had Kingsley's affection and approval. She depended on it. When he was feeling cheerful, he would look at his wife adoringly and say, "I have such a lovely life with you!" All was right with the world.

Jane was well acquainted with men behaving badly, especially as she tried to assert her position among London's male-dominated literary set. Once, while conducting what would be Evelyn Waugh's final broadcast interview (for the BBC, in 1964), Jane endured his belittling comments ("Ah, Miss Howard—and have you had anything to do with literature?") and dotty remarks to the camera crew: "When is Miss Howard going to take off all her clothes?" She was fond enough of men to overlook their more beastly moments, and for Kingsley she seemed to retain an infinite store of patience and forgiveness.

In the spring of 1965, Kingsley and Jane married at Marylebone Town Hall in London. The fawning media attention following the wedding was hard for Hilly to take—she admitted later that she was still, perversely, in love with Kingsley. She couldn't bear seeing photographs, gossip columns, and feature articles about the newlyweds. "They were always in the papers," Hilly later recalled in an interview. "You find yourself reading, 'I like to sleep on this side of the bed' and so on, and you think, 'aaarrrgh!'—rubbing our nose in it, you know." The morning of the wedding, Philip and Martin brought Kingsley and Jane breakfast in bed. (Sally continued to live with Hilly but visited at holidays.) "I'm your wicked stepmother," Jane told the boys gleefully. She was anything but.

A few months earlier, Philip had said to her: "We've been rotten to you." She could not disagree. Relations between them had been horrible, however kind she tried to be. Philip would always prove the more unruly and unforgiving child, and his anger toward her would never subside. With the feckless Martin, however, Jane was able to bond through literature. In an oft-told anecdote, she found him lounging indolently around the house one day, "boredom seeping from every pore." She asked her supine stepson what he hoped to do with his life.

"Be a writer," he replied.

"But you never read anything," she said.

She gave him a copy of *Pride and Prejudice*. About an hour later, Martin banged on the door of her study, demanding to be told the ending. "I've got to know," he said. "Does Elizabeth marry Darcy?" This gesture marked not only a thaw in her relationship with Martin, but his start as a passionate reader, a consumer of something other than comic books. (He had also dipped into some Harold Robbins and the "dirty" parts of *Lady Chatterley's Lover*.)

"Turned out bloody well really!" Jane said of Martin in an interview decades later. "What I was so pleased about was that he really appreciated [Austen] like a grown-up person."

Jane viewed the young man as lost and overindulged, but also incredibly bright and worthy of guidance. She was determined to help him. (Even Martin later admitted that by the time he had moved in with his father and Jane, he was "a semiliterate truant and waster whose main interest was hanging around betting shops.") She kept feeding him books—Dickens, Waugh, Fitzgerald, Greene—and he was hungry for more.

When Martin received news of a scholarship to Oxford, Jane felt a burst of maternal pride. He graduated with first-class honors in English.

"I have a huge debt to you which I shall work off by being an ever-dutiful stepson," he wrote to her. Although his father never offered much encouragement, Martin claimed to be untroubled by Kingsley's disengagement. He once noted that because "literary talent isn't inherited," such advice might have been hollow, anyway.

Kingsley once declared that his son was "the only young writer I think is any good," yet he also found Martin's books unreadable. He surely felt a mixture of irritation and paternal pride about his son's fame, which would come to rival his own. After all, Martin, like his father, made his mark young by publishing his first novel, *The Rachel Papers*, at the age of twenty-four. Martin once said he believed it was the only novel of his that Kingsley read all the way through. The summer after the 1978 publication of Martin's acclaimed third novel, *Success*, Kingsley complained in a letter to Philip Larkin: "Last year he earned £38,000. Little shit. 29, he is. Little shit." (He also once said that the beginning and end of *Success* worked, but the middle did not.) Of Martin's novel *Other People*, Kingsley admitted to a friend: "Tough going I find." He found fault with *Money*, saying that he "hated its way of constantly reminding me of Nabokov." And in an interview, Kingsley offered his candid response to *London Fields*: "In parts I found it difficult. I suppose I should have tried to read every page, but it was beyond me."

At least publicly, Martin was good-natured about Kingsley's resistance to his work. "It's natural to admire your elders and to despise your youngsters," he said in a *Paris Review* interview in 1990, five years before his father's death. "That's the way of the world. There was a brief period when my father would snipe at me in print and use me as an example of the incomprehensibility and uninterestingness of modern prose. Thanks for the plug, Dad. But that was just amusing, that was just in character for him. And I sniped back."

Martin admitted that the implications of his famous surname proved frustrating in many ways. Being the son of Kingsley Amis was no picnic. He once told a reporter that the name had provided "a slight boost" when he started out as a writer. "Then the culture changed: it became a curse," he said. "I was tainted by heredity—by inherited elitism. And so it became accepted that you could say whatever you fucking well liked about me because, so to speak, I didn't earn it."

In the mid-1960s, Jane's marriage was off to a happy start—but Kingsley's uxoriousness was not to last. For a while, though, they made a glamorous literary power couple, and in a 1963 letter, Kingsley had cheekily written to Jane that they should announce to the world "THAT THEY ARE THE MOST ATTRACTIVE, INTELLIGENT, FUNNY, SOPHISTICATED AND MUTUALLY SUITED PAIR SINCE THE RENAISSANCE."

They bought a thirty-room Georgian house with eight bedrooms, a detached cottage, and a barn. The secluded property included several acres, with a beautiful, sloping garden, a meadow, and cedar woods. They could barely afford the house but were overjoyed to have it. Jane's invalid mother moved in, and would remain with them until her death in 1971—and her much-adored brother Colin, known as Monkey, also lived with them for years. At first, Monkey could find little fault with his brother-in-law. "They were dotty about each other, as far as I could see," he said. Things were harmonious mostly because Jane accommodated Kingsley's wishes, day and night. The division of labor was clear: she took care of everything while his days were freed up for creative work. "He got up and wrote," Jane recalled. "Then he ate lunch, had a walk or sleep, and then he wrote again." It was an idyllic existence—for him. As a friend put it, "Jane cooked and Kingsley drank."

She had to take on traditionally "female" domestic duties, as well as "male" responsibilities such as changing light bulbs and fuses around the house. She scheduled her husband's medical appointments. She handled the household budget—he couldn't be bothered, though their finances were in a precarious state—and served as his chauffeur. (Kingsley refused to drive and was afraid to travel on the Underground. He said that he cured himself of this fear by never riding the Tube again.) She was his part-time secretary. She was not allowed to nag him about his drinking, which he considered an essential social lubricant. Alcohol was inseparable from pleasure. She wrote his thank-you notes. And because he hated "boring" dark socks, she knitted multiple pairs for him in gorgeous, striking colors. She met with their accountants and lawyers. She tended to her husband's panic attacks and phobias. He was a grown man terrified of being alone in the house at night, so the children took it upon themselves to "Dadsit" whenever Jane was out after dark. (This phobia would make its way comically into his novel *The Old Devils*.)

Jane bought all the groceries and cooked big family dinners. She loved cooking. Kingsley, however, could behave like a petulant toddler at mealtime. She decorated, furnished, and cleaned the house, while Kingsley's duties were limited mostly to mixing and serving drinks. Jane got out of ironing only by claiming she didn't know how to do it—a lie—but nothing else was deemed outside her purview. She was constantly, and understandably, exhausted and would often fall asleep, upright in a chair, after dinner.

Years later, in a letter to Philip Larkin, Kingsley would mock her for the disparaging things she said about him in an interview following their breakup: "[S]he said I stifled her creative talent by making her run the house," he wrote. "Yes, she never did anything but cook, and never cooked except when he had people, about twice a month." (This was not true.) After the word "cooked," he inserted an asterisk, and at the bottom of the letter wrote the phrase, "elaborately but not very well."

It was not enough that Jane had to care for her own family, and that Kingsley was so unappreciative of all she had to manage. He loved, and insisted upon, weekend houseguests, which meant that setting the dinner table for twelve was not uncommon. (One Christmas, there were twenty-five guests.) Kingsley loved being the center of attention, and he was good at it. He would drink, crack jokes, talk politics, and tell stories late into the night. "I think it was wonderful for everyone but Jane," recalled a friend. Visitors to the Amis-Howard home included John

Betjeman, Pat Kavanagh, John Bayley, Iris Murdoch, and Elizabeth Bowen. Cecil Day-Lewis, dying of cancer, came to live with Kingsley and Jane. He wrote his final poem there, and died in their home in 1972 at the age of sixty-eight.

Two decades earlier, Jane and Day-Lewis had an affair. At the time he was married to his second wife, Jill Balcon, who was Jane's best friend and confidante. When Day-Lewis began his relationship with Balcon, he was still married to his first wife, Constance, and had yet another mistress on the side. Jane once described him as an "exceptionally beautiful man, with a marvelous forehead creased and mapped like the tributaries of a river." She felt terribly guilty about having betrayed Jill, and managed, eventually, to reconcile with her.

By acquiescing in silence to keep the peace with Kingsley, Jane recognized that she was encouraging, as well as enabling, his unrelenting demands. "It's true to say that writers are selfish people," she once said. "All artists are, really. But it's not quite enough of an excuse." Any distress she felt was of no consequence to her crapulous husband. He was rigorous in his work, careful never to drink much until he had finished writing for the day. That meant that he was very drunk in the evenings—the only time the couple had alone together. "Kingsley felt women were for fucking and cooking," Jane once said. "He stopped wanting to fuck because if you get really very drunk all the time you stop being able to do it." As it happens, the bitter protagonist of Kingsley's 1978 novel, *Jake's Thing*, is a late-middle-aged Oxford don who has lost his libido and despises women.

Women prove troublesome and unruly in many of Kingsley's novels. In the bilious *Stanley and the Women*, the narrator's best friend is stunned to learn that "only" twenty-five percent of violent crime in England and Wales is the result of husbands assaulting their wives. "You'd expect it to be more like eighty percent," he says. ("Stopping being married to someone," Kingsley wrote, "is an incredibly violent thing to happen to you, not easy to take in completely, ever.") He dedicated the novel to Hilly.

That year, writing in the *London Review of Books*, Marilyn Butler—King Edward VII Professor of English Literature at Cambridge and rector of Exeter College, Oxford, the first woman to head what had been a men's college—minced no words in the opening line of her piece: "Like Norman Mailer in America, Kingsley Amis has made a career out of being nasty to women." Even in interviews, his misogynist streak came out: "It's nice to have a pretty girl with large breasts," he said in 1973, "rather than some fearful woman who's going to talk to you about Ezra Pound and hasn't got large breasts and probably doesn't wash much."

Jane always marveled at her husband's intense discipline in his work. Something was in the midst of production at all times. However extreme his hangover, however foul his mood, he ate breakfast each morning and got straight to work. As Martin later described it, Kingsley was a "grinder," trudging over to his desk no matter what. He also noted, with admiration, that his perfectionist father was adept at problem-solving when stuck:

> My father described a process in which, as it were, he had to take himself gently but firmly by the hand and say, Now all right, calm down. What is it that's worrying you? The dialogue will go: Well, it's the first page, actually. What is it about the first page? He might say, The first sentence. And he realized that it was only a little thing that was holding him up. Actually, my father, I think, sat down and wrote what he considered to be the final version straightaway, because he said there's no point in putting down a sentence if you're not going to stand by it.

Jane often felt too worn down by fatigue and insecurity to write. "He was incredibly disciplined about his work and was a marvelous example for me," Jane said wistfully, "although I didn't have the same time to do it." Her days were a series of missed opportunities. "Writing is a fraught activity for everyone, of course, male or female," Janet Malcolm wrote in *The Silent Woman*, "but women writers seem to have to take stronger measures, make more peculiar psychic arrangements, than men do to activate their imaginations."

Jane began to retreat. Her solace was gardening: it was private, all hers. Even though she felt guilty about indulging this passion—so much was expected of her—she carried on doing it. Gardening was easier and more pleasurable than writing. She could make something derelict grow, with satisfying results. In her writing, Jane often saw nothing but paths toward failure. She was terrified of the blank page. Although Kingsley had been encouraging of her work, he had broken ties with his previous agent, Curtis Brown, and signed up with Jane's agent, as well as the same publisher, leaving her feeling cast aside in favor of the bigger star. In the years she spent with Kingsley, her self-esteem sank ever lower. Once, when a therapist asked what Jane liked about herself, the best response she could summon was being "reliable." In contrast, Kingsley's amour propre was unwavering. He was neither haunted by guilt, nor prone to reprimanding himself. He was beyond reproach and would not be challenged. A former acquaintance recalled that when someone once admonished Kingsley for behaving rudely, he replied, "Fuck off. No, fuck off a *lot*."

Jane was often made to feel invisible in her husband's presence. There was a couple she and Kingsley used to stay with occasionally, and on each visit their hosts would insist with much fanfare that her husband sign his books and articles for them. She was never asked to do the same. Worse, Kingsley never talked her up as a writer. She admitted feeling like an "anonymous outsider" in such situations. Once, at dinner with the literary editor of the *Observer*, Jane mentioned that she had just finished writing her novel *After Julius*. "That must be a good thing," he said, and—as if she had just told him that she ordered bread rolls for the table—then turned to Kingsley to ask him about doing some reviewing for the newspaper. Jane also recalled that a friend of hers and Kingsley's once remarked that "no woman over thirty-five was of much, if any, sexual interest, and implied that such women weren't worth having any real conversation with." No wonder her self-esteem was so rocky.

After Jane found herself often sobbing in private, her doctor prescribed Valium. She was able to sleep at night. But the writing would not come, at least not at the rate Jane wished for. She could not possibly keep up the clockwork routine that Kingsley enjoyed—thanks to her. "I think I certainly had to be second fiddle," Jane said decades later, in one of her final interviews. "I really couldn't write very much when I was married to him because I had a very large household to keep up and Kingsley wasn't one to boil an egg, if you know what I mean."

During her eighteen-year marriage, Jane published three novels: *After Julius* (1965), *Something in Disguise* (1969), *Odd Girl Out* (1972), and *Mr. Wrong* (1975), a collection of stories. Not too shabby, but not so impressive when compared with what her husband was able to crank out in that time. Jane kept an erratic writing schedule at best, yet "if an idea lay in the back of my mind, little by little some flesh started to cover its bones." Although she yearned to be more prolific, the mountain of demands at home made that impossible. Her work, once described by a former lover as a cross between Nancy Mitford and Evelyn Waugh, was generally praised by critics, but also dismissed as "women's novels." (She described her readers as "women and educated men.") Despite having admirers such as Sybille Bedford and Hilary Mantel, she did not achieve the readership or acclaim she deserved. Jane was puzzled and hurt when Margaret Drabble omitted her name from the 1985 edition of *The Oxford Companion to English Literature*.

Contrast Jane's frustrating experiences with Kingsley's output, which was steady and prodigious: one novel after another came tumbling forth, sometimes two within the same year, as well as collections of poetry, short stories, nonfiction, and criticism. He edited anthologies and wrote for television and radio. While married to Jane, Kingsley published nearly twenty books. Following their divorce, he went on to publish several other novels, along with books in various genres. Jane could not blame him for having held her back—she had *chosen* to devote herself to Kingsley. This had been a pattern throughout her life: Jane's relationships with men consumed and distracted her. She could not forget something her mother once told her: "Never refuse your husband—whatever you feel."

IN THE SPRING OF 1942, JANE—ELEGANT, WITH HIGH CHEEKBONES, long blond hair, and long legs—had married Peter Scott, the thirty-two-year-old son of the Antarctic explorer Captain Robert Falcon Scott. She was nineteen years old, an aspiring actress, working in repertory theater, and flattered by the attention of a handsome older man: "He was the first person who noticed me, and I was grateful for that." She married him also to escape her own family. Born in London on March 26, 1923, Jane grew up in Notting Hill in a privileged household with multiple servants. Jane was the firstborn child, yet not quite: her mother Katherine, known as Kit, had given birth to a daughter previously, also named Jane, but the girl died soon after. Kit liked the name, so she saved it for her second daughter.

The family money came from a timber business that her paternal grandfather founded after World War I, and summers were spent at a sprawling country house in Sussex. Jane's maternal grandfather, Sir Arthur Somervell, was a composer, and one of her uncles was governor of the Bank of England. The family was as distinguished as it was unhappy. Kit was a great beauty, intellectual and well read. She had given up her career as a dancer with Diaghilev's Ballets Russes to marry Jane's father, David, a compulsive adulterer who would eventually leave Kit for his mistress. Jane, who described her father as "physically very brave and morally a coward," recalled that women "fell for him like rows of shingled ninepins."

JANE WAS AN ANXIOUS CHILD, BULLIED AT SCHOOL. BEGINNING IN ADO-lescence, she was educated at home by a governess—the same woman who had taught her mother. Jane recalled her elderly teacher as "large, fat and almost blind, but infinitely gentle," with an encyclopedic mind, and one of the ugliest women she had ever seen. Jane read all of Shakespeare and wrote poems, stories, and plays, selling her first play at the age of fourteen. Her mother offered little praise for her daughter's achievements, even though Jane had also impressively learned piano, needlework, painting, French, a bit of Latin and Greek, tennis, horseback riding, and more. Kit never gave Jane the unconditional love she longed for, and made no secret of favoring her two sons, Monkey and Robin. She later threw away Jane's letters and cards while keeping all the mail from her sons. Because Kit treated her daughter with such cruelty, Jane grew up with an intense fear of abandonment. "I was self-conscious," Jane later wrote, "with a desperate love for my mother that I felt was unrequited and the family thought was morbid."

Jane felt adored by her father, who was charismatic, athletic, gregarious, and always well dressed. At restaurants, the waiters "always liked and served him well." He taught Jane about wine, and gave it to her from the time she was four, and their frequent father-daughter outings, such as sailing or theatergoing, made her feel special. "With him I never felt plain or clumsy or intellectually not up to the mark: he was simply affectionate, easy, undemanding company," she recalled. But when she turned fifteen, their relationship took a turn that left her traumatized.

"I can't remember the exact circumstances of his first assault," she recalled in her 2002 memoir, *Slipstream*. One evening, when they were alone, her father commented on how quickly Jane was growing up. He grabbed her breasts and aggressively kissed her. Jane broke free of his grip and fled, but this would not be his last attempt. Soon Jane learned that she must never be alone with him. They did not speak of what he had done, and although he attempted subsequent displays of casual fatherly affection in the presence of his wife, Jane rebuffed him. She felt not only terror in his presence, but betrayal and hatred, and was too ashamed to report his behavior to anyone else. The damage was done. "This state persisted until I was married," she wrote. His repugnant abuse, along with Kit's open contempt for her daughter, would forever mar Jane's self-worth and relationships with men. Time and distance provided her with some measure of forgiveness—heroically summoned, it seems—and somehow in adulthood she settled upon a cordial, distant relationship with her father. "He loved me," she wrote, "and when I ceased to be a little girl, he simply added another dimension to his love. This was irresponsible and selfish, but it wasn't wicked." (Her take on his abuse is painful to read.) Jane had absorbed the message, from her mother too, that the body was disgusting, that sex was not an act of love, and "[t]his was to influence the next thirty years of my life." At the age of nineteen, she couldn't escape home soon enough.

NOT LONG AFTER JANE BEGAN DATING PETER, SHE WAS STARTLED TO learn that he was still mourning the love of his life, someone who had ended the relationship and married someone else. His lost love, he confessed, was a man. Peter wept as he poured out his misery to Jane. "You do understand, don't you?" he said. "You're so wise, so grown up for your age." She did, sort of. He said that he loved her. Then they had sex.

The following year, Peter and Jane had a daughter, Nicola. Jane was afraid of being alone with Nicola, did not like breastfeeding, and couldn't stand dealing with the dozens of diapers that had to be rinsed, soaked, boiled, and dried daily. She knew nothing of the overwhelming happiness that everyone insisted she was experiencing as a new mother. A congratulatory letter from the wife of one of her father's friends made her feel even more estranged from herself: "Now, at last you will understand that everything we have to go through in marriage with a man is recompensed by this great joy—the only reason for marriage." She had a brief affair with another man, Peter's stepbrother, Wayland, and for the first time she experienced physical desire. Confessing the affair to her husband, and ending it, did not make her love him more. With "dull predictability," she fell into several other affairs and suspected that Peter had been unfaithful too.

At the best of times, their marriage dwelt in benign amiability. She wrote at night, working on her first novel, partly to avoid sleeping with Peter. Hoping to sort through her feelings about the relationship, she sought the guidance of a psychiatrist and began seeing him twice a week. He seemed sympathetic toward her marital difficulties, and, as she began to trust him, she was "anxious to tell him everything and gain his good opinion." She realized that she was turning him into a father figure of sorts, but whatever the dynamic, she found it consoling and helpful. One day, though, she showed up at his office to find a plate of cakes and a bottle of wine. At the end of their session, the psychiatrist lunged toward her and attempted to force her into a kiss. "I love and adore you and want you," he said. She pushed him away and fled the office, feeling badly shaken up and afraid that he might come after her. The incident called to mind what her father had done. No one could be trusted. "Thereafter in my life," she recalled, "whenever real intimacy or trust seemed to loom, I withdrew to avoid any possible ambush."

IN THE FALL OF 1946, STILL IN HER EARLY TWENTIES, JANE LEFT PETER and her young daughter. "I was selfishly determined to be a writer, to put it first, and I knew that I had to do it alone," she admitted. (Decades later, Nicola would recall her mother as "a very beautiful stranger who would visit from time to time." She could not remember Jane ever having read to her or baked a cake for her birthday.) Jane moved alone into a small, depressing flat: "I remember my first night there, a bare bulb in the ceiling, wooden floors full of malignant nails, the odour of decay that seeped through the wet paint smell and the unpleasant feeling that everything was dirty except my bedclothes. Above all I felt alone, and the only thing I was sure of was that I wanted to write."

She visited Nicola regularly, "miserably aware of how unsatisfactory this was." Their relationship would require decades to mend, though it did, and they became close. In the spring of 1950, Jonathan Cape published Jane's first novel, *The Beautiful Visit*, just before her twenty-seventh birthday. Her advance was fifty pounds. Antonia White praised her in the *New Statesman* for her "true imagination and a kind of sensuous power." Jane attended her first publishing party, where she was excited to recognize the famous writers in the room by the jacket photos she'd seen on their books. In 1951, she won the John Llewellyn Rhys Prize, and one of London's top literary agents, A. D. Peters, offered to represent her.

That was also the year Jane and Peter divorced. She fell hard for a financier who bought her expensive gifts but had no intention of leaving his wife. Subsequent lovers included brilliant, high-profile men such as Arthur Koestler, who instructed Jane to get an abortion when she learned she was pregnant in the spring of 1955. (Abortion was illegal in England until 1967.) Her brief but thrilling affair with Laurie Lee, who was married to a woman half his age, ended amicably, and his last postcard to Jane read, "I still think of you with rapture." She was pursued by the besotted (and married) novelist Romain Gary, with his "dark hair, dark moustache, and mournful eyes set in a face of faintly olive-skinned pallor." He confessed that he had been in love with her from the moment they met—coincidentally, at a dinner with Koestler. Gary invited her to spend a week with him in Paris, where he introduced her to Albert Camus. The fling did not extend beyond the week, but Jane and Gary stayed friendly, and he went on to marry his second wife, Jean Seberg, in 1962. Jane also enjoyed the company of Kenneth Tynan for a few months, while his wife was in New York; they went out to plays, dinners, and parties together. Sexually, they were incompatible, and as Jane later admitted, "I didn't like all that spanking."

She was well aware of her inability to overcome a desperate need to be loved (or lusted after) by powerful men. "If a very attractive man makes a dead set at you and you're very lonely, it's very difficult to resist him," she once said. Oddly, she seemed to regard herself as a passive participant in these affairs, convinced that such flings "simply struck one—like lightning—and that one had no choice." In the absence of stable romantic relationships, she sought intimacy wherever she could find it: "Love, which still seemed to me the most important thing in the world, had eluded me; I seemed incapable of sustaining, inspiring or receiving it. This reinforced all my secret feelings of being worthless."

In 1956, Jane published her second novel, *The Long View*—a wrenching dissection of a failed marriage, told in reverse, from dissolution to meeting. The passport of her heroine, Antonia Fleming, depressingly states her occupation as "Married Woman." Jane later said of the novel, "The idea of stripping people down to their raw beginnings seemed to me to have interesting possibilities." The book, loosely based on her marriage, was well received. "Why *The Long View* isn't recognized as one of the great novels of the 20th century I will never know," wrote the British journalist and author Angela Lambert. "I don't think anyone has expressed so delicately the way that young beauty has been dominated and exploited. She has amazing intelligence—subtle, and painful." John Bayley called it a "technical triumph, of a very unusual sort." And in a 2016 tribute to Jane in the *Guardian*, Hilary Mantel wrote, "It is daunting to think that *The Long View*, so accomplished, so technically adroit, was only her second book." Praising Jane's early work, she wrote that "[Howard's] talent seemed so effervescent, so unstoppable, that there was no predicting where it might take her. . . . From the first, she was a craftswoman."

Yet the six-year lapse between novels was agonizing for Jane, who berated herself for being "lazy" and fixated on her romantic life. With her constant pursuit of intimacy, she had a hard time focusing on work. Her energy was scattered. "I was a tart for affection," she said. She craved the thrill of new relationships, admitting that "every time I fell in love with anyone, they used to make me a reading list, but I never caught up with it because I was in love with someone else."

In an interview she gave at the age of ninety, responding to a question about whether she was capable of being in love and writing simultaneously, Jane quoted from Byron's *Don Juan*: "'Man's love is of man's life a thing apart, / 'Tis woman's whole existence.' You have to put writing first and I can now, there's no earthly reason why I shouldn't. If I was mooning after someone and waiting for their letter I wouldn't be focused. I wasted a lot of my life on men, but I think a lot of women novelists have."

When she wasn't falling in love, men were desperately in love with her, beguiled by her husky voice and stunning beauty. "My view of myself was not beautiful," she said in an interview in 2012, at the age of eighty-nine (and still quite beautiful). "I thought these people liked me because I had a good mind. . . . That was an initial but basic error. They saw me not as a dumb blonde, but something like that." One man dropped his trousers on their first date, only to be politely rejected by Jane. When Jonathan Cape signed up her first novel, she later revealed that he offered her a strong martini because he insisted it was "very good for women who are menstruating." Then he chased her around a table, demanding that she submit to him before he would issue her work. (She refused, and he published her anyway.) Over the next few years, thanks to the attention around her second novel, her social life became a whirlwind. She found herself mingling with the cultural elite, invited to dinner parties and luncheons with luminaries such as Stephen Spender, Ian Fleming, Stevie Smith, Somerset Maugham, Ivy Compton-Burnett, and Oona and Charlie Chaplin.

In 1958, she married Jim Douglas-Henry. This union was more wretched than her first. Jane was feeling lost at the time, unhappy and unproductive, and tired of dead-end affairs. She had been writing short stories, freelancing for magazines, writing film scripts, and finishing her novel *The Sea Change*. She'd also had brief stints as an editor at the publishing houses Chatto & Windus and Weidenfeld & Nicolson. Jim was attractive, and, as Jane recalled later, "like all con-men, he was possessed of a considerable charm that he knew exactly how to use." In retrospect, Jane married him, as she put it, for "the deep, deep peace of the double bed after the hurly-burly of the chaise longue." By her mid-thirties, she had grown "exhausted by people wanting to go to bed with me after half an hour." She also wanted to have another child.

Jim, a member of a secretive philosophy group in London called the Ouspensky Society, had a violent temper and was emotionally abusive. He had no means of supporting himself, yet he possessed extravagant tastes and believed that Jane (with her prosperous background) had a trust fund. Nearly two months into their marriage, Jim ordered several bespoke shirts. He expected his wife, who was shocked at the expense, to pay for them, insisting she had the means. Jane could no longer comprehend why she had married him. Burdened with more financial responsibilities than she could have possibly anticipated, she took on projects to earn extra income. She wrote a film script and landed a regular spot on a TV show in Manchester, reviewing novels on-camera and interviewing authors. She enjoyed the work but, stuck in the "densely unhappy climate" of her life, felt herself drifting further away from her ambitions as a novelist. She resolved to find her way back and distance herself from Jim. Their union was unconsummated, and by 1962, it was over. Then came Kingsley.

EVEN DURING THE WORST OF TIMES OF THEIR RELATIONSHIP, JANE loved his ability to make her laugh. "Kingsley is terribly funny, and that is the biggest turn-on of all, isn't it?" she said. He was a brilliant mimic, a fantastic raconteur, and a great cultivator of family jokes. (Robert Graves once described Kingsley as "the only man who makes me sick—with laughter.") In the first few years of her marriage, Jane could not have hoped for more happiness.

At a certain point, though, it occurred to Jane that by serving as a model wife, she had not only put herself at a crippling disadvantage as a writer, but lost the interest of her husband. "I was encouraged, even expected to be responsible," she recalled, "but conversely nobody finds responsible people entertaining or desirable." She was convinced that Kingsley must have had one or two flings, though she didn't know for sure. (Martin believed that his father had been "more or less faithful" to her.) "Kingsley wanted someone to lean on, to run all the boring parts of his life," she recalled. "He'd been in love with me, and now he wasn't. Or perhaps it would be truer to say that he was beginning not to be."

This was around 1972. The atmosphere of their marriage was filled with gloom. Apart from Kingsley's fading libido, owing to his heavy drinking, the domineering aspect of his personality took on a more splenetic form. His appalling views on women, "Yids," "queers," and others became nastier, and Jane was convinced that her marriage was headed toward a bitter end. The strain was undeniable. An ever-dyspeptic Kingsley insulated himself with alcohol to keep his distance. As Jane noted, "One of the difficult things about living with someone who drinks is that they intensely resent you not doing the same." (Of dipsomania, Martin once wrote, "To make a real success of being an alcoholic, to go all the way with it, you need to be other things too: shifty, unfastidious, solipsistic, insecure and indefatigable.")

In a 1973 interview, Kingsley could just as easily have been speaking about himself as he expressed sympathy for the corpulent, adulterous protagonist of his 1963 novel, *One Fat Englishman*: "Yes I do, I do feel a lot of sympathy for him because, I think, he's awful all right, and he knows it, and this is no excuse. But it does point to a perennial human problem, I think, that I tried to pin down in Roger's character and experiences—that if one behaves badly, it's no help to realize it. Roger is a bastard to a very large extent, and he understands it, and yet he can't be different. One isn't asking for sympathy for him exactly, but we all have our crosses to bear, and being a bastard and realizing it is a kind of cross which he bears."

Even though Jane's marriage was no refuge, it was all she had. At any rate, she didn't want to be known as a three-time "bolter," and some small portion of love kept flickering, at least on rare occasions. She and

Kingsley relied on each other as sounding boards for their writing, ending their workdays by reading the results aloud, seeking counsel, offering critiques: "That word doesn't seem quite right," "that needs cutting," and so on. But Jane wasn't producing much. Although she had steady journalism work and various side projects, including writing for television and radio, her fiction was slow going. At one point, Jane was offered the opportunity to write a biography of the Queen Mother, and a friend even arranged for Jane to have lunch with her. Even so, Jane thought the biography project, however lucrative, would prove to be a "pointless exercise" and turned it down. She was desperate to finish another novel. Following the publication of *Mr. Wrong*, Jane recalled that she "seemed to dry up." She did not publish any fiction again until her marriage was over. (Her novel *Getting It Right* came out in 1982.)

The long dry spell was depressing. Jane admitted feeling like an "abject, unfruitful creature." As has been true historically for many women artists and writers, only a divorce or the death of a spouse liberated them to create and publish their best work—or any work at all. "I got a bit fed up with it in the end," Jane admitted later, "because I never felt, funnily enough, that he was a better writer than me—I felt that he was a different writer. But he received acclaim and money and interest on a scale which never happened to me." She recalled that whenever she would express her frustration with her husband, "He would say, 'It's got to stay like this,' and I would say, 'Why?,' and he would say, 'Because I'm older, heavier, and I earn more money.'"

Decades after her marriage ended, Jane summoned a day in 1976, when she was fifty-three, as having been her last truly happy time with Kingsley. They spent the weekend in Oxfordshire with John Bayley and Iris Murdoch, and afterward Jane felt she had caught a glimpse of the "old" Kingsley: "relaxed, affectionate, funny, communicative." That night she went to bed wondering if their lovely day "held the promise of endurance, of an honest and companionable future." It didn't. There were occasional, half-hearted attempts at change: "I'm afraid I wasn't a very good husband to you this morning," Kingsley jotted in a note after failing to accompany his wife to the hospital for a test, saying he would "try to do better." In another letter that year, sent while Jane was off visiting friends in France, the lust and tenderness of Kingsley's early writings were notably gone. Instead, this missive—as in others to follow—was merely a dry rundown of goings-on at home ("Monday nothing much but work") and medical updates ("Tomorrow I go to Clive jr because my loose tooth is really flapping in the breeze"). Short of describing his latest bowel movements, Kingsley's letter was as unromantic as could be.

As Martin wrote in his memoir, *Experience*, "the most incurious visitor, sticking his head round the front door for ten seconds," would have known that the Amis-Howard marriage was now dead. Jane began seeing a (female) therapist once a week in South Kensington, where she sought to work through her "swamp of grief." She described her marital misery and isolation in an interview many years later: "I don't think it's easy to live with someone who drinks too much, but in the end I couldn't live with someone who disliked me so much as well," she said. "You can go on living with someone who doesn't love you, but what is really killing is someone who dislikes you."

Jane and Kingsley ceased going out together, except when socializing with others, and stopped sleeping in the same room. (Martin remembered Jane "telling me more about my father's growing remissness in [their sex life] than I really wanted to know.") One morning, Kingsley came into the bedroom, kissed Jane, and put his arms around her. "I used to be so much in love with you," he said, and walked away. Jane felt as if she had seen a ghost.

In the fall of 1980, Kingsley published the poorly received *Russian Hide and Seek*. After he'd finished writing it, he expressed his unhappiness in a letter to Philip Larkin: "Don't know that I'll ever start another. Too much like hard work what? And anxiety-promoting. Like walking to Antarctica *and* being afraid *all the time* you're going to fall over and break your hip." On a brighter note, he mentioned that he "had a wank this morning."

Kingsley struggled to get his next book going. He abandoned one manuscript and began another. He felt despair about getting older (he was nearly sixty) and the loss of his once-potent sex drive. He was drinking more than ever, behaving badly at parties, and sometimes unable to recall the offensive things he had said. (Regardless, he would angrily deny whatever he was accused of having done.) Sometimes Kingsley drank so much that by the end of the night, he was too unsteady to walk, and he would crawl upstairs to bed on all fours.

One morning, Jane walked into the kitchen and announced that she was off to a "health farm" in Suffolk with a friend. Kingsley didn't bother looking up from his newspaper as she left. Jane was due back ten days later, but what arrived instead, on the date of her expected return, was a terse letter, hand-delivered by her solicitor. It read, in part: "This is to tell you that I'm leaving. You know that I have been—we've both been—unhappy for years. I've thought about this for a long time and have come to the conclusion that there isn't the slightest hope of things getting any better. They don't, they simply get quietly worse. . . . [I]t was not the *rows* that were the worst things—it was the awful sterile desert in between them that I can't take any more."

Adding that it was "the most agonizing decision," she said: "I have made it, and it is final." Still, she worried over how to make things less painful for him. "There is no good way of leaving someone," she admitted. She dreaded his response. The vitriol would come later and with tremendous force, but first, he begged for her return. In a state of extreme suffering, he pleaded for another chance. Enclosing a poem he'd written for her, he acknowledged that things had been difficult, and promised to drink less and be more present for her. Jane wrote back, asking him to give up drinking completely. If he could do that, she would return. (Kingsley mocked the ultimatum in a letter to Larkin, joking that Jane's second condition for coming back was "presumably that I saw off my head and serve it up to her with a little hollandaise sauce.") After realizing the futility of negotiating with Kingsley, she filed for divorce. She did so with no small amount of grief. "It was rather like being widowed," she recalled in an interview, "although in a sense worse because people said, 'Well you left him, didn't you? So it was your fault.' They didn't seem to recognize that you might have to choose between two bad things."

When Martin got the call from Philip that Jane had left their father, they swooped in at once. "It wasn't a question of two sons planning to console a father who had lost his wife," Martin recalled in *Experience*. "It was much more elementary. One or other of us had to be there all the time. Not round the clock but every evening, every night, every morning." Martin found his father "heartsick," rumpled and quiet, willing to explain the most basic aspects of Jane's leaving, "but nothing was ventured about his feelings, about love, about broken hearts, broken vows." Kingsley had been going downhill for some time, and now, "getting fat was more like a project, grimly inaugurated on the day Jane left him in the winter of 1980—a complex symptom, repressive, self-isolating. It cancelled him out sexually." Martin could not take sides in the split. He had a warm relationship with his stepmother and felt he had "lost all appetite for apportioning blame in matters of the affections—in failed unions, sunderings, divorces. The symbiosis, the dyad, it fails, and that's that."

On December 5, 1980, Kingsley wrote to Larkin, with whom he could always be candid and rueful, to indulge in preposterous revisionism. He did not mention Jane by name. The letter opened with an apology for having been out of touch:

> I haven't written any letters to anyone or done much of
> anything since my wife left me 23 days ago. Not with anyone,
> just buggered off. She did it partly to punish me for stopping
> wanting to fuck her and partly because she realised I didn't like

her very much. Well, I liked her about as much as you could like anyone totally wrapped up in themselves and unable to tolerate the slightest competition or anything a raving lunatic could see as opposition and having to have their own way in everything all the time. Well, I expect reading between the lines there you can sense that we hadn't been getting on too well of late. Yeah, but not having her around and trying to take in the fact that she never will be around is immeasurably more crappy than having her around. I've had a wife for 32 years.

A month later, Kingsley wrote to Anthony Powell that "things are not as good as they might be here. It looks like a final parting of the ways, a thought that arouses in me, among many other things, a profound sense of relief." After Powell took Kingsley out for lunch, Kingsley thanked him "for being so sympathetic to my tale of woe." One can only marvel at Kingsley playing the victim. Even more remarkable, in his 1991 *Memoirs*, Jane is hardly mentioned. When she does appear on the page, it is only in passing. There is no reflection on their marriage, no description of loss, no sense that she was a central figure in his life for nearly two decades.

The divorce came through in 1983. After her first two divorces, Jane felt her life beginning anew, but this one made her sink like a stone. Certain she would never again fall in love, she consoled herself with "the uncomfortable notion that solitude was probably good for writing." It was, but Jane suffered from chronic loneliness and found solitude debilitating.

Kingsley seemed to bounce right back. He was a survivor. After publishing the "gynophobic" *Stanley and the Women* in 1984, which Martin described in his memoir as "a mean little novel in every sense, sour, spare, and viciously well-organized," he wrote *The Old Devils*, for which he won the Booker Prize—beating Kazuo Ishiguro's *An Artist of the Floating World* and Margaret Atwood's *The Handmaid's Tale*. He was knighted in 1990: Sir Kingsley Amis, CBE. And unlike Jane, he was no longer living alone. As Kingsley reported to Larkin a year after Jane left him, he had found a couple to look after him for the rest of his days: "They are Hilly and her 3rd husband, Lord Kilmarnock. Nay, stare not so. Well, you'd be justified in staring a bit, but it was their suggestion, the boys are much in favour, it's the only way for me to have a bit of family, all that."

Philip and Martin figured this head-scratching ménage would last no more than a year, but Kingsley lived until his death in 1995 with Hilly (now Lady Kilmarnock), and her Scottish husband, Alastair Boyd (the seventh Baron Kilmarnock). The arrangement, though far from ideal, suited them all. Lord Kilmarnock had his title and seat in the House of Lords, but he was strapped financially. Kingsley bought a home in London for the couple and their young son, Jaime. The motley crew eventually moved into a bigger house, with separate living quarters for Kingsley. He paid the household expenses and provided a modest weekly stipend. In exchange, Hilly cooked his meals and served them on a tray. She made his bed, shopped for him, did his laundry, kept track of his medications, cleaned, and—rather uncomfortably— sat with him and watched TV in the evenings so he would not be alone and afraid. "We weren't allowed to watch anything on telly that he didn't want to watch, and I was more or less trapped there," Hilly later recalled. "I'd always say good-night at nine. I had to put my foot down."

She wanted to help Kingsley. In the aftermath of his second divorce, Hilly felt loyal to her ex—hating Jane for taking away Kingsley and judging her as having behaved very badly after leaving him. (There was much wrangling about divvying up the house, the money, and so on, and Kingsley believed Jane took advantage of him by demanding more than her fair share.) With the Kilmarnocks, Kingsley lived like, well, a king. He continued to let himself go, drinking heavily and popping at least six different pills daily. He broke his leg, his liver was shot, and he suffered from irritable bowel syndrome. He was "enormously fat," as he put it. This once-dashing man was in terrible shape. "When your personal life takes a downturn, you resort to comfort eating," he said in an interview. "Chocolate biscuits, cake. It began when Jane left me. Carbohydrates evidently have a tranquilizing effect. People who are depressed like curling up with a bar of chocolate."

Kingsley came to believe that leaving Hilly had been the biggest mistake of his life. As for Jane, he never forgave her, never spoke to her again, and told people that meeting her was the worst thing that ever happened to him. "Do I see her?" he said in an interview, a few weeks before his death. "No. It was bad enough being married to her." When he died in his sleep at a hospital on October 22, 1995, at the age of seventy-three, his last coherent words to his son Philip were said to have been: "For God's sake, you bloody fool, give me a drink." Hilly died in 2010, at the age of eighty-one.

Jane never fell in love again. In her early seventies, she became involved with a fan of hers, Fergus Brand, who heard her on a radio program and contacted her. Having obsessively researched her background and books, he conned his way into her life and borrowed a lot of money. They had a brief affair, and she found him "fantastic" in bed. He said that he wanted to marry her. Jane, recovering from cancer at the time, had been single for fifteen long years, and it had been even longer since she'd had sex. Her guard was down. It was only after Nicola did some digging into the man's past—a history rife with violence and lies—that his unsavory motives became clear. "It's very painful, very humiliating," Jane said of the experience, but she made use of it in her 1999 novel, *Falling*. The bestselling author Louis de Bernières commended her for getting "a jolly good novel" out of something so shocking. It was also adapted into a TV movie.

"I have had a life 'crowded with incident,' as Lady Bracknell would say," Jane admitted in an interview at the age of eighty-five. Kingsley had been her greatest love. As Martin once noted, his stepmother was a "disastrous chooser of men," and his father had been "the pick of the bunch, standing out from a ghastly galère of frauds, bullies, and scoundrels."

The best outcome of Jane's post-Kingsley life was her literary output. In her sixties, Jane produced a series of semi-autobiographical novels that she had started with Martin's encouragement. Known as The Cazalet Chronicles, these proved to be her finest works. Following three generations of a large, upper-middle-class family in Sussex, the evocative saga was based on the author's memories of her childhood. The series has sold millions of copies worldwide and was adapted as a BBC series and Radio 4 drama. In 2000, Jane was awarded a CBE. Her career was not nearly as prolific or lauded as she had hoped for, yet it spanned more than sixty years. It was something to be proud of. Rather than ruminating over her position as a "woman of letters," she focused on making up for lost time. The older she got, the more she longed for simplicity. "People have a very grandiose view of the world," she said. "It's easier to imagine yourself in an operatic version of real life—standing on the ramparts in a Puccini dawn, preparing to plunge to your death, instead of just getting on with it."

Jane died at home on January 2, 2014, at the age of ninety. In her final years, she lived in Suffolk, in a beautiful old farmhouse along a river. By then she was too frail to indulge in gardening and cooking, and no longer able to drive, but, she said, "I can still learn." She required a full-time nurse. "Sometimes I don't feel any age at all," she said. "I feel quite, sort of, naive and open to things." She had few regrets: "I think I've more or less paid for them." And she kept up a voracious reading habit—about seventy novels a year—and wrote for a few hours each morning, aiming for three hundred words a day. Despite a hacking cough and having to carry an asthma inhaler at all times, Jane remained a heavy smoker. A year before her death, Jane published her final novel, *All Change*, the fifth volume of The Cazalet Chronicles. The *Guardian* praised it as "ultimately a novel about constants—loyalty, kindness, compassion."

A critic in the *Telegraph*, noting that "the struggle of the female writer" was a poignant aspect of the story, wrote, "For too long Howard was written about as Kingsley Amis's wife and Martin Amis's stepmother. Much as might be said for both roles, they should never have defined her literary presence."

Toward the end of her life Jane had achieved a sense of genuine contentment and self-worth. "The most important things in life cannot be taught," she said. "But life is so organized that you get the hang of things just when you're on the way out. It seems frightfully unfair."

# PATRICIA NEAL
## and Roald Dahl

"I wish you were dead. I wish
something would kill you."

Packard, Kentucky, is a ghost town, long extinct. Only a few faded photographs are known to have survived. Set along the Cumberland Mountains, a range in the southeastern section of the Appalachian Mountains, Packard was founded as a mining camp around 1900 and thrived for nearly fifty years. Eventually three coal companies set up operations in the town, located in Whitley County, less than ten miles from the Tennessee border. There was a small schoolhouse, a boarding-house, a post office, a doctor's office, a general store, a Baptist church, and a community of a few hundred homes. The buildings and houses have long since been razed. A single pump provided well water for all the residents, and sanitary conditions were awful. There was no electricity or indoor plumbing in Packard until the 1930s. With daily life focused on mining operations, there were many periods of labor strife in which work stoppages, walkouts, and strikes were common. Women were for-bidden to enter the mine shafts. In 1922, Kentucky's governor ordered the National Guard, including two machine-gun squads, to Packard after aggrieved mine workers committed an act of arson to protest a dangerous working environment and poor wages. "We are bound to win," reported a local miner and union representative, "for the terrible conditions cannot be stood any longer." By 1946, mining operations ceased, and the town was abandoned.

Patsy Louise Neal was born in Packard at 4:40 on the morning of January 20, 1926. The town was "fertile and thriving" and "nurturing many families like ours on the deep veins of coal that wound down into the bowels of the earth," she recalled in her 1988 autobiography, *As I Am*. Patsy's mother, Eura Mildred Petrey, was the daughter of Pascal

Gennings Petrey, the local doctor, whose office was in the back of the general store. Patsy's father, William Burdette Neal, was a manager for the Southern Coal and Coke Company and regarded as a kind of god in Packard, referred to as the most popular man in town. Known as "Coot," he was one of six children born into a family that owned a tobacco plantation in Virginia and landed in Packard in 1914. Coot met Eura at a gathering of friends for a card game, and they got married in 1918. He was twenty-three, and Eura was nineteen. Six years later, on March 8, 1924, Eura gave birth to their first child, a daughter they named Margaret Ann. Two years later, along came Patsy Louise.

For the Neals, life in Packard was good. There were just three phones in town: one at the general store, another in Coot's office, and a third in the family's home. Posted above Coot's desk was a plaque: "Organization is the art of getting men to respond like thoroughbreds. When you call upon a thoroughbred, he gives you all the speed, strength of heart, and sinew in him. When you call on a jackass, he kicks." These were Coot's words to live by, and one day Patsy would inherit the plaque. After his office became short-staffed, Coot hired Eura to fill in as bookkeeper. As well as being a mother and housewife, Eura reported to the office daily and worked alongside her husband, who split his salary with her. Even though Eura was no longer a full-time housewife, the family's clothing was always washed, rooms were cleaned, and meals were cooked. The Neals were happily settled with a comfortable routine and a close-knit community. But in 1929, Coot accepted a better-paying job with his company at its main office in Knoxville, Tennessee, about sixty miles south of Packard. Patsy was just three years old when the family moved to what was then an industrial city—they knew no one and people were not very friendly. Adjusting to Knoxville life was difficult, which was why the Neals made the three-hour car trip "home" to Packard twice a month.

On December 22, 1935, there was a new addition to the family: William Peter Neal, known as Pete. Patsy saw her baby brother as "a real live doll of my very own." Although Patsy was desperate for Margaret Ann to be her friend, the age difference presented problems. Patsy recalled her sister's funny response upon meeting her for the first time: "When I was just born—I guess hours old—my sister, who was twenty-two months old, came into the room and she looked—of course no one told children about expecting a baby in those days—and . . . she took one look at me in the bed with my mother and she said, 'Well, if it isn't Bill!'" So for years afterward, "Bill" was Patsy's nickname. Whereas her big sister got to boss her around all the time, Pete served as Patsy's "tiny pupil." She got in trouble with her mother one day when Pete announced, "Fuck-oh-fuck," and promptly disclosed that "Pat-Pat" had taught this word to him. The children grew up playing imaginative games together, as well as baseball in an empty lot. Thanks to her cousin Jack, she was also introduced to her first bad habit: smoking. One day he stole a big box of cigarettes that belonged to their aunt. He, Patsy, and Margaret Ann snuck outside and took turns lighting up cigarettes, one after the other, and—after a single puff—throwing each one away. They did this with all one hundred cigarettes in the box. (Jack got a beating when his mother found out.)

At school, Patsy fell happily under the influence of a teacher, Miss Cornelia Avaniti, who gave dramatic readings around Knoxville, along with moralizing speeches on topics such as "the demon alcohol" that threatened to destroy family life. After hearing Miss Avaniti recite a monologue for a Christmas program at the local church, Patsy was hooked. "I was utterly thrilled," she recalled. "I could do that! I knew I could! This, I said to myself, is what I want to do all my life." She rushed up to her teacher at the end of the evening to say how much she'd loved the performance, and how she dreamed of doing the same thing but could never be as good. "Of course, you can, Patsy Lou," Miss Avaniti said. "I will probably be listening to *you* one day."

One night, Patsy overheard her father talking about a new drama school starting up in Knoxville, founded by the daughter of Coot's boss. Without realizing it, Coot had just sealed his daughter's fate. Ten-year-old Patsy wrote a note to Santa and placed it in her sock over the fireplace:

Dear Santa,
What I want for Christmas is to study dramatics.
*Please.*

She got her wish, and, with the encouragement of her new drama teacher, Patsy began performing monologues for neighborhood children and formed her own theater group, dancing, acting, and singing with other kids on various "stages"—the Neals' front porch, yard, and basement. After her grandparents died, visits to Packard were few and far between, and now Knoxville felt more like home. Patsy was a popular, confident girl, and as word spread about the talented young actress, she performed monologues at local venues, won a state award for dramatic reading, and even directed a high school production of *Jane Eyre*. Eventually she caught the attention of Malcolm Miller, the city's most important theater critic:

Knoxville High School's Patsy Neal made her debut with the Tennessee Valley Players and just about walked off with the show. She had grace and poise; her reactions were well timed and natural; her reading was nicely pointed, and her voice projection was splendid.

Miller sensed that Patsy should take her talent beyond Knoxville and told her so. He wrote to Robert Porterfield, the founding director of the Barter Theatre in Abingdon, Virginia, on her behalf, recommending Patsy as a summer apprentice there. Founded in 1933, the Barter was less than a decade old but had already developed an excellent reputation, and in 1946 it was designated the state theater of Virginia. The

Barter started during the Depression and got its name because of its proclamation that "with vegetables you cannot sell, you can buy a good laugh." The price of admission was either forty cents or an equivalent amount in produce, meaning that corn on the cob could get you in the door. Theatergoers paid their way with dairy and even livestock ("ham for *Hamlet*"). The Barter is still operating and thriving today.

In the summer of 1942, Patsy was sixteen years old and had just completed her junior year in high school. Coot and Eura, ever supportive of their daughter, gave Patsy a beautiful suitcase as a parting gift, and off she went—the first time she had traveled away from home by herself. Being among "real theater people," Patsy felt she was in the company of royalty. She started by moving props, serving as assistant stage manager, and then landing small parts and finally, a lead role. She also had her eye on one of the handsome young actors at the Barter, and she was curious about sex. One night she showed up late at the actor's room, nervous, and returned every night for more than a week. All they did was sit up talking, and Patsy—five-foot-eight, hazel-eyed, and strikingly beautiful—wondered what it might take to seduce the object of her affection. Once she arrived to find him already in bed, so she took off her shoes and boldly crawled into bed with him. Would it be okay if she stayed, she asked? Sure, that would be fine, but he was going to sleep. "Before I left the theater that summer, I learned that he did not like girls," she recalled. "I had heard about homosexuals at school but had never met one in Knoxville."

Patsy begged her parents to let her go to New York City to pursue her acting ambitions, but they insisted that she attend college first. She enrolled, reluctantly, at Northwestern University, where she modeled for the campus magazine, studied with a renowned acting teacher, and joined the university theater group. But the girl who believed she had been "born under a lucky star" suffered tragedy in the spring of 1944, when her father died of a heart attack at the age of forty-nine, the same year she lost her first boyfriend and a cousin in the war. She cut short her time at

Northwestern and bought a train ticket. With three hundred dollars in savings, she headed to New York in the fall of 1945.

"No one should come to New York to live unless he is willing to be lucky," E. B. White famously wrote, and Patsy was ready for some luck. Things fell into place for her quickly. She found a small, top-floor apartment on the Upper West Side of Manhattan with four roommates, three of whom had also attended Northwestern, and started making the audition rounds, "smile by smile, flirt by flirt. Flirting was a tool of the trade, and I was becoming an expert." She took acting classes, saw as many plays as she could, and worked at a Greenwich Village luncheonette, earning seventy cents an hour, almost six dollars a day. And she ate at places like the Horn & Hardart cafeteria and the Walgreen's Drugstore at the Astor Hotel—popular networking hangouts for out-of-work theater actors—where she could find scene partners or hear about auditions. At her apartment, the typical culinary options were cheese, crackers, donuts, peanut butter, popcorn, and tuna fish. Four beds were set up in one room, and the last girl home at night slept on the sofa. That girl was usually Patsy.

Money was tight, but Patsy was ambitious, and soon she officially became a working New York actress. Her first theater job was a production of *Seven Mirrors*, which also featured a young actress named Geraldine Page. She landed her first agent, Maynard Morris, who had recently discovered Marlon Brando. For $150 a week, she took on an understudy role for the hit Broadway production of John Van Druten's *The Voice of the Turtle*, as well as for the touring company, and the show's producer suggested a new professional name: Patricia Neal. She was nineteen years old.

By Christmas 1945, Patricia Neal had signed her first autographs and a lease for her own apartment on Morningside Drive. It was a fourth-floor walkup with cockroaches and a bathroom down the hall, but it was all hers. From there, she moved into a bigger, sunnier place nearby with another friend (and fellow actress) from Northwestern, Jean Hagen.

Patricia may not have had much money, but she was confident in her talent and the work kept coming. She received two Broadway offers at once: Richard Rodgers wanted to give her the lead role in his new play, *John Loves Mary*, and Lillian Hellman wanted Patricia for her new play, *Another Part of the Forest*. It was a prequel to her semi-autobiographical 1939 play, *The Little Foxes*, whose title had been suggested by Hellman's close friend Dorothy Parker. This was a tough choice, but Patricia settled on the Hellman play. (Luckily, Rodgers would come back to Patricia for the film adaptation of his play.)

She was excited to begin work on *Another Part of the Forest*, which the playwright would also direct. "I am getting $300 a week the first year and $460 the second if I am still in it," Patricia reported in a letter to her Aunt Maude, with whom she was close and who had supported her ambitions from the start. "If it is a hit, I can't get out for two years unless Mr. O'Neill wants me to do 'Touch of the Poet.'" As Patricia would learn, dealing with Hellman, a first-time director, was not easy, and Hellman did not even finish writing the last act until rehearsals were underway. Hellman's companion, the author Dashiell Hammett, was a frequent (and frequently drunk) presence at rehearsals, and he was openly smitten with Patricia. Hellman adored Hammett, no matter the state he was in or how badly he behaved, and the couple bonded in part by being active in left-wing literary circles. Hammett was later called to testify by the House Un-American Activities Committee, and he served six months in prison after being found in contempt of Congress. He was blacklisted for refusing to cooperate with Joseph McCarthy's witch hunt, and Hellman was blacklisted for her past involvement in the Communist Party. No matter how draining Hammett was on Hellman—financially, emotionally—she stuck by him.

"But Lillian's gentle, tender side was obvious to few," Patricia later recalled. "Most people saw only her impetuous temper and never the woman beneath the fire. Instinctively, I understood her and knew that when I got an angry swat, all I had to do was duck and wait it out." And

Hellman was quite fond of her, writing in her 1973 memoir, *Pentimento*, "It gives me pleasure that I found an unknown girl, Patricia Neal, and watched her develop into a good actress and woman." Not only did they remain friends for the rest of Hellman's life, but with a dinner invitation in 1952, the playwright would play a key role in shaping Patricia's fate.

*Another Part of the Forest* was well received in its out-of-town tryouts, with great reviews all around, and Patricia—playing the role of Regina, who had been portrayed by Tallulah Bankhead in *The Little Foxes*—was described by critics as "very beautiful and talented" and "a revelation," and praised for her "rich voice, flexible and full of expression." Then came Broadway. Opening night was November 20, 1946, and it was everything Patricia had dreamed of. "I knew for certain that the reason I wanted to be an actress was for that moment," Patricia wrote in her autobiography. "Applause was love. It was approval by everybody, and I bathed in it." *Another Part of the Forest* received mixed reviews, was a modest hit, and ended up running for 182 performances at the Fulton Theatre, now the Helen Hayes Theatre, before closing on April 26, 1947. (It was adapted into a film a year later.) But the critics loved Patricia. "Miss Neal contributes an extraordinarily vital and memorable stage portrayal," wrote Howard Barnes in the *New York Herald Tribune*. Hellman hosted a post-show party at her Upper East Side townhouse, where the cast waited for the reviews to come in. Patricia's mother and brother had traveled from Tennessee to New York for the premiere, staying at the Algonquin. "I was so fidgety and excited when the curtain rose that I hardly got the gist of the play," Eura later told a reporter for the *Atlanta Journal*.

After the opening night party, Patricia came back to the hotel, where Eura proudly told her daughter that she had received almost ninety congratulatory telegrams, not just from family and friends, but from luminaries such as Tallulah Bankhead and David O. Selznick. Patricia went to bed and awoke the next morning a Broadway star. "Overnight I was the toast of New York," she recalled. "It was thrilling to walk down the street for the first time in my life and have people, complete strangers, come up to me and say, 'You were wonderful in that play.'" A young actor who saw Patricia around this time described the actress as impressive, "just so beautiful, so healthy, so had-it-all-made." Indeed, she had been a struggling actress for a New York minute. Now there were tables waiting for her at Sardi's, A-list party invitations, and dinners with celebrities such as Gregory Peck. Hollywood producers came to woo her. The night of Patricia's twenty-first birthday on January 20, 1947, the cast got together to sing "Happy Birthday" to her, and Hellman brought a bottle of brandy and a birthday cake to her dressing room. She and her roommate, Jean, were able to upgrade to a beautiful apartment on Riverside Drive, where they stocked up on champagne and sent their laundry out. By the time the play closed that spring, Patricia was a media darling, with a *Life* magazine cover, features in *Vogue*, *Harper's Bazaar*, and *Redbook*, and an award from *Look* for Broadway's brightest newcomer. She also won the Drama Critics Award, the Donaldson Award (launched in 1944 and discontinued in 1955), the Theatre World Award, and on April 6, 1947, the very first Antoinette Perry Award—now more commonly known as the Tony Awards—for Best Performance by a Featured Actress in a Play. Other big Tony winners that night included Arthur Miller, Ingrid Bergman, and Agnes de Mille. (The "ladies" took home engraved silver compacts, while the men were given gold bill clips or cigarette lighters.) She joined the touring company production of *Another Part of the Forest*, which didn't last long, and took on a demanding summer stock schedule in Denver. She was delighted to receive a kind note from one of her idols, Eugene O'Neill, who expressed pleasure at her success and added, "This was no surprise to me as I know you will, one day, be one of our best."

Around that time, Patricia heard about a new workshop intended as a training ground for professional actors who were obsessively devoted to their craft. Called the Actors Studio, it was founded by Elia Kazan, Robert Lewis, and Cheryl Crawford. She felt honored to be invited to join, and found herself in a group with Marlon Brando, Sidney Lumet,

Montgomery Clift, and other young talents. She didn't get to study with her idol, Elia Kazan—a great disappointment, since she found Robert Lewis psychologically abusive—but remembered fondly how Kazan "spoke with fire. He had me in the palm of his hand." (She would have the opportunity to work with him later, and he was quite fond of her.) In any case, she could not put off Hollywood any longer.

On December 30, 1947, Patricia signed a contract with Warner Brothers after receiving offers and proposals from multiple film studios. "I wanted to be the greatest actress ever to appear on the screen," she later recalled. Knowing her mother was lonely back in Knoxville, she got them an apartment to share, along with her brother, where Eura would cook and take care of the house and Patricia would provide for Pete's education, just as she'd done since the death of their father. She was very comfortable financially: her new seven-year contract gave her a starting salary of $1,250 a week (rising to $3,750 in the final year), plus featured or star billing and the option to return to the theater twice during the term of the contract. Patricia's first project with the studio would be the comedy *John Loves Mary*, to be released in 1949, adapted from the Rodgers play. Warner Brothers hosted an extravagant New Year's Eve party, filled with movie stars, where a handsome man approached her. "I'm Ronnie Reagan," he said. "We're going to do this 'John Loves Mary' together. I'm very happy to meet you." (They would make another film together, *The Hasty Heart*, released in the fall of 1949.)

The screenplay for *John Loves Mary* was written by a married couple, Henry and Phoebe Ephron, whose daughters Nora, Delia, Hallie, and Amy would grow up to become notable writers themselves. "Everyone on the set was experienced but me," Patricia recalled in her autobiography. "But I was too excited to be afraid." Her quick rise to fame was impressive, but she would quickly learn that fame did not equate box office success. *John Loves Mary* got mixed reviews from critics, as did Patricia's performance. In the *New York Times*, Bosley Crowther wrote a harsh review, saying that the "brand-new Warner girl" had a lot to learn and "shows little to recommend her to further comedy jobs. Her looks are far more arresting, her manners are slightly gauche and her way with a gag line is painful." Yet this film would seem like a great success compared with her next one. Her personal life was about to unravel as well.

Warner Brothers had paid fifty thousand dollars to acquire the rights to Ayn Rand's 1943 novel *The Fountainhead*, and another thirteen thousand dollars for the author to write the screenplay, which required several rewrites. After some casting missteps and bridges burned—both Clark Gable and Humphrey Bogart had coveted the role of Howard Roark, and Barbara Stanwyck, Gene Tierney, and Lauren Bacall had been considered for the role of Dominique Francon—the studio hired Gary Cooper and Patricia Neal for the lead roles. Born in 1901, Cooper was one of Hollywood's biggest and most bankable stars, admired for his restrained acting style, and popular within the industry, with a reputation for being courteous, charming, and humble. He was also twenty-five years older than Patricia, married, and notoriously unfaithful. (Among other affairs, he'd begun a romantic relationship with Ingrid Bergman in 1942 while they filmed *For Whom the Bell Tolls*.) He and Patricia fell for each other the moment they met, but did not act on their mutual attraction until filming wrapped.

WARNER BROTHERS HAD SIGNIFICANT BOX OFFICE EXPECTATIONS FOR *The Fountainhead* and studio executives were invested in building Patricia's career. She admitted later that the intimacy and intensity of a movie set has a way of seducing everyone involved into thinking they are making great art. "Little did we know that we were heading over the cliff like lemmings into the passionate sea," she recalled. When the film opened in July 1949, less than six months after the disappointing *John Loves Mary*, it bombed at the box office and was panned by critics. ("'The Fountainhead' is a picture which you don't have to see to disbelieve," warned the *New York Times*.) No matter: her affair with Gary Cooper was just getting started—even as Kirk Douglas was the "public" beau arranged for her by Warner Brothers—and her film *The Hasty Heart*, shot in England, was a success upon its premiere in the UK in the fall of 1949. The audience gave it a standing ovation, and the film premiered in Los Angeles and New York that winter, also to wide acclaim. The following year, Patricia had three films released, and by this time, she felt that her double life with Gary Cooper had become "hellish." Deeply in love, she was frustrated that he would not leave his wife, Veronica, known as Rocky, a former New York debutante. Patricia told herself it was just a matter of time. But when Rocky confronted her husband about the affair, she mocked Patricia to him as a "southern cow" and told their young daughter, Maria, what her father had done. (Maria later spat on Patricia when she met her.) He admitted he was in love with Patricia, and the affair carried on. A highlight of their time together was Cooper taking Patricia to Cuba by chartered plane to meet his good friend Ernest Hemingway and his wife, Mary. (Patricia appeared in a film adaptation of one of his novels, though it was poorly received.) Meeting the great writer was a thrill for Patricia, but Mary, who was close to Rocky, disliked her and made no attempt to hide it. When Patricia asked Mary whether she enjoyed playing bridge, she replied dismissively: "I have so many books to read, I don't have time to play trivial games."

Not long afterward, Patricia received a telegram: "I HAVE HAD JUST ABOUT ENOUGH OF YOU. YOU HAD BETTER STOP NOW OR YOU WILL BE SORRY." It was signed "Mrs. Gary Cooper." Patricia began to see a psychiatrist. She was crying all the time, at unexpected moments, and yearning for a husband and a family of her own. She was also depressed after filming *Operation Pacific* with John Wayne, who was always in a foul mood on set, arguing with the director and behaving like a bully. Plus, Patricia was exhausted and bloated, her costumes ill-fitting. After going to see her doctor, she found out she was pregnant.

When she broke the news to Gary, both were excited until reality set in. He said he "knew someone," and made an appointment for her at a doctor's office in a shabby building in downtown Los Angeles. On a bright October day in 1950, he drove her to the small office, handed her an envelope of cash, and waited in the car while she got an abortion. "If I had let myself think about it," she recalled, "perhaps I might have been disappointed that Gary did not insist on coming inside with me." She described the traumatic experience in her autobiography:

> He did not say anything more than was absolutely necessary. I followed his instructions without a word. I remember he held a needle at bay while he filled the syringe. It was the longest needle I had ever seen in my life. I closed my eyes. The needle's impaling gift was supposed to relieve pain. I thought I would die. My body began to sweat from every pore. The most agonizing hour of my life commenced. All I could hear was the sound of scraping.

Patricia returned to the car to find him soaked in sweat, and together they wept all afternoon. Patricia later revealed that for decades to come, she often cried alone at night, grieving what she had lost. "If I had only one thing to do-over in my life," she wrote, "I would have that baby."

Meanwhile, the affair escalated from an open secret to a full-blown scandal, with the press following Patricia everywhere, hounding her for details on life as a home-wrecker. She was easy fodder for the gossip columns. Publicists fed her generic lines to give to the press: "We're just good friends"; "If I were in love with him, I'd be silly to advertise it. After all, he *is* a married man." She was astonished to learn that Gary told his wife about the abortion and realized then that he would never leave Rocky. As a Catholic, Rocky said she would not consider a divorce under any circumstances. She was well aware of her husband's previous infidelities, but Patricia was the first woman to represent an existential threat to her marriage. Gary, unwilling or unable to commit to one woman, never discussed the affair publicly, yet the strain and guilt had taken a toll. "There is something about the sadness that appears in Mr. Cooper's eyes, something about the slowness and the weariness of his walk, something about the manner that is not necessarily in the script, which reminds the middle-aged observer that Mr. Cooper had been at it a long time," wrote one critic of the actor's performance in the film *Dallas*.

He must have sensed that his relationship with Patricia could not carry on much longer, but he refused to give up the mistress he loved, and she refused to let him go. Even so, it was Patricia who suffered the consequences of his adultery, and she who was targeted for sanctimonious public censure. "No one ever came out and criticized me to my face," she recalled, "but it was more than low-key snubs at parties now." Although she received steadfast support from her friend Clark Gable, many people she believed were true friends broke off contact. After she and Gary were invited for dinner one night at Cary Grant's house, his wife at the time, Betsy Drake, called Patricia in distress to cancel at the last minute, explaining with regret that her husband did not want them there because it might draw unfavorable attention. Patricia also lost a role in a play by Eugene O'Neill, who adored her, because his wife insisted he drop her. And at a grand party at the film producer David Selznick's house, Patricia walked in with Gary and "I could almost smell the hypocrisy in the air as the women in the room quickly looked away. Most of them were also sleeping with lovers, with married men, but I seemed to make their guilt visible."

After her Warner Brothers contract expired, Patricia was not asked to renew. She had won critical accolades, but the studio's investment in their high-priced star had not paid off at the box office. She was stung by an outcome that had once seemed so promising, but following the collapse of the Warner relationship, her agents got her a three-picture deal at Twentieth Century Fox. On May 18, 1951, just days before Patricia finished shooting *The Day the Earth Stood Still*, her first film for the studio, the Coopers publicly announced a separation. "THE GARY

COOPERS PART: IS PATRICIA NEAL NEXT?" blared the headline of one gossip column. Rocky remained at the family home in Brentwood and Gary moved into the Hotel Bel-Air. By the fall, he was coping with health issues (including hospitalization for ulcers), depression over the breakup of his marriage, anxiety and guilt over his daughter, and a stalled career. (After being hired for *High Noon*, he learned he was the director's fourth choice after Marlon Brando, Charlton Heston, and John Wayne had turned down the role.) Patricia ended things with him in an anguished phone call, yet she kept hoping he would call back and beg for her return. She didn't think she could live without him.

The gossip columnist Hedda Hopper scored an exclusive interview with Patricia and asked about the possibility of a reunion with Cooper. Admitting she was "very much in love with him," Patricia said, "I have a lot of life ahead of me. And I want to live it with someone who is fun and untangled, someone with whom I can have a relationship that will be good—and permanent. Coop is wonderful. I never knew anyone like him. But he's a very complex person, as you well know. . . . It is, I assure you, over and ended forever." Asked how many times she had been in love, Patricia replied, "Only once." That number would stay the same until the day she died.

For Christmas 1951, on a publicity junket in Acapulco, Mexico, without thinking she went shopping for Gary—handmade silk shirts, sweaters, socks, and a set of miniature antique guns she knew he would love—and mailed the gifts to his home. Meanwhile, he sent Patricia a mink coat with a note: "I love you, my baby. Gary." It was a goodbye gift. Cooper, who was said to be shattered after their relationship ended, had reconciled with Rocky. The couple remained together until his death from cancer at the age of sixty in 1961. "To this day whenever I see Gary on the screen," Patricia wrote in her autobiography, "I fall in love with him all over again. Even the sound of his voice is enough to renew my passion."

In the aftermath of the breakup, Patricia wept and wept, lost almost twenty pounds, could hardly speak, and suffered from insomnia. It was a full-on breakdown. "I felt as if my life had burst apart from the inside," she recalled. "Everything that had given life any meaning for me was torn into shreds." Gossip columnists such as Walter Winchell and Louella Parsons kept the breakup saga going: Parsons claimed that Patricia had run off to Palm Springs to deal with weight issues, while Winchell wrote that "the Gary Cooper–Pat Neal finale has left her in tatters, her closest friends report." In an interview a few years after Cooper's death, Patricia described him as "the most gorgeously attractive man—bright, too, although some people didn't think so." Time may not have healed any wounds, but it did give her some perspective: "I got myself into a sticky mess which couldn't work, didn't work, and never should have worked."

By the summer of 1952, Patricia had appeared in fourteen films. But Hollywood, along with Gary Cooper, had broken her heart. It was true that many of her performances won praise, and *The Day the Earth Stood Still*—with her utterance of the iconic phrase *"Klaatu barada nikto"*— would be recognized later as a cult classic and one of the top science fiction films of all time. But upon its release, it was only a moderate success, and her other films had mixed results. Still, she was a first-rate actress and a tall, radiant beauty who was gorgeous onscreen. Of her high, wide cheekbones, the critic Brendan Gill once remarked that "the camera can sort of *pan across* a face of that kind."

Not long after her relationship ended with Cooper, Patricia fell into a rebound affair with Peter Douglas, a wealthy son of the United States ambassador to England. What began as a fling sparked by strong sexual attraction had, in her mind, developed into a relationship with deeper possibilities. But one night, Peter failed to show up for a date and didn't bother calling to explain. It was the final humiliation. Heartbroken, her Hollywood career in tatters, she decided it was time to rekindle her passion for the theater, a community that always embraced and celebrated her. In August 1952, after a visit to her sister and mother in Atlanta, where they were now living, Patricia headed to New York to begin her life again.

She landed in a suite at the Plaza Hotel, then settled in an apartment on Park Avenue and had her furniture shipped from Hollywood. She felt excited to be in Manhattan and realized at once that she had made the right decision. "At every turn I was reaching out to New York to say, 'Here I am!' and New York took my hand in the most amazing way." When she learned that Lillian Hellman, along with the producer Kermit Bloomgarden, was mounting a Broadway revival of Hellman's bold first play, *The Children's Hour*, she phoned Bloomgarden immediately and asked to read for it. He had produced *Another Part of the Forest*, as well as Arthur Miller's *Death of a Salesman* and other plays. When it debuted in 1934, *The Children's Hour* was declared "indecent" by the mayor of Boston, Frederick Mansfield, who issued a decree banning it from being performed in the city. Yet the succès de scandale was a Broadway hit with both critics and audiences, and it established Hellman, at the age of twenty-nine, as an important American playwright. "Whatever its minor imperfections may be," wrote Brooks Atkinson in his *New York Times* review on December 2, 1934, "*The Children's Hour* is stinging tragedy." The idea for the play actually came from Hammett, who told Hellman about a nineteenth-century case in Edinburgh in which a schoolgirl accused two teachers of having a lesbian affair, and the women spent the rest of their lives trying to clear their names.

Patricia's friends teased her for being willing to audition for Hellman— she was, after all, a *star*—but she had not lost any of her hunger or drive and was always willing to prove what she could do. She also felt confident that she could play either of the two women, Martha or Karen. "Five years of frustration and a broken heart exploded on the stage," Patricia recalled of her audition. Hellman, who planned to direct the play, and Bloomgarden said immediately that they wanted her, and that she could have either role. She chose Martha. (Kim Hunter was cast as Karen.)

In September, shortly before rehearsals were set to begin, Hellman invited Patricia over to her Manhattan townhouse for a dinner party. A handsome, blue-eyed, six-foot-six man caught her eye.

"Who is that tall man?" she whispered to Hellman.

"*Roald Dahl!*"

By chance or by plan, Patricia was seated next to Dahl, who made a terrible first impression. The Hollywood star, accustomed to being the center of attention, especially in the presence of men—and to others vying for her attention—had no idea who he was, but expected he would attempt to charm her all evening. She waited. His attention, however, was focused on the guest seated directly across from him, Leonard Bernstein. When Patricia tried to join the conversation, both men ignored her. She left the party furious: "I had quite made up my mind that I loathed Roald Dahl."

Yet he *had* noticed Patricia and secured her number from Hellman. "Jolly glad to find you home," he said when Patricia picked up the phone a day or so later, and he invited her out the following night. She declined. Two days later, Dahl called again, and they made a date. He took her to an Italian restaurant owned by John Huston's father-in-law, and she was charmed by the intelligence, confidence, and wit of her date. He had an interest in just about everything: painting, gardening, antiques, chess, wine, politics, theater, architecture, medicine, music. He was also a great storyteller. Patricia was still stuck in a deep depression, but she had to admit that Roald wasn't so loathsome after all. She liked him. One date led to another, and soon he began to stop by the theater after rehearsals so they could have dinner together. He later recalled his early impressions of Patricia: "She was in a depressed state when I met her. . . . She was reserved, holding herself in, obviously pretty shaken all around. . . . I think she planned to work hard as an antidote against her personal misfortunes."

By now, Patricia was well acquainted with Hellman's "blunt and sometimes brutal" directorial method, and she, unlike Hunter and others in the cast, was lucky to be spared much of the unpleasantness. On December 18, 1952, *The Children's Hour* opened at the Coronet Theatre, now the Eugene O'Neill Theatre, where it ran for 189 performances before closing on May 30, 1953. Writing about the revival in the *New York Times*, Brooks Atkinson remained a fan: "It is still a first-rate piece of theatre, and eighteen years have tended to make it more generally pertinent than it was originally. . . . As the two school teachers, monstrously slandered, Patricia Neal and Kim Hunter give discerning performances in vigorous and contrasting styles of acting."

By the time the play opened, Patricia and Roald were seeing each other every night. She wasn't so much swept off her feet as led away from her pain. And Roald was steady and persistent. At thirty-six, he was ready to marry, and at twenty-six, so was she. Just as Patricia was healing from heartbreak, Roald had relationship troubles of his own, though far less dramatic. He had been dating a Hungarian American divorcée, Suzanne Horvath, who had a child from a previous marriage. In the fall of 1951, not long after buying her a two-hundred-dollar Patek Philippe watch, he proposed—but by February 1952, he had cold feet about making a commitment, and the relationship ended that year. As someone who kept his feelings largely to himself, he never revealed why the relationship ended, only that Horvath broke up with him. He was not an easy man to be entangled with, romantically or platonically. In 1950, in a handwritten note entitled "Things I Hate," he listed, with great specificity, the objects of his abhorrence:

All piddling spindly tables, specially the kind that slide into each other—six of them.
Women who say "What are you thinking?"
Bookshelves with an unread look.
Men who wear rings that are not absolutely plain.
The larger the ring the worse it is. A diamond worst of all.
Men who wear bow ties, pointed shoes, shoes in two different

leathers, tie clips, sock suspenders.

Men who have four or five strands of hair and they let it grow long
and paste it to their domes.

Men or women who hold a cigarette between thumb and first
finger.

It seemed that Patricia came into his life at just the right time. "He knew what he wanted and he quietly went about getting it," Patricia recalled in her autobiography.

Roald (pronounced *Roo-all*, with the "d" silent) was born in Llandaff, Wales, on September 13, 1916, to wealthy Norwegian émigrés who named him after Roald Amundsen, the Norwegian polar explorer who had reached the South Pole in 1911. While Patricia's childhood in Kentucky had been fairly blissful, Roald's early life was marked by tragedy.

His mother, Sofie Magdalene Hesselberg, was in her twenties when she married Harald Dahl, who was in his forties. This was Harald's second marriage: his first wife, a Frenchwoman named Marie, died at twenty-nine in 1907, leaving him a widower with a young daughter, Ellen, and a son, Louis. By the time he married, Harald had made his fortune as the co-owner of a ship-brokering business in Cardiff, one of the largest cargo shipping centers in the world. He bought a beautiful house in the medieval town of Llandaff, and named it Villa Marie. Devastated after the death of his wife, Harald focused on his business and struggled to raise two young children with the help of Marie's mother, Ganou. After four lonely years, on holiday in the summer of 1911, he met Sofie and proposed to her within a week.

After they married, she became stepmother to Harald's children while starting their own family: daughter Astri was born in 1912, Alfhild in 1914, and son Roald in 1916, followed by Else in 1917. (Alfhild later recalled that Roald, as her mother's only son, was Sofie's "pride and joy" and that he received special treatment.) The following year, at the end of the First World War, the family moved to a grander house in the country—Ty Mynydd, a Victorian mansion with 150 acres of farmland and cottages for the household staff. Harald, an expert gardener and accomplished wood carver, bought paintings and antique furniture for the new house. He had an enthusiasm for beautiful things that would later influence Roald, who later bought and sold paintings, furniture, and more to supplement his earnings from writing. Harald worked long hours and was often preoccupied and withdrawn. Then came tragedy.

Roald was three years old when, in February 1920, his sister Astri died of appendicitis at the age of seven. As Roald later recalled, "Astri was far and away my father's favourite. He adored her beyond measure and her sudden death left him literally speechless for days afterward." Overwhelmed with grief, Harald came down with pneumonia and died in April. He was fifty-seven years old.

With her husband and oldest child dead, Sofie, thirty-five years old and pregnant at the time, sold the house and moved the family back to Llandaff, where she bought a modest redbrick Victorian house and gave birth to their daughter Asta that fall. Harald had left her more than £150,000, the equivalent today of millions of pounds, more than enough for the children to go to boarding school and live comfortably well into adulthood. Every summer, Sofie took her children to a remote island in Norway. On these annual getaways, Roald and his siblings learned to speak Norwegian, ate fresh fish and burnt toffee, swam in the ice-blue fjords, and listened with rapt attention to stories of trolls and witches.

Harald had been adamant about wanting his children to be educated in England, as he believed English schools were the best in the world. In 1925, when Roald was nine years old, Sofie sent him off to St. Peter's School in Weston-super-Mare, Somerset, which Roald later dubbed "Weston-super-Mud." He despised both the town and the school, and once described St. Peter's, which was demolished in the 1970s, as a "private lunatic asylum." At thirteen, he moved on to the Repton School in

Derbyshire, founded in 1557. By then his mother had moved the family to an eight-bedroom house in Bexley, Kent, with a tennis court on the property. At both schools, Roald was academically weak, caused in part by pervasive feelings of homesickness. A half-term report at St. Peter's had shown Roald to be an unremarkable student: English composition ("very fair"), maths ("only moderately good"), and "gradually improving" in French. In a half-term report at Repton, the boy who would grow up to sell more than 250 million books worldwide was described as "a persistent muddler. Vocabulary negligible, sentences mal-constructed." And in another: "I have never met a boy who so persistently writes the exact opposite of what he means. He seems incapable of marshalling his thoughts on paper."

While away at school, Roald sent letters to his mother once a week, sometimes more often, and kept them up well into adulthood. It was not until 1957, the year Sofie died, that Roald discovered his mother had saved every single one of his letters—twenty years' worth, more than six hundred of them—binding them carefully into neat bundles with green tape and leaving each one in its original envelope.

Although he understood his mother's decision to send him away to school, he missed her terribly, and as ever, he missed the father he barely remembered. Being trapped at Repton was endlessly dreary, whereas at home, Roald was much adored and often the center of attention— his siblings gave him the nickname "the Apple," as in the apple of his mother's eye. Sofie was, as he later recalled, "undoubtedly the absolute primary influence on my own life. She had a crystal-clear intellect and a deep interest in almost everything under the sun."

Roald later admitted that the account of his schooling years in *Boy: Tales of Childhood* was "coloured by my natural love of fantasy," and former classmates challenged the accuracy of some of his stories, including portrayals of faculty members and incidents of bullying. Tall and athletic, Roald was known for his cleverness, such as rigging up a mousetrap whose catchphrase was "Catch as Cats Can't." But he was always willing to invent details, to stretch the truth if it made for a better story. One former Reptonian recalled that the school was indeed a "tough place" with "rules and discipline tight, living really spartan, enforced by boys who did 90 percent of the beating, of which there was a lot." And Roald later described Repton as far worse than St. Peter's, with disciplinary beatings "more fierce and more frequent than anything I had yet experienced." Yet amid the miseries were aspects that made him happy: Roald became passionate about photography, even converting a bedroom at his mother's house into a darkroom for his hobby. Though deemed an unskilled writer by his teachers, he was, as he later recalled, "an avid and insatiable reader." Intensely competitive, he thrived at sports, playing hockey, football, golf, and cricket, becoming captain of the squash team and winning the school boxing competition in his final year. He also got hooked on gambling—poker, bridge, and other games—which would become a lifelong hobby. Above all, there was one aspect of Repton that made his experience slightly less of an ordeal: Cadbury's (now Cadbury), the British confectionery company, conducted a bit of market research by allowing the boys at Repton to sample and rate new chocolate products. Every boy was given a cardboard box with chocolates to test, along with a checklist to indicate their scores. The delightful tastings would shape Roald's lifelong love for chocolate, lead him to wonder about the factories where these sublime treats were made, and inspire a certain bestselling book.

As a child, Roald regarded authority figures with fear and distrust. In *Boy*, the author describes his first encounter with the headmaster of St. Peter's, casting him as predatory: "He advanced upon my mother and shook her by the hand, then he shook me by the hand and as he did so he gave me the kind of flashing grin a shark might give to a small fish just before he gobbles it up." For good measure, he adds—or perhaps invents—a few thug-like details: "One of his front teeth, I noticed, was edged all the way round with gold, and his hair was slicked down with so much hair cream that it glistened like butter." The moment the headmaster steps away to greet other incoming students, Roald recalls, "I began to cry."

As the historian and critic Jeremy Treglown notes in *Roald Dahl*, his 1993 biography of the author, "It is the fate of all schools that some of their liveliest pupils grow up to revile them." However exaggerated or misremembered were Roald's anecdotes, Treglown writes, the boy was struggling at school: "You can't calibrate psychological suffering any more than physical pain. To say that Dahl exaggerated is, at least partly, to point to the subjectivism of experience—and to the particular varieties of subjectivism which can turn people into writers of fiction. To Dahl, his experiences seemed real enough, and it is clear that he was lonely and insecure."

Another thing is clear: the memories were traumatic and had a profound influence on his work, elements of which were hard to separate from the sadistic behavior evinced in his personal life. Acts of violence, revenge, and sheer nastiness are rife in the author's books for children, including *Matilda*, *The Witches*, *The Twits*, and *James and the Giant Peach*—as well as in his adult fiction, in which sinister acts are often steeped in crude and disturbing misogyny. Yet if Roald saw himself as a tormented victim at school, some of his former Reptonian peers remembered him as a bully. In *Boy*, Roald is candid about the damaging effects of his boarding school days:

> By now I am sure you will be wondering why I lay so much emphasis upon school beatings in these pages. The answer is that I cannot help it. All through my school life I was appalled by the fact that masters and senior boys were allowed literally to wound other boys, and sometimes quite severely. I couldn't get over it. I never have got over it. It would, of course, be unfair to suggest that *all* masters were constantly beating the daylights out of *all* the boys in those days. They weren't. Only a few did so, but that was quite enough to leave a lasting impression of horror upon me.

It left another more physical impression upon me as well. Even today, whenever I have to sit for any length of time on a hard bench or chair, I begin to feel my heart beating along the old lines that the cane made on my bottom some fifty-five years ago.

In 1934, after Roald graduated from Repton, his mother hoped he would go to Oxford or Cambridge, but given his poor academic record there was no chance of that. He did not attend any university, regarding it as a waste of time. Instead, Roald opted for travel and adventure, deciding to work for the Shell Oil Company for £140 a year. Hoping to be based in Africa or Asia, he started off at the London office, where he kept on his desk a ball-in-progress, constructed from the silver wrappings of his daily postlunch chocolate bar. Four years later, the twenty-two-year-old finally got his wish for a posting abroad when he was sent to Dar es Salaam. Decades later, reflecting on his time there, Roald expressed a sense of shame about British imperialism in Africa. "It was only comfortable because we had masses of servants, which is not right," he said in a radio interview. "Of course, it's not right." In 1939, when the Royal Air Force came looking for wartime recruits, Roald eagerly signed up for duty. He believed the experience would be exciting, if nothing else, and he was keen to learn how to fly and shoot for free—but at six-foot-six, the dashing new fighter pilot had to crumple himself into the cockpit. He chronicled his RAF exploits during World War II—which proved exciting and dangerous beyond measure—in the suspenseful, entertaining, funny, and surprisingly poignant memoir *Going Solo*. On his first mission, he was forced to crash land in the Libyan desert, an episode that left him with a fractured skull, a smashed hip, and spinal injuries that would plague him for the rest of his life. The book's final scene describes a joyful return to his mother, who had fled Bexley to escape the bombing during the war and moved to a sixteenth-century thatched cottage in Buckinghamshire, about fifty miles northwest of London:

I caught sight of my mother when the bus was still a hundred yards away. She was standing patiently outside the gate of the cottage waiting for the bus to come along, and for all I knew she had been standing there when the earlier bus had gone by an hour or two before. But what is one hour or even three hours when you have been waiting three years?

I signalled the bus driver and he stopped the bus for me right outside the cottage, and I flew down the steps of the bus straight into the arms of the waiting mother.

Roald was not home for long. In January 1942, he was assigned a post as an assistant air attaché with the British Embassy in Washington, DC—where his colleagues included the embassy's information officer, (the future Sir) Isaiah Berlin, and where he befriended David Ogilvy, the future advertising mogul, and Ian Fleming, the future James Bond novelist. At that point, the thought of becoming a writer had never occurred to Roald, nor did he have any profession in mind. But with a chance meeting and a bit of luck, his literary career got off to an unlikely start.

While Roald was working in DC, the British novelist C. S. Forester was commissioned by the *Saturday Evening Post* to write a story about Roald's wartime adventures as a young pilot who had endured enemy fire, crash-landed in the Libyan desert, narrowly escaped the plane's flaming wreckage, and been "invalided" and discharged after suffering severe injuries. Roald was excited to meet a famous writer, especially having read all of Forester's books. Over a meal at a French restaurant, the novelist asked Roald to tell him the most frightening, exciting, or dangerous thing he had experienced as a fighter plane pilot and proceeded to take notes. But as Roald began to share his story, he realized it might be easier to write up some notes that evening and hand them off to Forester to rewrite as he wished and in his own time. He sat down that night to "put down the facts" with pencil and paper, and a glass of brandy by his side. "For the first time in my life," he later recalled, "I became totally absorbed in what I was doing." A few weeks later, he got a reply from Forester:

> Dear RD,
>
> You were meant to give me notes, not a finished story. I'm bowled over. Your piece is marvellous. It is the work of a gifted writer. I didn't touch a word of it. I sent it at once under your name to my agent, Harold Matson, asking him to offer it to the *Saturday Evening Post* with my personal recommendation.

The *Saturday Evening Post* accepted the piece, paid Roald well for it, and encouraged him to submit more stories to them. "I do hope you will," wrote Forester. "Did you know you were a writer?"

In DC, the young bachelor was flourishing socially, too. He came to the city to help represent British interests and serve as a liaison to representatives of Allied air forces, and women were drawn to him. In *The Irregulars: Roald Dahl and the British Spy Ring in Wartime Washington*, Jennet Conant chronicles his escapades—gathering intelligence for British higher-ups, including Winston Churchill, to influence American policy in England's favor and enjoying affairs with beautiful Georgetown society types. Among his conquests was Clare Boothe Luce, the wife of Time-Life owner Henry Luce. "I am all fucked out," Roald boasted to a friend, later seducing an oil heiress who was having an affair with Ian Fleming at the same time. He loved going to parties and found a father figure and patron in the newspaper magnate Charles Marsh, who was a few decades older. Roald was also invited to the White House, where he met the war correspondent Martha Gellhorn (who found Roald "very, very attractive and slightly mad") and her husband, Ernest Hemingway. He played poker with Senator Harry Truman, and he was introduced to Lillian Hellman.

In 1943, another happy accident occurred in relation to his writing. Walt Disney invited Roald to Hollywood, where he wanted to adapt a story Roald had published in *Cosmopolitan* magazine, "The Gremlins," as a full-length animated feature. The project fizzled out, but the twenty-six-year-old was put up in a luxury suite at the Beverly Hills Hotel and given a car to drive to the Disney studios each day. He got a consolation prize of sorts when his story was turned into a picture book, published in the United States by Random House. The book became a favorite of Eleanor Roosevelt, who read it to her grandchildren, and she invited Roald for dinner at the White House and subsequent weekend visits to the president's country home. The literary agent Ann Watkins signed up Roald as a client, and he went on to publish stories in the *Atlantic Monthly*, *Harper's*, and *Ladies' Home Journal*. (Watkins represented Ezra Pound, Carson McCullers, Frances Hodgson Burnett, and Ernest Hemingway, among others.) By 1945, having served the British Embassy followed by wartime intelligence work for the network of British Security Coordination (BSC), Roald had a clear vision of his future. It didn't involve furthering his education, working for the Shell Oil Company, or holding any proper office job. As he neared his thirtieth birthday, he knew he would make his living as a writer.

In 1946, after Alfred A. Knopf passed on the manuscript, Reynal & Hitchcock published *Over to You: Ten Stories of Flyers and Flying*, and Hamish Hamilton brought it out in England. Two years later, Roald wrote his first novel, *Some Time Never: A Fable for Supermen* (issued as *Sometime Never* by Collins in the UK), with the American edition published by Scribner's. But the editor who commissioned the book, the great Maxwell Perkins, died of viral pneumonia days after receiving the manuscript. Roald was devastated. He had wanted to be published by the man who discovered Fitzgerald and Hemingway. Scribner's released *Some Time Never* anyway, which depicted the end of the human race in the aftermath of a nuclear holocaust. The book was a flop. In a letter, Roald admitted to Ann Watkins that he felt "depressed about this writing business."

Roald's friend Charles Marsh swooped in to help by looping him in on some business dealings and even setting up a small trust for him. The help wasn't one-sided. Marsh had come to rely on Roald's excellent instincts to build his British antiques collection, and, with Roald's impeccable taste and knowledge of art, trusted the younger man to purchase paintings on his behalf—by Vuillard, Rouault, and others. Marsh referred to himself as Roald's "papa," and Roald once described Marsh, who died in 1964 at the age of seventy-seven, as his best friend.

Despite the recent disappointments with his work, Roald's career had by no means foundered. He was back in England when, in May 1949, after many rejections, he sold his first short story to the *New Yorker*. Roald clashed with the editor, Harold Ross, over proposed cuts and rewrites, and eventually, Ross backed down. With a few stories published in *Collier's* and another sold to the *New Yorker* in August 1951, Roald felt even more removed from the British literary establishment and unsure of his place in it. He had been unable to find a UK publisher for his second novel, which left him disheartened and drawn to the idea of living in New York. Marsh offered him a job working for his nonprofit foundation in Manhattan, secured a visa for him, and invited Roald to live in his townhouse on East 92nd Street rent-free. That's where Roald was staying the evening in 1952 when he met Patricia Neal.

As the two spent more time together, things were going well in their work lives, with Patricia immersed in *The Children's Hour* and looking forward to doing off-Broadway productions of *The Scarecrow* and *School for Scandal*, while Roald had drawn the interest of Alfred Knopf, who read one of his stories in the *New Yorker* and signed him up for a book of stories, *Someone Like You*, which was published to positive reviews in the fall of 1953. Patricia had already declined a casual proposal of marriage from Roald, but even if he was not earning much money and what she felt for him was not exactly love, "the complex Roald Dahl" was growing on her. "His intelligence and dependability made him very attractive," she recalled. "He was not the kind to stand me up. He had a charming and elegant side that I found captivating. And an absoluteness of judgment that was as fascinating as it was, at times, frightening. There was something very freeing about feeling someone strong at my side. Although I did not love him, I admired him deeply, and at that time in my life, admiration was more important than love." On June 16, 1953, Louella Parsons reported in her gossip column that Patricia Neal was "a very happy girl these days" with her constant escort, "Ronald" Dahl. "He's with Pat everywhere," Parsons wrote, "and she is again sparkling as she did when she first came to Hollywood." Patricia and Roald would marry in less than a month.

On May 23, 1953, Roald had written to his mother about the upcoming wedding: "She insists on a church, so if I can find one small enough and far enough away from the reporters etc., it'll be okay with me. . . . Charles has insisted on donating a huge yellow sapphire ring, about 20 carats, which is very decent of him." (The couple planned to travel to Italy and France for their honeymoon.) Three days later, he wrote to Patricia's mother:

Dear Mrs. Neal,

I know Pat has told you that she and I are now hoping to get married some time around the end of June, before we go to Europe, but I just wanted to write you myself and let you know how happy we are about it all, and how fortunate I think I am to be getting such a fine girl. It's going to be a bit strange to have a wife who earns more money than me, but that really isn't a problem and I'm confident that I'll always be able to support her myself with my own work whether she earns anything or not. After we return from Europe, and she goes on the road with the play [the touring production of *The Children's Hour*], I'll start looking around for a slightly cheaper, but also a larger, apartment and I hope you'll come and see us often when we're finally settled in.

Mentioning again his desire to evade press photographers for the wedding, he added, "maybe we can manage to be a bit secret about it when the time comes, and just slip in somewhere quietly with four or five friends at most." He ended the letter by saying, "All my sisters (4 of them) and my brother have been happily married for a long time now, so I'm hoping I can manage things as successfully as they. Pat seems happy and excited, and I certainly am."

She was neither happy nor excited and knew her fiancé "was not everyone's cup of tea." But Patricia was ready for marriage and she adored children, as did Roald. The troubled Dashiell Hammett, who had become a good friend, "was the first in a line of noteworthy prophets of doom where our forthcoming marriage was concerned," she recalled. The men argued one night at Hellman's and had not spoken since. "Don't marry him, Patsy, he's a horror," Hammett warned. "I can't understand why you're doing this." Leonard Bernstein took her aside one evening at Hellman's and whispered in her ear, "I really think you are making the biggest mistake of your life." She noticed that Roald was often rude, argumentative, and arrogant—perhaps a defensive response, stemming from insecurity over having never gone to university. At the dinner table, he was a master of one-upmanship and condescension, and, armed with his vicious misogynist streak, he took pleasure in telling inappropriate stories to shock female guests. Even in the early days of their relationship, Patricia knew that her future husband "seemed to feel he had the right to be awful and no one should dare counter him. Few did."

He disparaged the man who would become her agent and friend, Harry Orkin, complaining that Orkin was "loud-mouthed and Jewish." In the decades to come, Roald's antisemitism became uglier and more pronounced. In an interview in 1983, Roald told a journalist that "there's a trait in the Jewish character that does provoke animosity. . . . I mean there is always a reason why anti-anything crops up anywhere; even a stinker like Hitler didn't just pick on them for no reason." One night, in a drunken scene at London's Curzon House Club in 1979, Roald complained loudly that there were too many Jews in the club, with more insults about the restaurant's food. He was thrown out and his membership revoked.

Roald envied Patricia's success and her close friends, none more than the man who would make her heart ache for the rest of her life, Gary Cooper. "Whenever he saw his name in the paper he would question my feelings for Gary," she recalled. "I admitted that I loved Gary very much but hurried to add that our relationship could never have worked." Both things were true, yet it was also true that while Patricia was settling down for a "normal" life, it was not the one she wanted. "There's something in him I hate," she snapped to a friend after Roald behaved badly over dinner one night. Yet she vowed to remain faithful to Roald, and told herself that no matter what, there would no divorce. Love was irrelevant. Her commitment would be absolute.

She took solace in the off-Broadway plays she was appearing in, where she got to prove her mettle as a character actress and reunite with Eli Wallach and Anne Jackson, her friends from the Actors Studio. And she was impressed by a talented, good-looking young actor with a small dancing role: "I was sure James Dean had a great future ahead of him."

On July 2, 1953, Patricia and Roald were married at Trinity Church in Manhattan. She was twenty-seven, and he would turn thirty-seven in September. Back home that night with her husband, she cried in the dark. The next day, the *New York Times* issued a two-line announcement of their marriage with a headline that must have infuriated Roald:

## PATRICIA NEAL AND WRITER WED

Roald told Patricia on their wedding night that he loved her. This was to be the first of three times over the course of their thirty-year marriage that he would utter the words "I love you." On their honeymoon, Patricia learned that Roald found her nudity off-putting, and when he caught her preening in the mirror in their hotel room, he ordered her to put clothes on. (Gary Cooper had always loved the sight of her naked body.) Even though the marriage was off to a rocky start, Patricia believed Roald was the answer to all her problems. Over time, he would cause most of them.

Back in New York in the fall of 1953, the newlyweds settled into a two-bedroom rental near Central Park, planning to use the small second bedroom as a writing studio for Roald. He insisted that Pat sell off two of her paintings "because we could use the money." Patricia was earning more than her husband, but for Roald no amount of money seemed sufficient. "It was my money when we were [first] married," she said bitterly, decades later. "Roald didn't have any money at all." But she suspected that his controlling behavior was less about money than trying to make any evidence of her past (and past relationships) disappear. That might explain why he instructed her to sell a pair of diamond earrings Cooper had given her as a gift—but that was nonnegotiable. Rather than risk triggering her husband's temper, Patricia said she would consider it and Roald didn't bring it up again. But a few weeks later, after seeing a photograph in the newspaper of a smiling Gary and his wife, Patricia marched over to Harry Winston to sell the earrings. Upon learning from the jeweler that they were one of three pairs Gary had bought at the same time, she laughed and knew she had made the right decision.

On the Chicago stop of the traveling production of *The Children's Hour*, a young aspiring actor named Michael stopped by her hotel suite with a request. He had met her husband once and asked shyly whether Patricia might be willing to do a recording of one of Roald's stories for his theater group. The young man didn't strike her as talented, and she politely tried to discourage him. Seven years later, while she was in rehearsals as Helen's mother for *The Miracle Worker*—with Anne Bancroft as Anne Sullivan and Patty Duke as Helen Keller—the man came backstage to say hello. "I'm the fellow you told not to go into show business," said Mike Nichols, who was there with Elaine May.

While Patricia was on the road with *The Children's Hour*, she called her husband almost daily and spent the downtime in her dressing room knitting a scarf for him, knowing how much he loved cashmere. She returned home to hit another marital bump, but promptly swept it from her mind. It should have been another red flag. Roald mentioned that while she was gone, he had struck up a friendship with Gloria Vanderbilt. What did that mean? They met at a party, and the heiress was attracted to him, he said, but he claimed to have cooled things off right away by informing her that he was a married man. Why he was spending time with Vanderbilt in his wife's absence, he did not explain. It made no sense, but three months into her marriage, she trusted her husband, or had made up her mind to. Years later, Vanderbilt claimed that nothing physical had happened between her and Roald (though he supposedly tried to pull her into bed)—but she shared with Patricia the love letters Roald had written to her, detailing his fantasies about their relationship.

The first Christmas Patricia and Roald spent together further revealed incompatibility that would become glaring in the years to come. Over the summer, they had visited Roald's family at the end of their honeymoon, so they had agreed that the holiday would be spent with the Neals in Atlanta. During her England visit, Patricia was touched by how close the Dahls were, how magnetic and loving Roald was in the presence of children, and how much his mother doted on him—yet no one hugged or kissed Patricia to make her feel welcome, and Sofie came across as critical and stern. The new bride felt very much like an outsider. "We all sat down together to have our first meal," she recalled. "Nine sets of eyes were leveled at me."

Patricia might have guessed that visiting her family would not go over well with Roald, and he exceeded expectations. She had taken to his family even without a warm reception, but Roald did not bother to mask his contempt for hers. Finding them parochial and dull, he spent most of his time reading in the bedroom, appearing only at mealtimes (which he took as an opportunity to insult Eura's southern cooking). "My people were not rich and cultured in the way Roald appreciated," she recalled. "Mother and [Margaret] thought he was the rudest thing alive."

Not long after the Christmas trip, one night before bedtime Roald turned to his wife and, with no explanation, said he wanted a divorce. His demeanor was nonchalant, as though he'd asked for a cup of tea. They were less than eight months into their marriage. "But don't worry about it now," he added. "Just go to sleep." He rolled over and began to snore. A frantic Patricia left the apartment and wandered the streets all night, attempting to make sense of her marriage imploding and what might come next. "The fear of meeting violence on the dark city streets never occurred to me," she recalled. "Why was I so devastated? It was a loveless marriage, wasn't it?" She wed Roald hoping to find relief from the devastation of losing Gary, and to have the children she longed for. Yet she did find her husband extraordinary and did feel as though she needed him. She walked home at dawn, determined to fight for her marriage and make it work. Roald, saying his decision was not final, had a softer demeanor that morning and suggested his wife have a chat with Charles Marsh. Roald almost always kept his emotions to himself, but he often confided in his surrogate father. Among other marital problems, he told Marsh in a letter, was the issue of compatibility:

Whichever way I look at it and however hard I try to change my own mind, I still always come to the same conclusion— that I do not believe it is possible for us to live together in complete serenity. She is still far and away the nicest girl I know and is full of two great qualities—courage and honesty. But that doesn't necessarily mean that we shall feel comfortable and as it were complete in each other's company. It happens to be a fact that when we are alone together in the evenings I find myself feeling extremely uncomfortable because I keep wondering what she is going to do to amuse herself. I read. She doesn't. We talk a little—about theatrical people and the stage, but not much more than that. I know that she longs for the company of her own group of theatrical friends, who I cannot (although I have tried very hard) stand.

Patricia had a more hopeful perspective on her marriage, but privately she could admit certain things to be true: she was the breadwinner; her fame was emasculating; she was not a good housewife; her husband craved admiration; they did not love one another; the sex was great.

The couple separated briefly, and Marsh gave Patricia some simple advice: "You can make the money," he told her, "but Roald must handle it. Have one bank account and let him write the checks, and I guarantee you that your marriage will be fine." Additionally, he said, "You must do all the cooking. You must wash the dishes and do everything in the house. You must not lie in bed. You must work hard." Simply put, her domestic failures could not go on. Eura Neal had given her daughter similar advice: "Remember, Patsy, cooking meals and keeping a house is not a demeaning role but the privilege of a good wife, whether she works outside the home or not." For Roald, the model of an ideal wife was his mother, who ran a tight ship at home and devoted herself to nothing other than her children. He reported in a letter to Marsh that when Harald was alive, Sofie did what all good housewives do: "running a house, keeping it clean, and to a certain extent, serving the man." He was very disappointed to observe that "Pat is not able to bring herself to do this." He understood that his wife was "naturally absorbed in herself because she is a fine and successful actress, but I do not believe it is possible to be a successful wife and to be absorbed in yourself at the same time unless you are very clever indeed." Part of the problem was that when he was writing, his wife didn't seem to think he was doing anything. So she stayed in bed, talking on the phone, while he was forced to make the coffee and "get my own lunch out of a can of soup." All of this struck him as terribly wrong.

Patricia resolved to do better. Getting a joint bank account proved a wise decision and yielded immediate results: "Roald now felt he wore the pants in the family and that was all that mattered." He stopped giving her the silent treatment, as he had done for days at a time, and he was less rude with her friends. His spirits were lifted after learning that his macabre story collection, *Someone Like You*, was selling well for Knopf: the first print run of five thousand sold out in a week, and by April 1954, the book was in its fourth printing and a Book-of-the-Month Club selection. "If you want something good, get *People Like You*, I think it's called, by Roald Dahl," P. G. Wodehouse wrote in a March 21 letter to his friend Denis George Mackail, grandson of the artist Edward Burne-Jones. "I think he is a comer. He had a story in the *New Yorker* a week or two ago so good that I had to turn back and look at the cover to make sure this really was the *New Yorker* I was reading. I always thought a *New Yorker* story had to have no point whatsoever."

WITH HIS INTELLIGENCE AND WIT, ROALD CHARMED THE JOURNALISTS he met during his promotional tour for the book, and he won an Edgar Award from the Mystery Writers of America. Still, he continued to envy his wife's success and couldn't bear that she was the more famous half of the couple. It was her income from television, theater, and film that made it possible for him to keep working on his fiction at his own pace, without taking on a "proper" job—and he resented her for it. Worse, he was subjected to the ongoing humiliation of seeing his name misspelled in the press: Roger, Ronald, Raoul, and even Fouald. Most irksome was when he was not named at all but mentioned only as "the husband of Patricia Neal."

In the summer of 1954, the couple decided to buy a house in England, where they wanted to start spending their summers. His family found a Georgian fixer-upper farmhouse on five acres of land, called Little Whitefield (later known as Gipsy House, in accordance with the original deed). It had no electricity or central heating and was selling at auction for £4,500. Sofie paid for half of it, and Patricia paid for the rest from her savings. All the while, wanting more than anything to become a mother, Patricia kept playing the role of compliant wife—tidying the apartment, making breakfast for her husband, and taking on television work, along with two films, because Roald insisted they needed the money. She was also pregnant.

At the same time, Roald had written his first play, *The Honeys*, which was given a tryout tour in a few cities (New Haven, Philadelphia, and Boston), and starred Hume Cronyn and Jessica Tandy. The experience was not a happy one for Roald, but as ever, Patricia was a supportive spouse. "Although I always read his stories and gave him my two cents' worth, and he always evaluated the scripts offered to me," she recalled, "this was the first time he had crossed over the line into my territory, the theater, and he was having a perfectly dreadful time." A director was fired, Roald argued constantly with Cronyn, and new writers were brought in to rework the script. Then came a happy distraction.

Olivia Twenty Dahl was born in Manhattan on April 20, 1955. Roald flew to the hospital from Boston, where *The Honeys* was in production. He and Patricia named their daughter "Olivia" for the role Patricia played in *Twelfth Night* as an undergraduate at Northwestern, and "Twenty" for the date of the baby's birth—and the amount of daily expense money Roald was given during the tryout run of his play. Eight days after Olivia's birth, *The Honeys* opened on Broadway, but it was a failure and closed after thirty-six performances. While Roald sulked, Patricia got back to work: just days after leaving the hospital, she was asked to join the cast of a Broadway play, *A Roomful of Roses*, scheduled for the upcoming season. Although well received by critics, it was not a financial success. Still, Patricia was thrilled to be working again, exhausted but having a wonderful time. She had also reconnected with her peers at the Actors Studio, now under the leadership of Lee Strasberg, and began attending workshops again. She recalled that during one session, she sat near a young actor with the bluest eyes she had ever seen,

Paul Newman. Going back to work felt gratifying, but Patricia was especially proud of having become the wife her husband wanted her to be. "I rose early to bathe and feed my now six-month-old, walked her in the park, and did the shopping," she recalled. "I made breakfast and lunch for my husband, conferred with the nurse, cleaned the apartment, prepared supper, did the dishes and made it to the theater for an 8:30 curtain. And I made sure there was always plenty of time to discuss my husband's work with great appreciation."

Months later, the family moved to a much larger apartment at East 81st Street and Madison Avenue, and Patricia was back on Broadway for *Cat on a Hot Tin Roof*, directed by Elia Kazan, who invited her to be the lead in his next film, *A Face in the Crowd*, costarring Andy Griffith, Walter Matthau, and Lee Remick. "I wish I could feed her some magic pills that would rid her of this fierce driving ambition that all actresses seem to have," Roald grumbled in a letter.

Amid the busy work period, Patricia was pregnant again, and she, Roald, and Olivia returned to England so the baby could be born there. On April 11, 1957, nearly two years to the day of Olivia's birth, Chantal Sophia Dahl arrived in Oxford. Realizing the rhyme (and teasing potential) of her first and last name, Roald changed his daughter's name to Tessa. Settled in Great Missenden, Buckinghamshire, the family now identified as "country folk," Patricia said. On trips to London to see theater, they occasionally saw some of Patricia's visiting Hollywood friends, such as Bette Davis, but mostly life revolved around Roald's family and spending time at home.

Roald had a small cottage built on their property, which he used as a workshop for restoring antique mirrors. He also salvaged an old caravan from one of his sisters, which he turned into a playhouse for the children. He was a doting father, loved gardening (planting two hundred varieties of roses), and enjoyed adding beautiful furnishings and paintings to the house. He had a writing hut built in the apple and pear orchard, fifty yards from the house, where he worked daily from ten o'clock until noon and from 4 to 6 p.m. "Four hours a day," he once said, "is the creative maximum." He always wrote with a neatly sharpened Dixon Ticonderoga pencil on lined yellow paper. In a radio interview in 1970, he talked about the hut as an essential refuge from domestic life. "You become a different person," he said. "You are no longer an ordinary fellow who walks around and looks after his children and eats meals and does silly things. You go into a completely different world. I personally draw all the curtains in the room, so that I don't see out the window . . . Time disappears completely." He went on to describe the best artists as "ordinary people who have a secret compartment somewhere in their brain which they can switch on when they become quite alone and go to work."

On a side table in his hut, he kept the heavy (and still in progress) metallic ball of chocolate bar silver wrappings he started years ago at Shell Oil, as well as a jar containing bits of his own spine that were removed during an operation on his lower back. In the wintertime, with freezing temperatures outside, to keep himself warm Roald had an electric heater perilously rigged up to the ceiling with string. But no matter the weather, he stuck to his work routine, sitting in his wing chair, writing on a felt-covered lapboard he had made himself. His ashtray was always overflowing with cigarette butts, and the hut walls eventually turned sepia-stained from all the smoke. Now in his early forties, he had a striking resemblance to Virginia Woolf, Patricia recalled, "whom I always thought of as Roald Dahl in drag." Though he appeared rather shabby in his typical outfit of a striped shirt, cardigan, and gray trousers, Patricia noted that it was a "studied" look since the shirts were custom-made in Scotland, and the sweaters a fine cashmere.

It was left to Patricia to fund his sartorial preferences and much else. Luckily, she had steady work. Her next job was a BBC production of *The Royal Family*, enabling her to establish herself professionally in England. In September 1958, she was excited to make her West End debut, to great acclaim, in the role of Catherine Holly in the Tennessee Williams play *Suddenly Last Summer*. She later described it as the most thrilling acting experience of her life. The critic Kenneth Tynan, praising her "harrowing" performance, singled her out in his review in the *Observer*: "I must pause here to salute Patricia Neal, the American Method actress. The power and variety of her dark brown voice, on which she plays like a master of the cello, enable her to separate the cadenza from its context and make of it a plangent cry from the depths of memory." She was devastated to learn that Elizabeth Taylor was given her role in the film adaptation. But she started to pick up quality television projects in the States, along with more BBC work, and was relieved that her income was on the rise. As she later recalled, "Roald's writing was not yet pulling in very much." Over the next two years, he received multiple rejections from the *New Yorker*, which left him depressed. He sold some stories to *Playboy*, causing tension with Alfred Knopf, who disapproved of the unsavory magazine. But Roald kept busy working on what would become his first book for children, *James and the Giant Peach*, and in February 1960, Knopf published another collection, *Kiss Kiss*. The stories were grisly, malicious, and cruel. (Of Roald's adult fiction, Noël Coward once noted, "The stories are brilliant, and the imagination is fabulous. Unfortunately, there is, in all of them, an underlying streak of cruelty and macabre unpleasantness and a curiously adolescent emphasis on sex.") Regardless, *Kiss Kiss* became a *New York Times* bestseller and was well received in the UK, but Roald felt ignored by the English literary establishment, and believed he did not get the recognition from his country that he deserved. It was a chip on his shoulder for years to come. Foreign rights to *Kiss Kiss* were sold in Italy, Germany, Japan, and elsewhere.

On July 30, 1960, Patricia gave birth to her third child, Theo Matthew Roald Dahl. Over the next five years, Roald would publish two of the most popular novels in the history of children's literature and establish himself as one of the greatest and most imaginative writers for children of all time. During this period too, he and his family would face catastrophic suffering, grief, trauma, and loss.

Patricia and Roald adored their children—she described her husband as "a very maternal daddy"—and for Roald, becoming father to a son was particularly meaningful, having lost his own father so young. They were comfortable living on Manhattan's Upper East Side, with Roald using the apartment above, owned by the playwright Clifford Odets, as his writing space. They would return to England each summer and go on holiday in Norway, which they had established as a beloved family tradition. Raising the children had brought the couple closer, and at times Patricia felt genuine love for her husband. Olivia and Tessa were enrolled in a neighborhood preschool, and their mother was working steadily. By late fall, she finished filming a role in the movie *Breakfast at Tiffany's*, directed by Blake Edwards. Roald was generally less grumpy, having sold *James and the Giant Peach* to Knopf, and already completed a draft of a story he had been telling Olivia and Tessa, "Charlie's Chocolate Boy."

On December 5, 1960, the Dahls' nanny was pushing Theo in his pram along Madison Avenue and bringing Tessa home for lunch. When the light changed at East 85th Street, the nanny pushed the pram off the curb and was about to cross the street when a taxicab careened around the corner, crashing into the pram and hurling it forty feet into the side of a bus, with Theo still inside. His head was shattered. Patricia, shopping at a nearby grocery store, heard police sirens but did not know they were for her son. An ambulance rushed the infant to the emergency room at Lenox Hill Hospital, where he was expected to die. "The hours that followed were simply hell," Patricia recalled.

She and Roald kept a steady vigil at the hospital, and after a series of frightening complications caused by hydrocephalus (an accumulation of cerebrospinal fluid within the brain), Theo clung to life. His survival was a most miraculous gift for Patricia's thirty-fifth birthday on January 20, 1961, and by Easter, when her son smiled back at her, the worst seemed over. But Patricia and Roald were in a perpetual state of anxiety. Theo required constant attention, and the relapses he suffered were terrifying. A neurosurgeon placed a shunt in Theo's brain to help drain the excess cerebrospinal fluid and reroute it into a vein to be dispersed into the bloodstream. However, the tube's one-way valve kept clogging, resulting in scary episodes of fever, temporary blindness, and additional operations for Theo. Roald's relentless curiosity, knack for invention, and controlling nature proved a virtue as never before. Obsessed by the faulty valve and determined to develop a better, clog-proof device for his son, he worked alongside a neurosurgeon and a hydraulic engineer to invent what is now known as the Wade-Dahl-Till (WDT) valve. He had always been fascinated by medicine, and said that if he were not a writer, he would have been a doctor.

On top of caring for Theo, there were medical bills in the thousands of dollars, work to keep up with, and Olivia and Tessa to care for as well. Now more than ever, convinced that New York was not the right place to raise his family, Roald yearned for the comfort of Buckinghamshire and proximity to his family. Their cottage in Great Missenden seemed like the safest and most peaceful place in the world, and they returned to their country refuge by the summer of 1961. That year, *James and the Giant Peach* was published by Knopf, but in yet another snub by the London publishing world, no UK house wanted it. In the States, *James* was a modest success. "The book contains many words too difficult for 8- to 10-year-olds to read, but when read aloud by an adult with a dramatic sense, it will be received with rapt attention," wrote the critic Aileen Pippett in the *New York Times*. Roald dedicated the book to Olivia and Tessa.

As they adjusted to their insular life in Great Missenden, Patricia's love for Roald deepened. She was pleased to see her husband in his element—writing, gardening, refinishing his antique frames, and above all, caring tenderly for their son. "Theo was a centering force," she recalled, "not only for Roald and me but for our daughters as well." In an interview with *Housewife* magazine, she expressed her fondness for this "sleepy, leafy place," and said she was proud to be a good wife—her husband's "best and truest friend." With work being less of a priority, she refused to be away from her family for an extended period of time. "I was glad I had fought for this marriage," she recalled in her memoir. "I had not become the greatest actress in the world, but I had not been deprived of a career of some stature." Apart from a television play costarring Jason Robards Jr. that would take her to New York for a few weeks before Christmas, and a lead role in another BBC project, Patricia felt as though she was in early retirement. She had no regrets.

As Patricia kept busy being "mother, mistress, and manager at Little Whitefield," Roald adhered to his work schedule of two hours in the morning and two hours in the afternoon. He rigged up a wire to the light inside his writing hut, connecting it to a button outside the back door to the main house. Patricia would press it to summon her husband: one flash indicated a visitor, a phone call, or her need to speak with him. Two flashes was an emergency. Otherwise, he was not to be disturbed.

In the fall of 1962, Theo had made remarkable progress—enough that there was no need to use the WDT valve, yet his father's invention would be used to treat pediatric head injuries around the world, helping thousands of other children. Theo still struggled with his balance, but his speech improved and his parents saw him as a happy and adorable child. As Patricia recalled, it had been a "glorious" year all around: Olivia and Tessa were content at school, and Roald had submitted his manuscript for *Charlie and the Chocolate Factory* to his editor, Virginie Fowler. ("If she doesn't like it then I guess we will throw it away," he told his agent.) The Dahl home became known locally as a magical place for their friends to visit. In addition to the old-fashioned caravan set up in the garden, where the children could play, the girls' eccentric father was popular for handing out sweets to visitors.

One day in November, Olivia came home with a note from the school headmistress, notifying parents of a measles outbreak. Although there was no generic measles vaccine in the UK at the time, Roald knew that a gamma globulin injection could boost the children's immunity.

With his vulnerable immune system, Theo was given the shot, but a physician reassured Patricia that it would be fine to let Tessa and Olivia get the measles. "It will be good for them." Both girls did, and a few days later, Olivia had a fever and was covered in spots. She was lethargic, even as Roald tried to comfort her. A doctor made a house call, examined Olivia, and assured her alarmed parents that the illness was taking its usual course. Two days later, after falling unconscious and being rushed to a local hospital, Olivia died from measles encephalitis, a rare complication, at the age of seven. Whereas Theo's tragic accident had galvanized Roald into action to save his son's life, and to care for him in recovery, there was nothing he could do for Olivia. She was gone. "I wish we'd had a chance to fight for her," he wrote in a letter.

After the death of Olivia, Roald lost his will to live. Patricia, too, was shattered and could not help wondering whether God was punishing her for aborting her child with Gary Cooper. For Roald, the trauma was compounded by the memory of his sister Astri's death, also at the age of seven, from appendicitis. "Pat and I are finding it rather hard going still," he wrote in a letter to Alfred Knopf on February 4, 1963. Despite "that Nordic strain of deep restraint," as his wife called it, by April, Roald had to admit that he was absolutely incapable of writing: "I feel right now as though I'll never in my life do any more! I simply cannot seem to get started again." He shut down in every way. Olivia had been his favorite child, and he made Tessa feel that she would never measure up. Already traumatized after having witnessed her brother's accident, Tessa was made to feel like "a poor understudy, a very inferior replacement" by her father, as she recalled decades later: "'Why can't you be like her?' he screamed. I wet my bed. Tried hard to be someone else and 'they'— although I really mean my father—upped my medication. So I could not process grief or sadness or pain or any of the other natural emotions I should have had."

Rather than undergo family therapy, which Roald considered nonsense, he buried emotions and gave Tessa medication to deal with hers.

"Thus medicated, I plodded on," she recalled. "I had sleeping medicine too. Syrup in an Alice-like bottle." Finding her way in the family was a constant struggle, and Tessa was labeled as the fractious problem child. She had no sense of psychological safety: "Surrounded by sickness, brain injury and the knowledge that you were noticed only if you were very ill or dying—but better still dead. Also, knowing that any discomfort could be removed with medication, from Dad."

After Olivia's death, Roald and Patricia were toppled by a "landslide of anger and frustration," but Patricia had a different way of coping than her husband. She did as much as possible at all times, "like a mad-woman." No acting job was beneath her, and all household chores were worth tackling. She feared that if she did not keep her family going, emotionally and financially, they were doomed.

She took on a TV job strictly for the money, an episode of a popular medical series that paid well and covered the expenses for her family to fly out to Hollywood. "We feel like we have been living the Book of Job," Patricia told the columnist Louella Parsons. "Tragedy has welded us together. We don't want to be apart even for a short time."

Next, she landed a film role she was excited about. With just twenty-two minutes of screen time in the Western drama *Hud*, starring Paul Newman, she was unprepared for the critical raves about her perfor-mance when the movie opened in wide release on May 29, 1963. "Miss Neal, with her lovely mezzo voice and, one might say, lovely mezzo eyes, gives a performance of wit, womanliness, and reticent dignity," wrote Stanley Kauffmann in the *New Republic*.

*Hud* was a box office hit and nominated for seven Academy Awards, winning three, including Patricia Neal for Best Actress. She also received awards from the New York Film Critics Circle, the British Academy Film Awards (known as the BAFTAs), and the National Board of Review. "Not only did my whole industry think I was good enough," she recalled, "but now, finally, a fabulous new career was just around the corner. And we'd make a fortune." Film and theater offers began to roll in, and her career seemed to have reached its pinnacle. Roald was thriving, too, with the publication of *Charlie and the Chocolate Factory*. The first printing of ten thousand copies sold out within a month. (The 1972 follow-up, *Charlie and the Great Glass Elevator*, was also a best-seller.) Although children adored Roald—he received hundreds of fan letters each week—some adults complained about the nastiness in his work. Roald was unrepentant and dismissive of the criticism. "Some librarians order 40 copies of my books," he said in an interview, "but there's a certain bunch of American lady librarians who flay me for what they consider the violence in my children's stories. Silly bitches have no sense of humor."

*Charlie and the Chocolate Factory* also proved controversial for the depiction of the Oompa-Loompas. Transported from Africa to run the factory, singing and dancing as they worked, and subjected to scientific experiments, these characters were slammed as racist stereotypes, and the NAACP called for a ban on the upcoming film.

The biggest blessing of all for the couple was Patricia's pregnancy. (She was unable to attend the Academy Awards ceremony because it came a month before her due date.) On May 12, 1964, Ophelia Magdalena Dahl was born, and for the first time in a long time, Patricia felt lucky. With two catastrophic events behind her, she believed, once again, the worst was over. That fall, in an interview with *Parade* magazine, she talked about counting her blessings in her career, while her husband offered his own take: "She's not obsessed by her career," he said. "She's far more interested in her home and her children. And that's why she's content to live tucked away in a village in England." He went on, oblivious to how his wife might feel: "Most American girls are proudly independent and rebellious, and when I first married Pat I thought it would be difficult to train her, but it hasn't been," he said. "In England, you know, a family is lost if a woman is allowed to take charge of everything, and I think the American wife is very much inclined to do this. It makes her miserable. She would much prefer not to, but she can't help it, because so many American husbands abrogate their rights and duties. I do not. Pat does all the cooking, and we have a nanny to help with the children when Pat's filming."

After Ophelia was born, Patricia took on her next film job, *In Harm's Way*, costarring John Wayne, Kirk Douglas, and Henry Fonda. The director, Otto Preminger, paid for the whole family to join Patricia on the shoot in Honolulu. It lasted just seventeen days, and Patricia was amused to have made a great sum of money so easily. They returned home to Great Missenden in time for Christmas, with her next project already lined up.

On Valentine's Day 1965, Patricia began work on the John Ford movie *Seven Women* for Metro-Goldwyn-Mayer. The Dahls relocated to Los Angeles for the shoot, renting Martin Ritt's Pacific Palisades home while he was away in Ireland. Patricia was thirty-nine years old and pregnant with her fifth child. "Time was running out and I wanted all the children I could have," she recalled. The project came just as Roald received news that Chatto & Windus had rejected *Charlie and the Chocolate Factory*. It was another slap in the face from British publishing, where he seemed unable to get any respect. As Patricia stayed busy in a whirlwind of rehearsals, costume fittings, and catching up with friends in Hollywood, Roald worked on a story that he would sell to *Playboy* after it was rejected by the *New Yorker*. "The Last Act" shows him at his most malevolent, imagining a gynecologist who rapes a widowed menopausal woman whom the doctor had once been in love with. It later appeared in Roald's 1974 book *Switch Bitch*—a collection of stories with a vengeful, nasty take on sex. In any case, "The Last Act" is a rather interesting window into Roald's apparent frame of mind at the time: bitter, anxious, and full of fury.

On February 17, after filming her first big scene in *Seven Women*, Patricia returned home in the evening, drank a martini, and went upstairs to bathe Tessa. A few minutes later, Patricia called out to say that she had a pounding headache, and that she was hallucinating and feeling queasy. Roald helped her into bed. While he was on the phone seeking advice from the neurosurgeon with whom he had developed the WDT valve, his wife lost consciousness. As Patricia later learned, she had two strokes and was admitted to the intensive care unit at the UCLA Medical Center, where she suffered her largest cerebral hemorrhage and lapsed into a coma "like an immense vegetable." United Press Syndicate (UPI) ran her obituary on the wires, and a number of newspapers picked up the story. "If we operate she will probably not survive," the doctor told Roald, who asked what would happen if they did not operate. "Then she will die for certain," he replied. Roald gave his consent to move forward, and at midnight, a medical team attempted to save Patricia's life with a seven-hour-long operation to remove the blood clots from her brain and stop the hemorrhaging from a broken blood vessel. "I'm not sure if I've done you a favor," the lead surgeon told Roald afterward.

Ten days later, Roald wrote a rather clinical report to his eighty-year-old mother in a letter, giving a blunt play-by-play of the emergency and Patricia's subsequent condition. "This morning's spinal tap showed the fluid becoming far clearer and less bloody," he wrote. "And now all we can do is wait and see." She opened her eyes occasionally, and her face appeared "normal." Noting that "the hemisphere where the bleeding took place is the speech control," he speculated that there could be permanent damage, but "that, of course, is looking far ahead. The first thing is to get her back to consciousness."

On March 10, 1965, Patricia awoke from her coma with aphasia, blurred vision, and paralysis on her right side. When receiving visitors, including Lillian Hellman, Cary Grant, and John Ford, she smiled but did not quite know who they were. Intensive physical therapy began immediately, and each day a needle was inserted into Patricia's back to draw spinal fluid for testing. Roald stayed at his wife's bedside, determined that she would walk and talk again. The friends he permitted to visit had been alarmed at the sight of Roald shouting in his wife's ear, and even slapping her in the face, to provoke a response.

A month after going to the hospital, Patricia could bend her leg and she had regained her voice, but only through song. With a friend, she sang "Oh My Darling, Clementine," and a few other favorites. On the evening of March 17, Patricia was released from the UCLA Medical Center, wearing an eye patch and a brace on her right leg. "The doctors didn't believe she had a chance," Hedda Hopper reported in her gossip column. "It's possible that she may have a full recovery."

Two days later, alongside a piece on the escalation of the war in Vietnam, with the landing of US combat troops, the *Los Angeles Times* ran a front-page article, "Patricia Neal, Partly Paralyzed, Five Months Pregnant, Husband Says," accompanied by a large photo of a smiling eight-year-old Tessa Dahl, holding her ten-month-old sister, Ophelia. In the article, Roald, "breaking a month-long silence concerning Miss Neal's condition," praised the lifesaving care his wife had received at the hospital—"Neurosurgery of the very highest order, swiftly and meticulously accomplished"—but said it was too soon to know whether his wife would fully recover and have the baby. Yet he described "a lot of laughter and excitement" at home as Patricia was reunited with her children, and said she was "exceedingly cheerful" and "fully able to comprehend and obey orders." He added that a nurse was staying at their temporary house in Pacific Palisades. Speech and physiotherapists would visit regularly until the family returned to England.

Patricia was inundated with hundreds of well-wishes, flowers, and gifts from friends in Hollywood and beyond, including Judy Garland and Frank Sinatra, and even a wire from her former elementary school classmates in Knoxville, Tennessee. The director Robert Altman, who had once invited Roald to write a screenplay with him (though the film was never made), came over to cook a meal for the family. Mel Brooks and Anne Bancroft invited Patricia and Roald over to their house just a week after Patricia's release from the hospital. "We expected Pat to arrive in a wheelchair," Brooks reported to Louella Parsons for her column, "but Pat was walking and got around unaided all over the house." She could not follow a word of the conversation all evening, but was pleased to be among friends.

Despite Roald's sunny portrayal of family life to the *Los Angeles Times*, the reality was different. Patricia was lethargic, depressed, exhausted, and lonely. Once, when she tried to reach for Ophelia, her hand would not cooperate, and the infant howled in terror. Patricia burst into tears as the nanny picked up Ophelia to soothe her.

Even the smallest, most ordinary actions proved a monumental struggle for Patricia—getting a drink of water, slipping on a sweater, brushing her teeth—and she was frustrated by her dependence on others. Some visitors spoke to her in baby talk, which made her furious. At times, she wished herself dead. Later she recalled her despair: "The fog of unconsciousness that held you prisoner from the outside world was, in fact, a blessing in disguise," she wrote in her autobiography. "First you're like a soul with no body, but the soul is drugged. Then the soul awakens into a body you cannot command. You are a prisoner in a private hell. Everybody is just pushing you around. They push your arms and your legs, your body. They say things, shout things, look at you with expectation, and you don't know what they want."

The Neal-Dahl marriage had entered a new phase, wherein the husband became bully, tormentor, and protector, and the wife patient, warrior, and victim. When Patricia wanted something, Roald would place the object just beyond her reach and withhold it until she was able to say the correct word. Her syntax was jumbled, and even when she knew the name of something, she was not always able to utter it. (She could not recall her husband's name and took to calling him Papa, after Hemingway.) Friends who saw her around this time described Roald in various ways—dog trainer, stage manager, drill sergeant, traffic cop—as he goaded and humiliated his wife into recovery, step by step. When Eura finally came to stay with them, moving into the guest house, she was appalled to witness Roald's imperiousness toward her daughter, but said nothing. Patricia knew better than to expect sympathy or tenderness from her husband. He was adamant about not giving her any "special treatment"—no matter that she was pregnant, recovering from her stroke, and half-paralyzed. At night, needing the bathroom, Patricia would scoot along the floor in the dark, awkwardly hoist herself onto the toilet seat, and struggle to use her left hand to flush. She dared not disturb her snoring husband for help. In the mornings, she learned to wake by herself at 7:30, get dressed, put on her leg brace and shoes, and make her way downstairs.

Roald had an obsessive approach to Patricia's recovery. One day, when he brought tea to her and an old friend, the actress Gloria Stroock, he spoke to his wife in "a hard, emotionless tone," badgering his wife to ask for sugar, as Stroock recalled: "I must say I admired his fierce, unrelenting approach, but as I left, I could not help but think it reminded me of the way one trains a dog. Sugar? Sugar? You say sugar and you get a pat on the head. I wondered if the Patricia Neal I had known could submit to that."

If his methodology was punitive, it was also effective: Patricia later recalled that after Theo suffered brain damage, Roald decided that his son would not fall behind developmentally, and sure enough, the boy—having undergone eight operations—was reading beautifully at four and a half. She took inspiration from Theo, "an active and outgoing child, undeniable proof of the brain's magic gift for healing." Rather than being perplexed or frightened by his mother's newly strange and limited vocabulary, Theo appeared delighted to watch his mother learning her ABCs. One day, while Patricia was working with her speech therapist, Theo bounded into the room with his flash cards and began to quiz his mother: SISTER, CAKE, ORANGE, TROUSERS. But while Theo had found a playmate on whom to practice matching pictures with object names, Tessa suffered from trauma. "In our family," she later recalled, "you got attention only if you were brain-damaged or dead or terribly ill. There was no reward for being normal." Scarred by the knowledge that Olivia had been the love of her father's life, and that both girls got measles but only Olivia died, Tessa recounted decades later, in a 2012 interview with the *Daily Mail*: "In 24 hours [my mother] went from being a ravishing, glorious movie star to a monster with no hair, tubes coming out of each orifice and unable to speak," she said. "After she came round from her coma, Dad took me to see her, without any warnings. I was horrified but said nothing. I fed her but expressed no real emotion. I was petrified. We drove away from the hospital and never spoke of it."

It was impossible to remember a time when the family had not lived in a state of crisis—first Theo, then Olivia, and now Patricia. Along with managing the stress of each day, the family was drowning in monthly expenses in California, with debts piling up to the point that Roald feared their savings would be wiped out. To bring in extra money, he took on a journalism assignment he did not want, writing about his wife's illness for the September 1965 issue of *Ladies' Home Journal* (with the dramatic cover line "Patricia Neal's Struggle to Live"). By mid-May, after doctors determined that Patricia was well enough to travel, it was time to return to England. In a piece that appeared on the wires on May 14, Roald made a bold announcement: "She's going to walk on the plane, and she won't need any help. We're going to have a short press conference so everyone can judge for himself how well she's recovered." (Cary Grant drove the Dahls to the airport.)

Upon landing at Heathrow, Patricia was overwhelmed by the welcome she received. The reception area was packed with photographers, hundreds of fans, and family and neighbors there to embrace her. She sobbed with joy and relief. At home in Great Missenden, baskets of flowers and homemade food arrived for Patricia, and she recalled that neighbors, helpers, and friends kept saying how beautiful she looked—but one later confessed to Patricia that she had been startled by the sight of her and wept after leaving. It was painful for anyone to see Patricia, iconic star of stage and screen, wearing an eye patch, face fallen, haggard, and inexpressive. "There was no way to put lipstick on," she recalled. "I couldn't find my mouth."

With terrier-like tenacity, Roald subjected Patricia to a brutal regime of six-hour-long lessons daily with a rotating team of volunteers. Despite being advised by doctors that one hour a day of rehabilitation would be sufficient, and that more might prove harmful, Roald ignored their guidance. "Surely one hour a day is not enough," he said later. "What in the world are you going to teach a child if she only goes to school for an hour a day? That is what Pat was like then—a child. She didn't even know her ABCs." Fearing his wife would become an "enormous pink cabbage," he set about creating his own program, overseeing it like a sadistic puppeteer. "Unless I was prepared to have a bad-tempered, desperately unhappy nitwit in the house," he said, "some very drastic action would have to be taken at once."

Constant stimulation was the key to keeping her motivated. Idleness would have a deleterious effect on her recovery, so she was not allowed to "sit and stare," as she later recalled. Hard work alone would save her, Roald said, and he made her life a boot camp, with reading, writing, and spelling lessons and rehabilitation exercises filling her days nonstop. She was learning how to cook again, do basic arithmetic, and play simple games such as dominoes and tic-tac-toe. No one was permitted to "rescue" Patricia by helping her navigate a flight of stairs or step out of a car. Roald showed no mercy as his wife struggled for words, lost her train of thought, and read like a toddler. Each day he would assess her progress in quantitative terms: she was forty-two percent better than yesterday, and fifty-one percent better than the previous week. He was not nursing his wife back to health so much as forcing her to get well. "God, I was so sick of his percentages, his plans, his programs, his world," Patricia recalled. "He was a hero, and I was hating him." Roald was repelled by her sorrow, regarding it as a sign of weakness and self-indulgence. It was something to be conquered, or at least ignored. "Daddy got so caught up in making things better," Tessa once recalled in an interview. "He used to say, 'You've got to get on with it.' . . . He used to shout, 'I want my children to be brave.'"

Six years later, in a lecture at the Speech Rehabilitation Institute, Roald defended his harsh tactics. "When you're talking about real life as opposed to vegetable life, you're in a crisis and you don't stop to enquire whether the patient is comfortable or not," he said. "Nothing was smooth or easy. In fact, at one time I took [Patricia] to a psychiatrist to make sure she didn't intend to carry out her threats of suicide." (What Roald failed to mention, however, was his cruel response to Patricia at the time: "We've got knives that will do you up fine," he said, laughing. "And there are my razor blades. Or else you can lock yourself in the car and turn on the engine.")

Still in her thirties, Patricia had lost her eldest child, her career, her independence, and her beauty. She had surrendered her roles as wife and mother. Roald's dominance was absolute: he severed ties to their life in New York by giving up the Manhattan apartment. He had an extension built onto Gipsy House for the new household staff, drove the children to school each day, and arranged play dates. He chose the wine for supper and planned meals with the cook. No one needed Patricia. She was made to feel like an outsider in her own family, and the children, deprived of a mother in good health, turned to Daddy for play, security, comfort, everything. Patricia worried that between having the nanny and Roald, Ophelia did not even know Patricia was her mother. One of the lowest points came when she overheard Roald tell the children that Mummy could do things for them if only she *wanted* to.

On August 4, 1965, six months after an artery burst open in Patricia's brain, Lucy Neal Dahl was born. Both mother and daughter were healthy and fine. In the delivery room with Roald was a journalist, Barry Farrell, and a photographer, both from *Life* magazine to cover the big event. Four years later, Farrell would turn his article into a book, *Pat and Roald*, published by Random House and accompanied by intimate photographs of the family. (The cover of the ninety-five-cent mass market Dell paperback featured an illustration of a smiling Patricia with the tagline, "The magnificent story of a woman's triumph—the moving human drama of Patricia Neal and the man she loved, the child she bore, and the career she saved.")

News of the birth hit the wires quickly, with the media calling Lucy "the miracle baby." (And she was, really.) Roald was attentive, if not affectionate, while visiting Patricia daily in her small, flower-filled room to help her write thank-you letters and ensure she was well cared for. Before leaving the hospital, Patricia at last had the brace removed from her right leg. She was able to walk unaided, slowly and haltingly, with Roald behind her, sternly urging her along, step by step, like a military commander. Back home, Patricia was tutored each day by a local acquaintance, Valerie Eaton Griffith, who would become a dear friend. These sessions proved transformative. When they met, Patricia's vocabulary was limited to strange words and phrases—cold coffee was "evil," and she would "jake my dioddles" if she couldn't have a cigarette. (Taking careful notes, Roald later used some of his wife's lingo in his 1982 book *The BFG*.) Often Patricia would give up and say, "My mind is gone." Valerie understood how lonely, vulnerable, and beaten down Patricia felt: "You were not getting the respect of a normal human being," she told her. Patiently and lovingly, she helped Patricia learn again how to handle money, solve crossword puzzles, express herself, and bring herself back to life. Patricia was getting sharper by the day. At this point, she almost had no choice—apart from being a famous actress, she had also become Trauma Survivor, someone "whose progress was important to the morale of others," she recalled. Every week, newspapers and magazines from around the world wanted to interview this inspiring marvel of human resilience. Letters flooded in too, not just from friends but from fans who offered support, wanted advice, or requested an autograph. She was pleased to use her typewriter again, slowly tapping out letters with her left hand. "Imagine my long-awaited pleasure when I pecked out, 'DEAR SIR LAURENCE. THANK YOU FOR YOUR KIND LETTER,'" she recalled in her memoir.

Patricia won a BAFTA for Best Actress in a Leading Role for *In*

*Harm's Way*, and she made the difficult trip to London to attend the ceremony and accept the award in person. At home, she still felt as though she had no authority, but at least she could read to her children again and play with them. Although there were no arguments with Roald, "this was primarily because I did everything he told me without question." On New Year's Day 1966, he announced to the press that his wife said she felt confident about working again within the year. (She had not said that.) With her weak memory, Patricia knew she could not possibly remember lines, and she still walked with a bad limp. She resented the pressure from her husband to return to work. Meanwhile, as Roald neared his fiftieth birthday, apart from the strict household supervision, his singular focus was on making money—lots of it—which he achieved after being hired to write the screenplay for the next James Bond film, *You Only Live Twice.* He was paid more than Patricia had earned in her entire career, and his drafts were sent to London via a chauffeur-driven Rolls-Royce.

In 1967, Patricia made her first big public speaking debut at a fundraiser for brain-injured children at the Waldorf Astoria in New York ("An Evening with Patricia Neal"), where she was to deliver a fifteen-minute speech. She didn't want to do it and did not think she could, but with Roald's bullying and Valerie's gentle coaxing, she practiced and practiced until she could give the speech with fluency and confidence. At the Waldorf, Patricia was amazed to find flowers and messages filling her suite, and within a few days she did dozens of interviews with journalists eager to inquire about her comeback. Before Patricia spoke at the dinner, Rock Hudson introduced her to a standing ovation, and when she finished her remarks, many in the audience wept and cheered for her. Overjoyed by the response, she realized then that "Roald the slave driver, Roald the bastard, with his relentless scourge, Roald the Rotten, as I had called him more than once, had thrown me back into the deep water. Where I belonged."

In the spring of 1968, Patricia began filming *The Subject Was Roses*, based on the Pulitzer Prize–winning play by Frank Gilroy and costarring Martin Sheen (playing her son) and Jack Albertson as her husband. What felt like an embarrassment of riches—she adored her supportive costars, who assured her that she could not fail—was compounded by more good fortune: Katharine Hepburn, whom she admired, heard from mutual friends how much Patricia wanted to meet her, so she paid a surprise visit to the grateful and delighted fan.

Once production was underway for *The Subject Was Roses*, photographers and TV cameras followed Patricia on the shoot and would not leave her alone. She did interviews for magazines, newspapers, television, and radio. Having become a spokeswoman for other stroke victims— some in wheelchairs, others learning to walk or talk again—she felt obliged to talk with reporters. Patricia wanted to show the world that it was possible to thrive, and to recover one's former self, after a harrowing medical ordeal. She had survived a stroke that nearly killed her. Now she was a film star again. When *The Subject Was Roses* premiered in New York on October 13, 1968, Patricia entered the theater with Roald to a standing ovation. The film received mixed reviews after its release, but Vincent Canby of the *New York Times* wrote that Patricia "gives the movie an emotional impact it wouldn't otherwise have." She was nominated for an Academy Award for Best Actress.

That year Roald met Robert Gottlieb, the new head of Knopf. (In his 2016 memoir, *Avid Reader*, Gottlieb called out Roald, along with V. S. Naipaul, as "a first-rate writer whom I came to dislike.") Although Gottlieb was not an editor of children's books, he had to take on Roald after it became clear that the arrogant author would not work with anyone lower on the totem pole. Even though Gottlieb enjoyed spending time with "the tremendous charmer," and "even more, his beautiful and tragic wife," he was stunned by Roald's abusiveness toward the staff: "So demanding and rude that no one wanted to work with him," Gottlieb recalled in his book. "Secretaries were treated like servants, tantrums were thrown both in person and in letters, and when Bob Bernstein, as head of Random House, didn't accede to his immoderate and provocative financial demands, we sensed antisemitic undertones." After years of Roald's "erratic and churlish" behavior, a contract dispute, and the author's threats to leave Knopf, Gottlieb terminated the relationship with a don't-let-the-door-hit-you-on-the-way-out letter, signing off "Regretfully, Bob." The irascible author may have been good for the company's bottom line, but he was impossible to deal with. "No matter how you spin it, Roald Dahl was an absolute sod," the British journalist Kathryn Hughes once wrote. "Crashing through life like a big, bad child, he managed to alienate pretty much everyone he ever met."

Although the release of *The Subject Was Roses* was a moment of great triumph for Patricia, she felt shaky much of the time and still had a faulty memory. Once she called her friend Paul Newman to congratulate him on his latest film and said, "Oh, what *is* your name?" when he picked up the phone. She did not work for another three years, and told reporters that she considered herself a mother and housewife—albeit one with a cook, a maid, and a secretary who also served as her driver. Meanwhile, Roald checked out of their marriage in ways both subtle and overt. Patricia felt less like his wife than one of the children, all competing for Daddy's attention. She often made candid and unfiltered remarks, such as admitting in an interview that she did not love Roald when they got married. He traveled often, and before one trip he told Patricia that because he would be extremely busy, she should not attempt to reach him. He would phone her if he had a spare moment. Not long after, a letter arrived in the mail, addressed to Roald from a woman he said he had met on his trip to Hollywood. If he was unfaithful to Patricia, she didn't have the presence of mind to delve into it. (During the marriage, he was said to have had many flirtations and at least a few affairs, even after his wife's stroke.) In a profile in the *Guardian* in 1971, the journalist Tom Hutchinson observed that Patricia "laughs often, with a barmaid vitality that never suggests the way life has mauled her." Discussing the early days of her marriage, she said, "I was a typical American wife. Worse,

I was a spoiled Hollywood actress. I never got him breakfast, never did any of the things that a European wife does to keep her man. He was all set to leave me." She added: "I guess I just had to save that marriage. But I still don't get him breakfast."

Because Roald's career was thriving, work provided an easy excuse for neglecting his wife. The Dahls became wealthy ("He was now the prosperous one," Patricia recalled) and had the first indoor swimming pool in Great Missenden. They owned expensive antiques and paintings by Matisse, Picasso, Bacon, and others.

In addition to his work on *You Only Live Twice*, Roald wrote the screenplay for *Chitty Chitty Bang Bang*, another adaptation of an Ian Fleming novel. (Neither experience ended well for Roald, who hated to collaborate and could not hide his disdain for a highly collaborative industry.) He was now an internationally famous author, with the film rights to *Charlie and the Chocolate Factory* sold in 1969. Although he had taken an initial stab at the screenplay, someone else was brought in to rewrite it, and he hated the finished movie. Still, when it came out in 1971 (as *Willy Wonka & the Chocolate Factory*), it made the author even more famous. By then, more than 600,000 copies had sold in the United States (and more than 250,000 copies of *James and the Giant Peach*). One day, after Tessa gave copies of her father's books to a friend, the girl's father happened to look through them. He was Rayner Unwin, of Allen & Unwin, publisher of J.R.R. Tolkien, and he did not know that Roald's work had been rejected by nearly every UK publishing house. Unwin offered Roald a book deal that led, finally, to the success in England that he had craved for so long. What he still lacked, however, was approbation from the literary mainstream. As an author of children's books, Roald felt very much like a second-class citizen, and no matter how rich and famous he became, he never overcame his bitterness and insecurity.

Over the next several years, as his marriage was failing beyond re-pair, he wrote what would become some of the most popular and best-selling children's books of all time, including *Fantastic Mr. Fox* and *The*

*Witches*. The appeal was easy to understand. "In every one of the books, he's on the side of the child," observed former UK Children's Laureate Michael Rosen. "He's thinking all the time about children's desires, but he also creates characters that allow children to experience their conflicted feelings about adults." Of course, the much-loved author—genial, charismatic, and funny in public—was hell at home. "Success did not mellow my husband," Patricia later recalled. "Quite the contrary, it only reinforced his conviction that although life was a two-way street, he had the right of way."

In 1972, General Foods hired Patricia to become the spokeswoman for Maxim Coffee, giving her a lucrative one-year contract and the possibility of an extension. She was forty-six, and Roald was in his late fifties. Both were asked to sample the product beforehand to make sure they liked it. (The company wanted a celebrity endorsement that seemed authentic.) Also, coffee had to be a "husband-pleaser," as Patricia recalled, and "Maxim felt *I* was the lady who could best convince American women that I would *never* do anything my husband did not like—including giving him a lousy cup of coffee." The campaign was a success. There was just one little problem, but it wasn't so little, and Patricia did not yet know it was a problem.

Her name was Felicity Crosland (née D'Abreu). Born in Cardiff, Wales, in 1938, she was young, elegant, and beautiful, recently divorced with three daughters. Known as Liccy, pronounced "Lissy," she could trace her lineage on her mother's side back to the Middle Ages. ("Her blood was tinged with blue," as Patricia later wrote.) Liccy was the granddaughter of Sir Richard Charles Acton Throckmorton, tenth baronet, and one of her ancestors, Bess Throckmorton—a courtier to Queen Elizabeth I—secretly married Sir Walter Raleigh after becoming pregnant with his child.

Liccy was hired to work on the commercial by David Ogilvy's advertising agency, which was handling the General Foods account. The director asked Liccy to help Patricia sort out her wardrobe for the shoot. Warm and eager to please, Liccy appeared at the Dahls' doorstep one day to deliver a selection of dresses and outfits for Patricia to choose from. Roald, however, was the one to approve everything. Soon Liccy began spending more time at the house, bringing gifts for the children and making herself useful. Patricia, believing she had found a new friend, often invited Liccy to join them on trips to London. At the Curzon House Club, she learned that Liccy shared Roald's love of gambling, especially blackjack, "and she usually wound up a winner."

Roald was exhausted from running the household, tending to the children's needs, and managing his work. He also suffered excruciating back pain and lingering headaches from his wartime injuries, which worsened over time, as well as other health issues. (In 1977, he needed hip replacement surgery.) Plus, his role in Patricia's extraordinary recovery attracted a lot of attention, with stroke patients and their families constantly writing to seek his advice. He decided to help Valerie Eaton Griffith turn this guidance into *A Stroke in the Family*, which was published in 1970. The book was highly regarded and led her to establish the Chest, Heart and Stroke Association in England.

Everyone in the family looked to Roald for stability. "He liked to give, but he didn't like to be demanded of," Lucy recalled. Theo later said that "Dad had a good temper and a bad temper. . . . you didn't want to get on the wrong side of him." (He also once described his father as "a wasp's nest.") Roald began to lash out more often, treating Patricia's friends rudely and humiliating his wife during bridge games. (He was fiercely competitive.) He criticized her so-called shortcomings—accusing her of black moods, self-absorption, intellectual laziness, and more. There were frequent rows between Roald and Patricia, and more drinking. ("Daddy was a mean drunk," Tessa recalled later.) Roald admitted that he had a short fuse and was far from perfect. "My faults and foibles are legion," he wrote in 1972. "I become easily bored in the company of adults. I drink too much whisky and wine in the evenings. I eat far too much chocolate. I smoke too many cigarettes. I am bad-tempered when my back is hurting. I do not always clean my fingernails. I no longer tell my children long stories at bedtime. I bet on horses and lose money that way. . . . I am going bald." Yet even the faithful Valerie Eaton Griffith had to admit that Patricia was also not easy to live with: "[She] began to behave badly. She was intolerant, she would yell at people, she would crave attention so that she'd overdo almost everything in an actressy way and make it very difficult for people to live and be peaceful in that house."

Soon after Liccy and Roald met, they began an affair. Decades later, asked by a reporter whether she felt guilty about her relationship with Roald, Liccy replied, "Yes and no. It was a particularly difficult situation because Pat had a stroke and was not well. I don't know how he managed to bring up these children, run a house, do the school runs and write this major volume of work. He was so worn out, so needing to be looked after, which of course Pat couldn't do. So there was a terrible pain about that."

In 1974, when Patricia returned home from shooting another round of Maxim commercials in New York, she was startled by her husband's coldness. "I lit up a cigarette," she recalled, "as I now did too many times a day and chalked it off to a bad mood." When Roald announced that Liccy and her daughters would be joining the family on their summer vacation, he added that they were going to the Spanish island of Minorca, not the usual trip to Norway. Patricia had no say in the matter. And after Liccy had a tonsillectomy, Roald informed his wife that Liccy would be convalescing at Gipsy House. One night, Patricia heard Roald leave their bed, but she rolled over and went back to sleep. "No woman, except perhaps one who has been through this, could believe how blind I was," Patricia later wrote. "It's really crazy, but I simply did not want to know what was going on."

Tessa knew. In a disturbing account later given to biographer Jeremy Treglown, she recalled overhearing her father on the phone one night, clearly talking with a lover. At the time, she was a teenager suffering from drug addiction and an eating disorder. When she confronted Roald, according to her recollection, he replied in a rage: "You've always been trouble, you've always been a nosy little bitch. I want you to get out of this fucking house now." This ugly encounter was followed by threats and manipulations from both Roald and Liccy, Tessa said, so she kept their secret—perhaps hoping it would bring her closer to her father. (Theo, Ophelia, and Lucy had no idea about the affair.)

After Patricia confronted Liccy and Roald, life carried on just as it had. Patricia and Roald went through their days like zombies—"He was bored, and I was ignored"—but nothing was talked about and nothing changed. She felt she was going crazy. She knew now that her husband must have cheated on her repeatedly during their marriage, and now Liccy might end it.

Patricia tried awkwardly to "make nice," even hosting a dinner party for her husband's mistress. She received a letter of apology from Liccy, expressing sadness for the pain she had caused and saying she was going away for a while. Around that time, a reporter asked Patricia whether she was happy. "Who's really happy?" she replied. "Let's just say it is enough not to be unhappy and let it go at that."

Later in 1975, while Patricia was in California shooting an episode of *Little House on the Prairie*, she received a letter from Roald. It was structured in six numbered points. The first two assertions rang hollow: "1) I love you. Surely you know that. 2) I would never think of leaving you." While admitting he was "fond" of Liccy, he insisted, "It is not sex. You think it is. I promise you it isn't." He mentioned that he would "probably look occasionally for her companionship," and asked his wife to reject any feelings of jealousy if "now and again, but not very often, I meet Liccy and have lunch with her." Citing his exceptional height as an impediment to feeling energetic, he noted that he was "a huge fellow physically," and "huge fellows, I mean really huge ones of 6 foot 5 or 6 inches, do grow physically tired earlier than others. Certainly, I feel pretty tired a lot of the time these days."

It was an astonishing letter, both for the author's audacity and for his inability to perceive how it might land. He continued building his case in a plainspoken way, as if his have-cake-and-eat-it-too solution made perfect sense:

5) I see no reason in the world why a man of fifty-nine should not love his wife and also be allowed to feel strongly about another woman. It would be strange if he didn't.

6) All of this is obviously a rotten deal for Liccy, and I sort of hope that she won't put up with it for long. There is no future in it for her. In time, she is bound to meet someone else and that will be the end of that. But it would be wrong and cruel and unkind for me to push her right away myself. I have told her long ago that there is no chance of me ever leaving you. She knows it.

Patricia spent much of her time over the next few years away from Great Missenden. Aside from some acting jobs, "My major performance was as Patricia Neal." She was a sought-after speaker on the lecture circuit, appearing at stroke centers, fundraising for stroke victims, and more. In 1978, the Patricia Neal Rehabilitation Center opened in Knoxville, Tennessee, becoming a leading facility in rehabilitating stroke, spinal cord, and brain injury patients. (It is still in operation today.) She continued giving interviews to the press, which often summed up her life using some version of the phrase "dogged by tragedy." With the production of a CBS-TV movie, *The Patricia Neal Story*, based on Barry Farrell's book and starring Glenda Jackson as Patricia, journalists and gossip columnists were eager for Patricia to comment on the television portrayal of her story, and to reflect on her struggles. "The first thing you have to do after suffering a stroke is to tell yourself you won't give up, that you don't want to die, or be cared for like a baby the rest of your life," she said at Sardi's in the fall of 1981, talking to a reporter from the *New York Times* and mentioning that her husband had "browbeat me with love and patience" into walking and talking again. Patricia's mother, interviewed by a local TV critic, bluntly criticized Dirk Bogarde's performance as Roald in *The Patricia Neal Story*. Noting that the actor portrayed Roald as a saint, Eura said: "He's far from it. I think it showed Mr. Dahl a little kinder and more patient than I remember him to be."

With her hectic speaking and media schedule, Patricia was constantly on the go. Roald encouraged her travels. He wrote fond letters from home, even as he remained smitten with Liccy and secretly met her at every opportunity. When he could not see her, such as when Patricia was home, a frustrated Roald would drive to a public phone box to call her.

The distance between Patricia and Roald was apparent in many ways. Both gave up the pretense of trying to connect. Patricia had fallen in love with Martha's Vineyard years earlier, and when she learned of a historic Greek Revival house for sale in Edgartown, she bought it in 1980, sight unseen, for four hundred thousand dollars. (The original owner, Captain Valentine Pease of the whaling ship *Acushnet*, is said to have been an inspiration for Herman Melville's Captain Ahab.) The following summer, Roald came over to see her. Upon returning home to England, he wrote a letter to Patricia saying how unpleasant the brief visit had been for him, and that he had no intention of coming back. In an interview the couple gave to the *Boston Globe* in 1981, they made no effort to hide their mutual contempt. "People get tired of being with each other for years—day in, day out," Roald snapped. "They need some time away from each other." Patricia chimed in: "Men are such conceited asses," she said, and then cheerily mentioned the dinner party she would be hosting the following evening. "Cagney will be there," she said. "Hellman, too." The reporter observed that Patricia smiled broadly, but "the smile does not synch with what seems to be a great well of sadness in her eyes."

Patricia stayed on in Edgartown and was glad to have an ocean between her and her husband. She kept busy with acting work, receiving lifetime achievement awards and other honors and traveling to see friends and family. One of her great consolations around this time was reconciling with Rocky Cooper, Gary's widow. (Patricia had already received a kind note of forgiveness from Rocky's daughter, Maria, after the stroke.) Shortly before the holidays, Patricia was surprised to receive a letter from Roald, letting her know that she did not need to return to England for Christmas. How bizarre, she thought. Of course she would go home. But when she arrived, Roald was colder than ever. That night, Ophelia burst out with the news that "Daddy is still seeing Felicity Crosland." Patricia recalled crying and ranting, which frightened her children.

Later that night, after Roald fell asleep, an enraged Patricia crept into bed and whispered into her husband's ear: "I wish you were dead. I wish something would kill you." The next day, Roald bought a one-way plane ticket for Patricia to New York and drove her to Heathrow Airport, accompanied by their weeping children. Going through the gate, she looked back and saw that "Roald's head was thrown back and he was roaring with laughter." (However, Ophelia later said she remembered her father being distressed and unhappy.) In any case, the children were caught in the middle of a messy and painful situation. Ophelia later said that "all of us realized that [our father] had found the love of his life with Liccy, and there's always a sense of relief when that happens."

After staying with friends, Patricia bought an apartment on the Upper East Side at 45 East End Avenue, in a co-op designed by Emery Roth & Sons that overlooked the East River. Rather than stash away her many awards and Hollywood memorabilia, she displayed them prominently throughout the apartment. On July 5, 1983, her marriage was officially over. Reuters ran a three-line story with the headline "Patricia Neal Divorced." Now, at the age of fifty-seven, she had to figure out how to live the rest of her life without the man she had been with for thirty years. Writing her autobiography, *As I Am*, must have been cathartic. The book became a bestseller and received critical praise.

On December 15, 1983, three days after Liccy's forty-fifth birth-day, Roald and Liccy married at Brixton Town Hall in London. In an interview years later, she said, "We never thought we could get married; we thought we'd keep it secret. No divorce in the world is happy and I think a husband falling for a younger woman must be the worst of all." To Roald, she was "everything a wife should be," meaning that she gave up working and made their home at Gipsy House comfortable and peaceful, so he could focus on his writing. Roald, whose American publisher was now Farrar, Straus and Giroux, still retreated to his writing hut seven days a week. He may have been happy and in love, but that didn't mean he was easy to live with. Roald always became grumpy when finishing a book. "I remember saying, 'But you should be pleased you're reaching the end!'" Liccy once recalled in an interview. "And he used to say, 'You don't understand—it's the fear of never writing another one.'"

The couple had only seven years together. On November 23, 1990, Roald died at seventy-four from a rare form of leukemia at John Radcliffe Hospital in Oxford. He was buried in Great Missenden, near Gipsy House, and his granddaughter Sophie (daughter of Tessa) remembered him with great fondness: "He knew the history of every single chocolate bar, when they were invented, who they were invented by, what year," she said in a 1997 interview with the *Independent*. "When he died, we buried him like a Pharaoh with all his favorite things around him—red wine, cigarettes, his snooker cues, and the most enormous box of chocolate bars, Twixes, Kit-Kats, Mars Bars, everything, just to keep him going till he got to heaven."

Months before her husband died, Liccy was already in a state of grief: her twenty-seven-year-old daughter, Lorina, died of a brain tumor. Liccy kept going by tending to Roald's colossal legacy, and among other endeavors started the Roald Dahl Foundation in 1991 (later renamed Roald Dahl's Marvellous Children's Charity) to support thousands of children in the UK living with serious illnesses. Asked by a reporter in 2008 what life was like without her husband, Liccy replied, "It's hell."

The summer before Roald's death, there had been a reconciliation of sorts with Patricia, who joined the family at Gipsy House for Theo's birthday celebration. At the end of her memoir, Patricia was generous toward her former husband. "If I had not married Roald Dahl," she wrote, "I would have been denied my children, even my life, because he truly saved me, and I will be forever grateful to him for that."

There would be no second husband for Patricia, and the only love of her life was long dead. What she had now was peace and closer relationships with her children. For her seventieth birthday in 1996, they threw her a grand party at the Carlyle Hotel in New York, packed with celebrity guests and friends. The lifetime recognition awards kept coming, along with occasional acting parts, including the title character in Robert Altman's 1999 film, *Cookie's Fortune*. She even appeared in a BBC documentary on the life and work of Roald Dahl—and a few years later she traveled back to Great Missenden to participate in a charity event with her family, reading from Roald's works to raise funds for the foundation in his name. But her main purpose, she felt, was channeling her energy to give hope and inspiration to other stroke survivors. "Notice I say *survivors* and not *victims*," she once said. She was happier than she had been for a long time.

In 2002, I interviewed Patricia Dahl by phone before the Tennessee Williams & New Orleans Literary Festival, an annual event held in the city's French Quarter. I was too young and foolish then to fully appreciate my conversation with a living legend, but she was an attentive listener, extremely kind, and generous with her time. Having read her autobiography, I shyly asked a question about her marriage to Roald Dahl. She paused and let out her wonderfully husky laugh. "Oh, *honey*," she said, "have you got all day?"

On August 8, 2010, Patricia died of lung cancer at her home in Edgartown at the age of eighty-four. Many of the obituary headlines contained similar phrases about how the actress had endured tragedies and achieved triumphs. The *Vineyard Gazette*, her local newspaper, praised the celebrity resident for her humility, optimism, and down-to-earth demeanor. She had spent every year on Martha's Vineyard from June through Thanksgiving, and her funeral was held at a church in Edgartown. The *Gazette* obituary included quotes from her interviews with the newspaper over the years. "I'm not wise, just very hard to beat," she said in an article in 2000. "I intend to live until I die." Locals paid tribute with their Patricia Neal anecdotes, such as an appreciation from a woman whose sister had a cerebral hemorrhage at thirty-six. The woman's family spent summers on the Vineyard, and one day she told her sister that they would be having tea with Patricia Neal. "I don't know how I became so bold, but I wrote to Ms. Neal and asked if this could be possible. To my surprise, she did invite us to her home. That summer we sat in her house and had tea with her. She was so gracious and she gave my sister so much hope. . . . [My sister] is doing well and is an artist. My family will always remember how kind Patricia Neal was to us and feel we have lost a friend."

Perhaps most poignant of all was a statement from Tessa, Theo, Ophelia, and Lucy in the *Gazette*: "She faced her final illness as she had all of the many trials she endured: with indomitable grace, good humor, and a great deal of her self-described stubbornness. We are grateful for her extraordinarily full life, which included a long and illustrious career on both stage and screen and was filled with loving friends and family spread across the world. . . . Last night she told us: 'I've had a lovely time.' So have we."

In the years after her divorce, Patricia learned how to thrive on her own and savored her freedom. "I really adore life now," she told a reporter in 1999. "I even adore the fact that you never know what's going to happen in life from one minute to the next. Now I'm just going to continue to do the best in this life. I don't conk easy."

# ACKNOWLEDGMENTS

My deepest gratitude to Tina Bennett for all that she's done for me over the years, and for stepping in once again to support this book. I'd be lost without her generosity, wisdom, and guidance. Thanks very much to Sophie Lambert at C&W and Helen Manders at Curtis Brown, and to Molly Wright at ICM for helping us move things along at every stage. I'm grateful to Terry Karten, to whom this book is dedicated, for her patience, encouragement, and love. Thanks to Rebecca Holland, senior production editor and superhero, and everyone at HarperCollins— especially Joanne O'Neill, Nancy Singer, Becca Putnam, Shannon McCain, and Heather Drucker. Above all, thanks to Sarah and Oscar for everything, every day. And to Freddy, still and always.

# SELECTED BIBLIOGRAPHY

I read hundreds of archival articles from newspapers, magazines, and academic journals in the course of my research, in addition to the sources below. I have also cited books that provided additional context, even though I did not quote directly from them. Any errors or omissions are wholly unintentional and will be corrected in future editions.

Abbott, Elizabeth. *A History of Marriage: From Same Sex Unions to Private Vows and Common Law, the Surprising Diversity of a Tradition.* New York: Seven Stories Press, 2011.

Amis, Kingsley. *The Letters of Kingsley Amis.* Edited by Zachary Leader. New York: HarperCollins, 2000.

———. *Memoirs.* London: Hutchinson, 1991.

Amis, Martin. *Experience: A Memoir.* London: Jonathan Cape, 2000.

Baker, Michael. *Our Three Selves: The Life of Radclyffe Hall.* London: Hamish Hamilton, 1985.

Calvino, Italo. *Letters, 1941–1985.* Translated by Martin McLaughlin. Princeton, NJ: Princeton University Press, 2013.

Castle, Terry. *Noël Coward & Radclyffe Hall: Kindred Spirits.* New York: Columbia University Press, 1996.

Chadwick, Whitney, and de Courtivron, Isabelle, eds. *Significant Others: Creativity and Intimate Partnership*. London: Thames and Hudson, 1993.

Cline, Sally. *Radclyffe Hall: A Woman Called John*. London: John Murray, 1997.

Conant, Jenet. *The Irregulars: Roald Dahl and the British Spy Ring in Wartime Washington*. New York: Simon & Schuster, 2008.

Coontz, Stephanie. *Marriage, a History: From Obedience to Intimacy or How Love Conquered Marriage*. New York: Viking, 2005.

Cooper, Artemis. *Elizabeth Jane Howard: A Dangerous Innocence*. London: John Murray, 2016.

Dahl, Roald. *Boy: Tales of Childhood*. London: Jonathan Cape, 1984.

———. *Going Solo*. London: Jonathan Cape, 1986.

———. *Love from Boy: Roald Dahl's Letters to His Mother*. Edited by Donald Sturrock. London: John Murray, 2016.

———. *Someone Like You*. New York: Alfred A. Knopf, 1953.

———. *Switch Bitch*. New York: Alfred A. Knopf, 1974.

———. *The Wonderful Story of Henry Sugar*. New York: Alfred A. Knopf, 1977.

Dellamora, Richard. *Radclyffe Hall: A Life in the Writing*. Philadelphia: University of Pennsylvania Press, 2011.

Doan, Laura, and Jay Prosser. *Palatable Poison: Critical Perspectives on* The Well of Loneliness. New York: Columbia University Press, 2001.

Doherty, Maggie. *The Equivalents: A Story of Art, Female Friendship, and Liberation in the 1960s*. New York: Alfred A. Knopf, 2020.

Dundy, Elaine. *Life Itself!* London: Virago Press, 2001.

———. *The Dud Avocado*. New York: NYRB Classics, 2007.

———. *Elvis and Gladys*. Jackson, MS: University Press of Mississippi, 2004.

———. *The Old Man and Me*. New York: NYRB Classics, 2005.

Farrell, Barry. *Pat and Roald*. New York: Random House, 1969.

Ferrante, Elena. *Frantumaglia: A Writer's Journey*. Translated by Ann Goldstein. New York: Europa Editions, 2016.

Glasgow, Joanne, ed. *Your John: The Love Letters of Radclyffe Hall*. New York: New York University Press, 1997.

Hall, Radclyffe. *Adam's Breed*. London: Virago Press, 1985.

———. *A Saturday Life*. London: Virago Press, 1989.

———. *The Unlit Lamp*. London: Virago Press, 1981.

———. *The Well of Loneliness*. New York: Anchor Books, 1990.

Hardwick, Elizabeth. *Bartleby in Manhattan*. New York: Vintage Books, 1984.

———. *The Collected Essays of Elizabeth Hardwick*. New York: NYRB Classics, 2017.

Hartog, Hendrik. *Man & Wife in America: A History*. Cambridge, MA: Harvard University Press, 2000.

Heilbrun, Carolyn. *Writing a Woman's Life*. New York: W. W. Norton, 1988.

Howard, Elizabeth Jane. *Getting it Right*. London: Hamish Hamilton, 1982.

———. *Mr. Wrong*. London: Jonathan Cape, 1975.

———. *The Beautiful Visit*. London: Jonathan Cape, 1950.

———. *The Light Years*. New York: Washington Square Press, 1995.

———. *The Long View*. London: Jonathan Cape, 1956.

———. *Slipstream: A Memoir*. London: Macmillan, 2002.

Johnson, Diane. *Lesser Lives: The True History of the First Mrs. Meredith and Other Lesser Lives*. London: William Heinemann, 1973.

Lahiri, Jhumpa, ed. *The Penguin Book of Italian Short Stories*. New York: Penguin Books, 2019.

Leader, Zachary. *The Life of Kingsley Amis*. London: Jonathan Cape, 2006.

Lucamante, Stefania, and Sharon Wood, eds. *Under Arturo's Star: The Cultural Legacies of Elsa Morante*. West Lafayette, IN: Purdue University Press, 2006.

Malcolm, Janet. *The Silent Woman: Sylvia Plath & Ted Hughes*. New York: Alfred A. Knopf, 1994.

Malcolm, Janet. *Two Lives: Gertrude and Alice*. New Haven: Yale University Press, 2007.

Middlebrook, Diane. *Her Husband: Hughes and Plath—A Marriage*. New York: Viking Penguin, 2003.

Morante, Elsa. *Aracoeli*. Translated by William Weaver. Rochester, NY: Open Letter Books, 2009.

———. *Arturo's Island*. Translated by Ann Goldstein. New York: Liveright, 2020.

———. *History: A Novel*. Translated by William Weaver. Lebanon, NH: Steerforth Press, 2000.

Moravia, Alberto, and Alain Elkann. *Life of Moravia*. Translated by William Weaver. Lebanon, NH: Steerforth Italia, 2000.

———. *The Time of Indifference*. Translated by Tami Calliope. Lebanon, NH: Steerforth Press, 2000.

———. *The Woman of Rome*. Translated by Tami Calliope. Lebanon, NH: Steerforth Press, 1999.

Neal, Patricia. *As I Am: An Autobiography*. New York: Simon & Schuster, 1988.

O'Brien, Edna. *Country Girl: A Memoir*. London: Faber and Faber, 2012.

Ormrod, Richard. *Una Troubridge: The Friend of Radclyffe Hall*. New York: Carroll & Graf, 1985.

Pierpont, Claudia Roth. *Passionate Minds: Women Rewriting the World*. New York: Alfred A. Knopf, 2000.

Rose, Phyllis. *Parallel Lives: Five Victorian Marriages*. New York: Alfred A. Knopf, 1983.

Santamaria, Abigail. *Joy: Poet, Seeker, and the Woman Who Captivated C. S. Lewis*. Boston: Houghton Mifflin Harcourt, 2015.

Schiff, Stacy. *Véra: Mrs. Vladimir Nabokov*. New York: Random House, 1999.

Shearer, Stephen Michael. *Patricia Neal: An Unquiet Life*. Lexington: The University Press of Kentucky, 2006.

Shellard, Dominic. *Kenneth Tynan: A Life*. New Haven: Yale University Press, 2003.

Simon, Linda. *The Biography of Alice B. Toklas*. Lincoln: University of Nebraska Press, 1991.

Souhami, Diana. *The Trials of Radclyffe Hall*. London: Weidenfeld & Nicolson, 1998.

Sturrock, Donald. *Storyteller: The Authorized Biography of Roald Dahl*. New York: Simon & Schuster, 2010.

Treglown, Jeremy. *Roald Dahl: A Biography*. New York: Harcourt, Brace, 1994.

Troubridge, Una, Lady. *The Life and Death of Radclyffe Hall*. London: Hammond, Hammond, 1961.

Tuck, Lily. *Woman of Rome: A Life of Elsa Morante*. New York: HarperCollins Publishers, 2008.

Tynan, Kathleen. *The Life of Kenneth Tynan*. New York: William Morrow, 1987.

Tynan, Kenneth. *The Diaries of Kenneth Tynan*. Edited by John Lahr. London: Bloomsbury, 2001.

———. *He That Plays the King: A View of the Theatre*. London: Longmans, Green, 1950.

———. *Letters*. Edited by Kathleen Tynan. London: Weidenfeld & Nicolson, 1994.

Tynan, Tracy. *Wear and Tear: The Threads of My Life*. New York: Scribner, 2016.

Weaver, William, ed. *Open City: Seven Writers in Postwar Rome*. Lebanon, NH: Steerforth Italia, 1999.

Wodehouse, P. G. *A Life in Letters*. Edited by Sophie Ratcliffe. New York: W. W. Norton, 2013.

Wolitzer, Meg. *The Wife*. New York: Scribner, 2003.

Woolf, Virginia. *Essays on the Self*. London: Notting Hill Editions, 2014.

Yalom, Marilyn. *A History of the Wife*. New York: HarperCollins, 2001.

# INDEX

# PHOTO CREDITS

# ABOUT THE AUTHOR

CARMELA CIURARU is the author of *Nom de Plume: A (Secret) History of Pseudonyms*, as well as several poetry anthologies. She lives in New York City.